STUDIES IN EVANGELICALISM
edited by
Kenneth E. Rowe &
Donald W. Dayton

1. Melvin E. Dieter. *The Holiness Revival of the Nineteenth Century.* 1980.

2. Lawrence T. Lesick. *The Lane Rebels: Evangelicalism and Antislavery in Antebellum America.* 1980.

3. Edward H. Madden and James E. Hamilton. *Freedom and Grace: The Life of Asa Mahan.* 1982.

4. Roger H. Martin. *Evangelicals United: Ecumenical Stirrings in Pre-Victorian Britain, 1795-1830.* 1983.

EVANGELICALS UNITED:

Ecumenical Stirrings in Pre-Victorian Britain, 1795-1830

by
ROGER H. MARTIN

Studies in Evangelicalism, No. 4

The Scarecrow Press, Inc.
Metuchen, N.J., & London
1983

Portions of Chapters Three and Four and of Chapter Nine were published respectively in The Journal of Ecclesiastical History (Volume 31, July 1980, Number 3, pages 283-300), and in Church History (Volume 46, December 1977, Number 4, pages 437-452). They have been reprinted here by permission of The Cambridge University Press and The American Society of Church History.

Library of Congress Cataloging in Publication Data

Martin, Roger H., 1943-
   Evangelicals united.

   (Studies in evangelicalism ; no. 4)
   Includes index.
   1. Evangelical Revival--Great Britain. 2. Church union--Great Britain--History--18th century. 3. Church union--Great Britain--History--19th century. 4. Ecumenical movement--Great Britain--History--18th century. 5. Ecumenical movement--Great Britain--History--19th century. 6. Great Britain--Church history--18th century. 7. Great Britain--Church history--19th century. I. Title. II. Series.
BR758.M27 1982   274.1'081   82-10784
ISBN 0-8108-1586-9

To my Mother and Father

CONTENTS

Editors' Note   vii

Preface   ix

Abbreviations of Archival References   xii

PART I: INTRODUCTION

Chapter 1: Unity--The Elusive Dream   2
Chapter 2: The Scattered Bones of Ezekiel's Vision   23

PART II: THE LONDON MISSIONARY SOCIETY

Chapter 3: Bigotry Is Dead   40
Chapter 4: A Mission for All Evangelicals   61

PART III: THE BRITISH AND FOREIGN BIBLE
           SOCIETY

Chapter 5: Disciples on the Road to Emmaus   80
Chapter 6: With the Torrent of a Vesuvius   99
Chapter 7: Schism   123

PART IV: THE TRACT AND JEWS SOCIETIES

Chapter 8: Pure Good-natured Christianity   148
Chapter 9: The British Israel   174

PART V: CONCLUSION

Chapter 10: 1830 and After   194

Appendix: Evangelical Biographies   205

Index   219

The current resurgence of Evangelical religion has highlighted the important role of this force in the formation of American and British culture. This series will explore its roots in the Evangelical Revival and Awakenings of the 18th century, its 19th-century blossoming in revivalism and social reform, and its 20th-century developments in both sect and "mainline" churches. We will be particularly concerned to emphasize the diversity within Evangelicalism--the search for holiness, the Millennial traditions, Fundamentalism, Pentecostalism, and so forth. We are pleased to publish Roger H. Martin's study of ecumenical stirrings in pre-Victorian Britain as number four in the series. This work extends the range of our series by focusing on the British roots in the development of Evangelicalism.

A graduate of Drew and Yale Universities, Mr. Martin received his doctorate from the University of Oxford. He was an administrator and Assistant Professor of History at Middlebury College in Vermont before joining the Divinity School faculty at Harvard University where he is currently Associate Dean.

Donald W. Dayton   Kenneth E. Rowe
Northern Baptist Theological   Drew University
   Seminary   Madison, New Jersey
Lombard, Illinois

The fifty years or so between the last decade of the eighteenth century and the third decade of the nineteenth, interposed as they were between the Evangelical Revival and the Oxford Movement, have unfortunately received little attention from British church historians and students of the ecumenical movement.   Yet it was during these years that British Christians--Anglicans and Dissenters alike--participated together for the first time in an interdenominational movement that made an important contribution to the ecumenical movement of our own era.   A great deal of interest has recently centered on the four major institutional embodiments of this early experiment in ecumenicism.   The London Missionary Society, the Religious Tract Society, the British and Foreign Bible Society, and the London Society for Promoting Christianity Amongst the Jews between them marshalled together an army of missionary advocates drawn from almost every county, town and hamlet in Great Britain.   Yet when reference is made to these organizations, it is usually to the religious and social impact they had on non-Western cultures in the mission field itself.   Mention is hardly ever made of the impact they had on the church in Britain, one which, initially at least, may have been greater than on the heathen.   This book is a modest attempt to correct this imbalance.

A subsidiary but equally important focus of this book has been more precisely to define the term "evangelical." Too often, nineteenth-century British evangelicals are seen as a rather amorphous group of seemingly like-minded Christians.   In real life, however, they were often as different as they were alike.   They could, when they wanted to, unite around common beliefs in order to achieve common objectives. But sometimes distinctive theological and denominational differences found within the various evangelical communities could also separate and divide.   A study of the pan-evangelical era brings to light some of these similarities and differences and better enables us to discuss British evangelicalism, at least within the nineteenth-century context, with a bit more precision.

Because of the wide scope of the period under study and the restrictions of time and space, there are by necessity at least two limitations to a book this size. In the first place, it uses for illustrative purposes the four major pan-evangelical institutions of the day, drawing most of its information from their archives. Some mention is made of the various other interdenominational organizations that flourished during this period, but a thorough examination of these must await future studies which it is hoped this book might inspire. Secondly, the book is restricted to the thirty-five years between 1795 and 1830. The year 1795 is a natural starting-point because it was then that the first major pan-evangelical institution of the period--the London Missionary Society--was founded. The year 1830 is a somewhat arbitrary termination-point since forms of evangelical cooperation continued into the nineteenth century and beyond. But by this time, most of the original fathers of the pan-evangelical era had either died or retired from the management of their respective organizations with the result that much of the early enthusiasm for church union that they had nurtured had passed with them into history.

Though the author claims sole responsibility for the ideas and concepts expressed in this book, mention must be made of the people who generously contributed their time to its making. Thankful appreciation must, of course, be extended to the General Secretaries of the various organizations mentioned in the book, who readily made available for examination their respective archives. But several individuals merit special recognition. The late Rev. Ernest Payne read sections of the book which he originally examined as an Oxford doctoral thesis, and made several valuable contributions. Kathleen Cann, Archivist of the British and Foreign Bible Society did likewise. The gratitude I owe to Dr. John D. Walsh of Jesus College, Oxford, cannot be expressed in words. It was under his supervision that a much lengthier doctoral thesis on the same subject was completed. I have continued to benefit from his suggestions and criticisms. Finally, I would like to thank the Teaching Resources Committee and the President and Fellows of Middlebury College for providing, while I was a member of the History Department, a stipend and leave to spend a summer in Oxford and London completing research. To all of these people, and to my wife, Susan, whose patience and support was generous, I am deeply grateful.

Roger H. Martin
Cambridge, Mass.
Fall 1982

Angus	Angus Library, Regent's Park College, Oxford
B. M. S.	Baptist Missionary Society, London
Bodl.	Bodleian Library, Oxford
B. S.	British and Foreign Bible Society, London
C. M. S.	Church Missionary Society, London
L. M. S.	London Missionary Society (Congregational Council for World Missions), School of Oriental and African Studies, University of London, London
L. S.	London Society for Promoting Christianity Amongst the Jews (Church's Ministry Among the Jews), Bodleian Library, Oxford
M. C. A.	Methodist Church Archives, John Rylands Library, Manchester
M. M. S.	Wesleyan Methodist Missionary Society, School of Oriental and African Studies, University of London, London
R. T. S.	Religious Tract Society (United Society for Christian Literature), Guildford, Surrey

PART I:

INTRODUCTION

Chapter 1

I.

The sources of the modern ecumenical movement are
many and diverse.   But paramount among them may be reckoned the great upsurge in missionary activity in late eighteenth-
century Britain, which effectively brought many different Christians together into a union of common purpose and mutual respect.   This was largely an evangelical affair, distinguished
by the great missionary, Bible and tract societies they founded
between 1795 and the turn of the century.   But it profoundly
influenced the course of British ecumenicism for years to come
and quite properly should be seen as a forerunner of the ecumenical movement of our own era.   This book is about the
people who founded and sustained this movement.   It is also
about the successes and failures of the interdenominational institutions that gave the movement its character and purpose.

While the concept of church union is hardly an evangelical invention, [1] our story must begin with the great Wesleyan
and Whitefieldite revivals of the mid-eighteenth century, for
it was out of the Methodist campaign to convert a nation to
"vital religion" that the modern-day ecumenical impulse in
perhaps its earliest form was generated.   As we shall see in
this chapter and the next, the road to unity was an uneven
one involving centripetal as well as centrifugal forces that
would unite like-minded Christians and then suddenly pull them
apart again.   The Revival began in a spirit of cooperation.
But even in the euphoria of the early 1740's, dormant theological and denominational differences threatened to erupt into
open conflict as finally happened with devastating effect in
1770.   In that year the so-called Calvinistic Controversy
reared its ugly head separating Calvinistic evangelicals from
their counterparts in the Arminian or Wesleyan camp.   On
another front, Anglican evangelicals, during the latter part

2

of the eighteenth century, slowly drew apart from their Nonconformist brethren over the issue of church order. But
evangelicals shared more in common than they perhaps realized and by century's end a somewhat fragile unity prevailed,
setting the stage for the great era of pan-evangelicalism which
is the subject of this book. Even then, unity would prove to
be an elusive dream, only incompletely realized by the mid-
nineteenth century when sectarianism and denominationalism,
not ecumenicism, were in the ascendant. Let us then briefly
examine the early eighteenth-century Revival and the complex
and sometimes contradictory forces that helped to shape the
coming "Age of Pan-evangelicalism."

        In theory at least, the early Evangelical Revival pro-
fessed what John Wesley called "the Catholic spirit." This
was a revival, said one evangelical in 1739, in which "all
controversial points were left alone, and Christ alone was
preached."[2] Indeed, it was never the intention of the Revival's leaders to create new denominations. William Seward,
a close friend of George Whitefield, the head of what soon
would become the Calvinistic branch of the Revival, echoed
Whitefield himself when, reporting on a revival in Wales, he
wrote:

> I told them I did not desire them to leave [their]
> Church but to attend it closely--and that I only
> wanted to bring them to Jesus Christ and then if
> they were fully persuaded in their own mind let
> each remain in the communion in which he was
> called. If he was called a Churchman let him re-
> main; if a Quaker, a Baptist, or Presbyterian let
> him remain so. [3]

To Seward and other evangelicals, denominational labels were
only of secondary importance. What mattered was the individual's awareness of the living Christ.

        John Wesley, Whitefield's friend and leader of the
"Arminian" branch of the Revival, also deplored party though
unlike many evangelicals, his remaining High Church principles somewhat dimmed his "catholic spirit." Fifty years
after the Revival commenced, Wesley still claimed that the
original design of the Methodists was "not to be a distinct
party, but to stir up all parties, Christians or heathens, to
worship God in spirit and in truth." He hastened to add, however, that his societies were particularly concerned to stir up
the Church of England, a qualification that would never have

been made by George Whitefield. [4] If Wesley was prejudiced
toward the Church of England, Whitefield moved with remarkable freedom between Churchmen and Dissenters, among the
various denominations in America, and even among the Arminian societies of Wesley. [5]

The Moravians then resident in England also claimed
to be not only an historic church but, far more, a "vital
leaven" set on stirring up the existing confessions of Christendom. Borrowing heavily from the seventeenth-century
Pietistic tradition of Jacob Spener, the ecumenical principles
of the Moravians were brought to England by Nicholas Zinzendorf, the central figure of the German movement. Zinzendorf,
himself an ordained Lutheran, claimed that the principal doctrine of Christianity around which all denominations would unite
was a simple, loving trust in "the lamb of Christ." Since in
the Father's house there were many mansions, so on earth it
was God's will that there should be a multiplicity of distinctive "schools of Wisdom." Zinzendorf built on Spener's concept of ecclesiolae in Ecclesia, or a communion of churches
within the Invisible Church. The "Unity of Christ" therefore,
was not an organic union based on the destruction of denominational peculiarities but rather a unity transcending all ecclesiastical and theological divisions. Zinzendorf intended the
Moravians in England and elsewhere to be a religious society
encompassing all Christian denominations. Their mission, he
said, would be to "gather together in one the children of God
that were scattered abroad" and to make visible "that great
Invisible Church of Christ."[6]

Theological and denominational labels, therefore, played
a minor role during the initial honeymoon period of the revival. In its first exhilarating phase, the suddenness of the
awakening, the sense of millennial expectation it aroused, the
freshness of the evangelical experience, created a powerful
sense of fraternity among the converts of the movement. Arminians and Calvinists, Churchmen and Dissenters, achieved
an unprecedented level of unity. Methodist societies in England and Wales were largely free of party labels until 1740,
but even after this date many of them remained organizationally undenominational. [7] The distinctions between theologies,
parties, or even between social classes seemed trivial compared with those between the regenerate and the damned. As
Joseph Milner, the great Evangelical Anglican later remarked:
"Insignificant indeed are all the distinctions of another kind
compared with these, converted or unconverted ... heirs of
heaven or heirs of hell."[8] In its infancy, the Revival was

far less a matter of organizational allegiance, more an open,
expectant and spontaneous attitude to life and religion.

II.

Though the concept of unity was central to the Evangelical Revival, it continually proved frustratingly elusive
for there were also centrifugal forces at work, some theological and others of a denominational nature, that would
serve to separate rather than unite evangelical Christians.
These forces were never strong enough completely to ex-
tirpate the pan-evangelical urge, but they bear mentioning
as illustrations of recurring problems that would resurface
in one form or another throughout the period under study.

After 1740, for example, there was serious disagreement between John Wesley and the Moravians at the Fetter
Lane Society where the quietism of the Moravian leader,
Philip Henry Molther, had led Wesley to suspect the Ger-
mans of antinomianism. Some Moravians in turn had serious doubts about Wesley's doctrine of Perfection. Furthermore, the strong personalities of Wesley and Zinzendorf increasingly came into conflict with each other. The split
between Wesley and the Moravians was perhaps precipitated
by the publication of Charles Wesley's hymns on "The Means
of Grace," which were circulated by him "as an antidote to
stillness." Consequently on July 16, 1740, it was decided
that Wesley should no longer preach at Fetter Lane, and
this action led to his separation one week later and the establishment of the first Wesleyan society at the Foundery.

There was also growing discord between Wesley and
George Whitefield. Whitefield had not been a strong Calvinist prior to 1740, but extensive travels in America brought
him into contact with sophisticated Calvinistic theologians
like Jonathan Edwards, who slowly converted him to a stronger predestinarian position. This never ceased to irritate
the Wesleys who were strong Arminians and between 1740
and 1770 there was an uneasy peace between the Arminian
and Calvinistic camps of the revival which periodically broke
out into open controversy and hardened the boundaries between the two. Arminians feared that predestination encouraged fatalism and led believers into an antinomian care-
lessness for the moral law. Calvinists, on the other hand,
held that the admission of an element of free will into justification detracted from glory and sovereignty of God and

qualified that fundamental axiom of Reformed theology, the
doctrine of total depravity. Though Arminian Wesleyans and
Calvinistic Whitefieldites still tried to recapture the "catholic
spirit" of the first days, they found it elusive. In 1764, for
example, John Wesley attempted to bring together evangelical
clergymen in a union "offensive and defensive, of all soldiers
of Christ," but only three clergymen bothered to reply to
his irenic circular. [9] The distinction between mere "opinions" which should be tolerated by evangelicals as non-es-
sentials, and the "fundamental doctrines" shared by all children of light was not easily maintained in practice. To a
large extent, theological distinctions were now used to legitimate the clash of rival organizations, hungrily competing in
some areas for members in a limited market and engaged
in periodic "sheep-stealing" raids into each other's terri-
tories. [10]

These smoldering animosities flared up in 1770 with
the publication of the famous minutes of Wesley's Conference
and generated the so-called Calvinistic Controversy which
rent the "Gospel World" for at least a decade and embittered
relations between evangelicals even into the nineteenth century. At that Conference Wesley persuaded his preachers
to approve a minute which not only warned the Connexion
against incipient Antinomianism, but declared that it was
false to believe that man could do nothing in order to secure justification. When made public, the minutes fell into
the hands of Lady Huntingdon, Whitefield's patroness, who
misinterpreted them as a direct attack on Calvinism and a
denial of the sovereignty of God. Consequently, she closed
the undenominational college at Trevecca to Arminians even
after Wesley's preachers had signed a declaration at the
Bristol Conference in 1771 declaring the doctrine of justification by works "as a most perilous and abominable doctrine." A very bitter pamphlet war ensued between both
theological camps over the doctrine of free-will and predestination which degenerated into a vindictive campaign of personal abuse when the Calvinists August Toplady and Rowland
Hill entered the fray.

Nor was doctrine the only fault-line between evangelicals. Issues of church-order played an increasingly important role in distancing Methodists from evangelical Anglicans. The early "Gospel clergymen" had often shown few
scruples about field preaching or fraternization with Methodists and evangelical Dissenters, but these attitudes slowly
changed. Evangelical parish clergymen began to take an

increasingly strict interpretation of their duty to give full
canonical obedience to the established Church.   "Irregular"
and "half irregular" clergymen became increasingly rare,
regulars the norm.   Why was this?   Partly because evangelical clergymen became concerned at the way in which
their own casual itinerancy built up Nonconformity at the
expense of the Anglican church.   William Grimshaw, a first
generation evangelical clergyman, for instance, proudly told
John Newton at the end of his life that he knew of no fewer
than five Dissenting congregations in which the minister and
most of the members were awakened under his ministry.[11]
To second and third generation evangelical clergymen, however, Grimshaw's boast was more an object of embarrass-
ment than self-congratulation.   In 1788, Miles Atkinson,
representing a new breed of "regulars" complained that "the
people of the Godly ministers go over to the Dissenters."
"Can this be wondered at," Atkinson questioned, "when these
very ministers in all their private ministrations and often
their public ones, forsake the mode of worship in the Establishment, and adopt that of the Dissenters and even encourage the people when they have not faithful preachers
in the church to go and hear the Dissenters?"[12]

Atkinson was referring to a number of very real
problems that his generation had inherited from their forefathers.   First, there was what Charles Smyth has labelled
the "problem of continuity."[13]   An evangelical clergyman
would build up a great and fervent congregation but then die
or remove to another parish.   As likely as not, his replace-
ment was an "unconverted" incumbent whose ministry drove
the faithful either to form a new schismatic chapel or to
join one or another of the local Dissenting meetings sometimes, as in the case of Henry Venn, with the encouragement of their old pastor.   The frequency of this process
worried later evangelical Anglicans.   So did what John
Walsh has called the "problem of the eloquent convert."[14]
A parishioner of humble means and little education would
be called, under the preaching of an evangelical clergyman,
to enter the Anglican ministry, but because he did not possess a university education or the means of getting one, his
bishop would refuse to ordain him, and he would seek ordination in an evangelical Nonconformist denomination.   Secondly, field preaching broke down the protective walls of
church order and provided Nonconformity with a host of converts.   As Charles Simeon put it, "the clergymen beats the
bush, and the Dissenters catch the game."[15]   By the late
1780's, when a revived Dissent was once again pressing for

the repeal of the Test Act, and in the 1790's, when it began
to whisper menacingly of disestablishment, evangelical clergymen felt guilt and anxiety at the unforeseen results of their
irregularity and the reaction towards "regularity" consequently intensified.   Since evangelical Anglicans felt themselves
to be loyal members of the national establishment as well
as members of the Invisible Church of Christ, itinerancy
was frowned upon.   If the world was still Wesley's parish,
the parish, more than ever before, was becoming the well-
defined world of the newer breed of evangelical churchman.

There were other issues that increasingly separated
regular evangelical clergymen from their Nonconformist and
Methodist evangelical brethren.   As they became respectable,
beneficed churchmen, they increasingly disowned the enthusiastic doctrines of their forefathers and irregular con-
temporaries.   Unlike the Methodists who taught that instantaneous conversions were normative in Christian experience
and that man's heart was often drastically re-directed toward God before his mind had absorbed the full significance
of the "doctrines of grace," the regulars taught that grace
was mediated by quiet and rational means, and that the
Holy Spirit worked first in the intellect and only afterwards
in the affections.   Instantaneous conversion, consequently,
was not necessarily the correct pattern of Christian experience. [16]   Evangelical clergymen also frequently rejected the
belief of many Methodists that a strong feeling of assurance
was a normal, perhaps even necessary concomitant of justification, teaching instead that simply by relying on the atonement of Christ, Christians could be in a state of salvation
although they possessed no assurance of it.   The regulars
believed that Methodists of all varieties had placed too much
emphasis on emotionalism: salvation by feelings was not a
proper foundation for sound Christian doctrine.

A final factor making for regularity among the Anglican evangelicals and separating them from their allies in
the Gospel was their increasing articulation in associations
and groups.   A number of clerical societies, like those at
Elland, Rauceby, and in London, brought clergymen into
closer fraternity.   Here, matters of faith, order and pastoral practice were hammered out and codified for the direction of members.   Future clergymen were recruited for
the Anglican ministry and financed through a course at Oxford or Cambridge.   Propriety chapels and advowsons were
purchased to insure ministerial continuity and to prevent the
drain to Dissent.   Most importantly, these societies, con-

nected together by correspondence, became almost a quasi-
denomination for Evangelical regulars. This development
significantly affected the future role of evangelical churchmen in pan-evangelical societies, for the clerical societies
not only united the regulars, but created an internal cohesion
that insulated them to some extent from complete involvement with evangelicals outside the Anglican fold. As we
shall see, this increased the reluctance of many evangelical
churchmen to participate with other evangelicals in the pan-
evangelical movement of the late eighteenth century.

III.

It was perhaps surprising that the divisions of the
Calvinistic Controversy in the 1770's and the issues that
separated Churchman from Dissenters and Methodists did
not permanently destroy the conception of pan-evangelicalism which survived to burst out again in the 1790's. That
it survived at all was due to George Whitefield more than
any other man. Though he died in the year the Calvinistic
Controversy broke out, he left behind him both within the
old Dissenting denominations he had helped to revive, and
the new evangelical societies he had helped to create, an
evangelical "catholic spirit" which inspired a later generation to rediscover something of the accord of 1739. It is
to George Whitefield, therefore, more than to John Wesley
or the regular evangelical Anglicans that we must look for
the wellsprings of the late eighteenth-century pan-evangelical
impulse.

Wesley's first concern, as we have seen, was with
the Church of England. If he was patently prejudiced toward Anglicanism, he was more or less latently prejudiced
against Dissent--witness his habit of terming the Baptists
"Anabaptists"! This blunted the impact of his ministry on
Dissent and helped to create barriers between Wesleyans
and evangelical Nonconformists which lasted for over a century. Whitefield, by contrast, was ecclesiastically far less
prejudiced, at least within the context of the revival.[17] Sharing a common Calvinism with the Dissenters, he was far
more cordial in his relations with them than Wesley. Because he did not try to force them into the Anglican mold,
they received him more eagerly than any other churchman.[18]
It was indeed by the ministry of George Whitefield that many
first generation evangelical churchmen and Dissenters were
awakened and by them the Whitefieldite heritage was trans-

mitted to Calvinists of the second and third generations--
those who produced the great united evangelical societies of
the 1790's. [19] The missionary-minded, undogmatic Calvinism that was the doctrinal cement of pan-evangelicalism was
largely inspired by Whitefield.

It is something of a paradox that Whitefield's failure
to unite properly his own societies assisted the union of
evangelicals within the pan-evangelical societies of the late
eighteenth century. Both John Wesley and George Whitefield
disclaimed any concern for party, but Wesley built up a
Connexion of formidable cohesion and loyalty which was compared with the Jesuit order, and his control over it earned
him the sobriquet "Pope John."[20] Indeed, the loyalty, cohesion, and discipline of his Connexion was such that it effectively insulated Wesleyanism from any deep involvement
with Christian societies beyond its fold.[21] Whitefield, however, abided by his "Catholic" principles and remained the
generous, roving evangelist rather than the ecclesiastical
leader. He did not have the time nor the inclination to gov-
ern societies properly, even those that he had created.[22]
When Whitefield died, he left behind him far more spiritual
children in evangelical Dissent and the Church of England
than in his own small and loosely-associated societies. Yet
in his weakness as a party leader lay his strength as the
inspiration of pan-evangelicalism. His type of broad, emotional, missionary Calvinism was the common denominator
among many different chapels and societies. His spiritual
children, though scattered in many different "causes," recognized in him a common paternity. By his itinerancy,
Whitefield had kept many groups of Christians in fraternal
association. In a real sense, George Whitefield could justly
be claimed as the spiritual founder of the London Missionary
Society and the other great pan-evangelical societies of the
late eighteenth century which will be examined in this book.

At least three new denominations that would later
figure prominently in the pan-evangelical impulse owed
their foundations in part to George Whitefield. Lady Huntingdon had founded, at least with his initial help, her famous connexion of chapels into which she hoped to place evangelical clergymen. But as the Connexion matured and developed, Nonconformists were also allowed to participate.
In 1781, she was forced to license her chapels under the
Toleration Act thereby pushing the Connexion into practical
Dissent even though the forms of the Church of England were
still used in worship. Connexion chapels were ministered

by the itinerant preachers who received their appointments
from the Countess herself and, when she died, from a central board of trustees.   A preacher would remain in an as-
signed chapel for a short period of time before moving on
to the next appointment elsewhere.   Each chapel, in turn,
would contribute to the itinerant's upkeep.   Lady Huntingdon
owned only seven or eight chapels outright, but many more
were informally linked with her name. [23]

The English Calvinistic Methodists and the Whitefieldites, on the other hand, evolved out of the societies that
Whitefield himself had established in his life time.   After
1770, they joined together into a very loose federation which,
unlike the Countess's Connexion, did not adopt a uniform
system of administration or worship.   Some chapels were
independently governed by a board of trustees which appointed
a permanent pastor.   Others were supplied by an itinerant
ministry.   While most of the chapels closely followed the
forms of the Church of England, some were not as strict in
their forms of worship and often followed the practice of the
Independents.   Though each chapel managed its own affairs,
members considered themselves bound together by common
interests.   Their ministers, for example, participated in
each other's ordinations and helped out in times of need
and crisis. [24]

The Welsh Calvinistic Methodists were largely indi-
genous in origin, owing their existence to Welsh leaders
like Howell Harris and Daniel Rowlands, yet they too had
close connections with Whitefield, and their societies were
for a time in close association and union with the English
Calvinistic Methodist societies.   Indeed, during Whitefield's
absence in America between 1743 and 1748, the direction of
his English preachers was given over to Howell Harris. [25]
Formal ties between the Welsh societies and the Church of
England continued far longer than their English counterparts
and it was not until 1811 that they formally separated into
a denomination modelled on the Presbyterian system of
church government.

Many Independent and Particular Baptist chapels, as
we have seen, owed a great deal to Whitefield's ministry,
but unlike the newer denominations they remained unorgan-
ized except by way of regional association.   The small number of English Presbyterians who had not fallen into Unitari-
anism and the evangelical Presbyterians in Scotland, both of
the Church of Scotland and Seceders, likewise were profoundly influenced by George Whitefield.

Many of the evangelical Anglican clergy--the "Gospel clergy"--had also been greatly influenced by both Wesley and Whitefield. Whether Calvinists or Arminians, several were, like them, highly "irregular." Henry Venn, John Berridge, William Grimshaw, and others left their parishes periodically to itinerate on extended "Gospel rambles." But, as we have seen, most second generation evangelical churchmen reacted against the irregularities of their forefathers and patterned their ministries on the accepted order of the established church. Still, a small remnant of ecclesiastically "left wing" evangelical churchmen carried on the "irregular" tradition of Wesley and Whitefield well into the nineteenth century. These included famous men whom we shall later meet, such as John Eyre, curate of Weston in 1779 and then Cecil's curate at Lewes in 1781; David Simpson, the assistant curate of St. Michael's in Macclesfield; Robert Hawker, vicar of Charles near Plymouth; Thomas Haweis, rector of Aldwinckle from 1764; and Rowland Hill, minister of Surrey Chapel in London. Most of these men were Calvinists though some, like Robert Hawker, tended to Hypercalvinism. One or two, such as David Simpson, were associated with Wesley. But all shared a common "catholic" view of the church. David Simpson, for example, could say:

> I confess, though a clergyman of the Establishment, I see no evil in joining for public worship or social intercourse, with any of the denominations of Christians. I hear what passes with candour, join where I approve, and reject whatever appears contrary to Scripture, and the plain dictates of sound reason and common sense. I am well aware this comes not up to the full standard of orthodoxy. But if such conduct constitutes a bad churchman, I feel not anxious to be accounted a good one. [26]

Because of this spirit, "irregular" evangelical churchmen moved with great ease between Church and Dissent.

The sense of denominational identity sat lightly on those who moved within the Whitefieldite Calvinistic milieu. This is illustrated by the astonishing facility with which they migrated from one denominational grouping to another. This denominational mobility is perhaps best understood by examining the spiritual biographies of the men who led the pan-evangelical movement of the late eighteenth century. We know who these people were, yet in so many cases,

it is difficult to determine to which denominations they were
affiliated. John Ball of London, for example, was called
at various times and in various places a Calvinistic Methodist and an Independent. Joseph Brooksbank, also from London, was listed as an Independent and a Minister in Lady
Huntingdon's Connexion. Thomas Haweis was both a trustee
of the same Connexion and an Anglican clergyman. Matthew
Wilks, at various times in his life, was a Calvinistic Methodist, a member of Lady Huntingdon's Connexion and an Independent, while Rowland Hill of London and Archibald Douglas
of Reading had such varied denominational backgrounds that
even their closest friends could not determine exactly where
they stood on matters of church polity.

Another indication of the degree to which Calvinistic
denominations were fluid at this time is the number of what
Ruth Rouse calls "Borderland Churches," or churches that
defied a denominational label. [27] Perhaps the most famous
undenominational church that appeared in the 1780's was
Rowland Hill's Surrey Chapel built for him in 1782. It was
open to preachers of all denominations, enjoying at various
times sermons from the Baptists John Ryland, Sr. and Samuel Medley; the Anglicans John Newton, Henry Venn, and
John Berridge; and the Independents Joseph Slatterie and
William Jay. [28] The home of Robert Haldane at Airthrey,
with its temporary chapel fitted out in the stable, became
for several years Surrey Chapel's counterpart in Scotland. [29]

Denominational mobility was perhaps nurtured in many
leaders of pan-evangelicalism by the circumstances of their
Christian upbringings. For instance, Edward Williams, the
great Rotherham Independent and tutor of so many evangelical
Nonconformists, was brought up an Anglican, came under the
influence of the Welsh Calvinistic Methodists, and was eventually ordained an Independent minister. [30] Thomas Raffles
of Liverpool, a future director of the London Missionary Society, was brought up by his mother (a Wesleyan Methodist),
baptized an Anglican, educated at a Baptist boarding school,
and eventually became an Independent minister. [31] Some
second and third generation evangelical clergymen also had
mixed religious educations. William Goode, the future vicar
of St. Andrew's, London, and a Bible Society advocate, was
brought up in a family that had migrated from Church to
Dissent. In later youth, he and his brother John met with
another friend, the future Oxford Baptist James Hinton, for
prayer and Bible reading. After attending the undenominational seminary at Newport Pagnell, William decided to be

ordained a clergyman in the Church of England though his
brother remained an Independent and later took a church at
Spitalfields, London. 32   John Eyre, the future Anglican Secretary of the London Missionary Society and editor of the
Evangelical Magazine, had a similar background.   Brought
up in a very liberal Calvinistic family, John later opted for
the Church of England while his brother Thomas became
deacon of the Particular Baptist church at Launceston.   Many
more examples of early "liberal" Calvinistic families, all
nurtured in the Whitefieldite tradition, could be cited which
would illustrate even further why some evangelical Calvinists
were highly receptive to pan-evangelicalism in the late eighteenth century.

IV.

Though the years between 1770 and 1780 were bitter
and divisive ones for the evangelicals, they were more united
than they were perhaps aware.   As we have already seen,
in this troubled decade Calvinists were pitted against Wesleyans in the theological controversy ignited by the Wesleyans doctrinal minutes of 1770.   Many Anglican regulars
in their quest for ecclesiastical respectability had severed
ties with evangelical brethren outside the establishment.   As
we shall see, Particular Baptists had closed their communion
tables to non-Baptists.   But even in the midst of controversy
and division and largely because of the Whitefieldite inheritance, there always existed centripetal forces of unity and
reintegration that would eventually bring into harmonious relations not only the Calvinists, but other evangelicals as well.
The "Gospel World," for all its bickerings, was a cultural
and ideological entity, rather like the "left" in the modern
political world.   Its unities of thought and outlook were always present and capable of reasserting themselves in a
propitious climate.   Evangelicals realized, for example, that
they shared an experience which marked them off decisively
from all others and ranged them together in the fellowship of
the Invisible Church of Christ to which all "vital" Christians
belonged.   This evangelical experience was not a matter of
theological reflection, but rather a general experiential crisis,
rooted in a deep-seated sense of sinfulness and spiritual in-
sufficiency and a thirst for assurance and personal salvation.
This experience had been shared not only by the Puritans,
but by a host of others throughout Christian history.   Joseph
Milner, whose Church History (first published in 1794) traced
the evangelical succession through the centuries, wrote:

> How uniformly similar are the dealings of God in
> the Kingdom of grace in all ages. The experience
> of Augustine, a Christian who lived in the latter
> end of the fifth century, is precisely the same as
> that of any Christian in the eighteenth. The phrase-
> ology may differ ... but it requires no uncommon
> discernment to see that it is the work of the same
> God, leading to the same ends.[33]

In the changeless nature of a Christian experience shared by
an army of Christians past and present, drawn from many
churches and denominations, evangelicals found a sense of
spiritual security. Nonconformists and Churchmen alike re-
joiced to find that others had fought through the same spiritual and temporal conflicts as themselves. John Newton
once told his congregation that "my sentiments are confirmed
by the suffrage of thousands who have lived before me, and
with many with whom I have personally conversed in different places and circumstances, unknown to each other; yet
all have received the same views because taught by the same
spirit."[34]

If theologies could divide, experience could unite.
Even in doctrine, evangelicals sensed that they were closer
together than they realized in the heat of controversy. They
held in common not only the biblical Word but the leading
doctrines it contained, including original sin, justification
by faith, and illumination and sanctification by the Holy Spirit.
But the central doctrine that transcended in importance all
of the others was justification by faith, the articulus stantis
vel cadentis ecclesiae of Nonconformist as well as Anglican
belief.[35] John Wesley agreed with Whitefield that the difference between evangelicals was small compared with their
agreement on justification by faith.[36] Joseph Milner, a Calvinist, spoke of justification by faith as the "distinguishing
doctrine of Christianity, without which indeed, the Gospel is
a mere name.... What are all the ideas of Christian government and discipline," he asked, "what all rites and cere-
monies ... what a thousand such subjects, compared with
the article of Justification?"[37] Most evangelicals, regard-
less of their theological biases, would have heartily agreed.
Here Anglican evangelicals felt more in common with their
Methodist or Dissenting brothers in the Gospel than with
their High Church colleagues of the cloth. They had experienced the same salvation. They believed in the same
essential theological doctrines. Though episcopalians, they
did not hold with High Churchmen that episcopacy was the

esse of the church. It was ancient, apostolical, beneficent,
but not of dominical authority. For evangelical Anglicans,
the "Church of Christ" was the visible body of all regenerate
believers. It alone could be held to be one, holy and catholic. If they did not like Dissent, they could not completely
condemn it, for they realized that between Church and Dissent
stood no substantial spiritual gap. Evangelical churchmen,
therefore, experienced a conflict of mind and heart. They
knew in their minds that they were respectable and loyal
members of the national establishment, but they also knew
in their hearts that they were evangelicals sharing with
other evangelicals a common faith and experience that transcended denominational barriers and theological parties.
This conflict of mind and heart--the problem of divided loy-
alties--was later overcome by what Geoffrey Best has called
the principle of "practical inconsistency."[38] Evangelical
churchmen allowed in their scheme of things an established
church which they conceived to be the "ideal" visible church.
But without repudiating their loyalty to the national establishment, they also acknowledged the existence of an invisible
church that transcended denominational barriers. The interests of the Church of Christ, wherever they appeared
manifest in the world, claimed prior allegiance.

By the 1780's, a realization of these shared funda-
mentals began to reassert itself and a reaction began to set
in against the acrimonies of the Calvinistic Controversy.
Evangelicals saw that they had perhaps placed too much
emphasis on circumstantials, not enough on essentials. The
death of August Toplady in 1778 coincided with a relaxation
of the "rigors of Calvinism" and a reappraisal of the Moderate Calvinism which had been held by many Dissenters and
not a few evangelical Anglicans. The roots of Moderate
Calvinism run back to the early seventeenth century and beyond.[39] At the Huguenot Academy of Samur in France,
Moyse Amyraut and John Cameron had developed a "hypothetical universalism" which veered away from the rigidities
of the conservative Calvinists. In England, moderates like
Davenant, delegate to the Synod of Dort, held similar theories. The Anglican Homilies and Articles seemed to countenance a milder and more ambiguous form of predestination
which appealed strongly to many evangelicals.

Eighteenth-century evangelicals were usually restless
under the Calvinistic label. They resented the assertion
that they subscribed ex animo to the whole of Calvin's In-
stitutes, still more to the implication that they were the

doctrinal heirs of those who had beheaded King Charles I.
They were embarrassed by the general belief that they regarded man as a mere automaton and God as the author of
sin.   It was particularly in the theological writings of second and third generation evangelicals like the Anglican Charles
Simeon, the Baptist Andrew Fuller, and the Independent Edward Williams that Moderate Calvinism was developed in
forms yet more moderate. 40

The moderates wished to dissociate themselves from
what they believed were three unscriptural doctrines, viz.
particular redemption, limited atonement, and predestined
reprobation.   Particular redemption and limited atonement
taught that Christ's blood was shed only for the elect.   The
moderates wanted to stress, however, that Christ shed his
blood for all men.   The atonement of Christ, they believed,
was a "general benefit" for which no man would be excluded
save from unbelief.   But this was not exactly Arminianism
or Universalism, for if the benefit of Christ's Passion was
of infinite sufficiency for all mankind, it did not follow that
the whole world would effectively partake of it.   Even though
the merits of Christ were enough to assuage the sins of the
whole world, these merits would be appropriated only by
those who possessed the saving faith to lay hold of them,
and only to the elect was this saving faith given.   In other
words, if in one sense there was general redemption, there
was in another sense particular election.   Grace, though
sufficient for all, proved efficient only for the elect who
possessed special or prevenient grace which allowed them
to repent and believe.   But the Moderate Calvinists felt no
constraints in offering salvation to all mankind since it was
for all that Christ had died.   Unlike the "no offer of grace"
theology of the Hypercalvinists, the exponents of hypothetical
universalism combined acceptance of predestined election
with belief in the indiscriminate preaching of the Gospel to
all unbelievers.   They dissociated themselves firmly from
the idea of predestined reprobation which appeared to make
God the author of sin.   If man's salvation was of God, his
damnation was his own fault conditioned upon disobedience
and foreseen by his Creator.

Moderate Calvinism served at least three irenic functions.   First, it provided second and third generation evangelical Calvinists with the kind of theological unity that Whitefield had provided for the first.   Simeon, Fuller, and Williams were all basically in agreement on their Calvinistic
beliefs.   Second, by softening the harshness of the predes-

tinarian scheme, Moderate Calvinism eventually brought the
Arminian and Calvinistic camps closer together than they
had ever been since the early years of the Revival. This
is not to say that all was peace between Calvinists and Wesleyans, but much of the bitterness of the 1770's was greatly
tempered by a new era of theological moderation. Finally,
the moderate position gave impetus to the growing missionary
urge. The Moderate Calvinists believed that none could with
certainty know who the elect were--that pertained to the secret counsel of God. He knew for certain, however, that
on the basis of the revealed will of God, it was his duty "to
go into the world and preach the Gospel to every creature."
This command was fully obeyed in the foundation of numerous foreign and domestic missionary societies at the end of
the century.

There were other currents that led to a perceptible
softening of doctrinal rigidity. Among the Baptists who stood
aloof from their non-Baptist brethren on the question of en-
try into the covenant of church membership, there was a
parallel movement toward moderation. The old controversy
between Baptists and paedobaptists had been two-fold. Did
Christ institute believer's adult baptism in the form of im-
mersion, or the baptism of children in the form of sprink-
ling? Was spiritual regeneration separate from, or con-
tingent upon the baptismal act? These theoretical issues
had divided Baptists and non-Baptists for ages, but it was
on the practical level of worship and ritual that the controversy had been most serious. Since the Lord's Supper was
the highest statement of fellowship for all Christians, it was
important to the Baptists to admit to the communion table
only those who had been baptized as believers. Consequently, prior to about 1780, paedobaptists had been barred from
the communion table in most Particular Baptist meetings.
This appeared to some tantamount to an assertion on the
part of the Baptists that they did not recognize most Protestants as Christians.

The controversy over open communion lay dormant until 1772
when Daniel Turner of Abingdon and John Ryland, Jr. of
Northampton published statements favoring open communion,
and they were followed by Robert Robinson of Cambridge and
Robert Hall then in Bristol. [41] What brought these men to
a moderate position on communion is uncertain. Perhaps
the influence of evangelicalism on a younger generation of
pastors had something to do with it. All we know is that
there came into being a new breed of "open communionists"

who, in the tradition of Bunyan, welcomed other evangelicals
to their table. The impact of this irenic theological development, as we shall see, was very important for the future
pan-evangelical impulse.

    Before concluding this chapter, it must be pointed out
once again that the growth of fraternity among evangelicals,
even at a later period, did not go unchallenged. Among
many Nonconformists one can detect a conservative reaction
against what seemed to them an indiscriminate and premature abandonment of the denominational traditions and beliefs handed down from their Puritan forefathers. In the
rush towards a more "catholic spirit" there seemed grave
danger of becoming denominationally nondescript and theo-
logically lax. Like the Anglican "regulars," so the Nonconformist conservatives were anxious to preserve their
sense of historic identity. Walter Wilson, the London Independent, expressed this feeling sharply some years later.
"By giving way too much to that laxity of principle, and
indiscriminate zeal which distinguished the Methodists," he
wrote, "Dissenters have lost that peculiarity of character
for which their forefathers were so eminent."[42] Though in
some ways sympathetic to the pan-evangelical feeling, Wilson defended the denominational conservatives who had pre-
served their own heritage and had not been stampeded into
a hurried acceptance of a fashionable but "spurious" and
imprecise evangelical pietism.

    This reaction was most evident in the Particular
Baptist camp. Open communion, it seemed to many conservative "closed communionists," was an untenable position
because it denied basic Baptist principles. To open the
communion table to non-Baptists, they argued, was to recognize ipso facto the validity of infant baptism and by implication to deny the doctrine of the baptism of believers.
The fact that there still were many prominent closed communionists at the end of the eighteenth century explains why,
to a large degree, the Baptists (like the "regular" Anglicans) tended occasionally to dissociate themselves from the
pan-evangelical movement and why, when pan-evangelical societies were later formed, they were at first reluctant to
patronize them.

    This type of reaction was not powerful enough to re-
strain the spirit of unity which began to well up in the 1780's,
but as we shall see it continued to harass the course of evangelical union and in the early nineteenth century helped to

produce the Congregational and Baptist Unions which were in part a reaction to pan-evangelicalism and an assertion of denominational loyalty. For the time-being, however, pan-evangelicalism was in the ascendant to give birth to a host of interdenominational societies and associations. To this development we shall now turn.

NOTES

1. For a discussion of early union movements see D. Bahlman, The Moral Revolution of 1688 (1957); G. V. Portus, Caritas Anglicana (1912); J. Woodward, An Account of the Rise and Progress of the Religious Societies (1701).
2. J. Humphreys, Experience (1742), 27.
3. MS Bangor 34: "Journal of an Early Methodist," 24 August 1740 [Courtesy of J. D. Walsh].
4. J. Wesley, Journal (N. Curnock, ed., 1909), VII, 486.
5. W. E. Collins called Wesley the "founder of undenominationalism." It would have been more accurate to give this appellation to George Whitefield. See W. E. Collins, Typical English Churchmen (1902), 218.
6. Cited in A. J. Lewis, Zinzendorf the Ecumenical Pioneer (1962), 119. Cf., E. Zorb, "Count Zinzendorf: An 18th Century Ecumenist," The Ecumenical Review, IX (1957), 419 f.
7. A. H. Williams, "The First Methodist Societies in Wales," Bathafarn, XV (1960), 34 f.
8. J. Milner, Practical Sermons (4th ed. 1821), II, 250.
9. W. J. Townsend, et al., A New History of Methodism (1909), I, 320 f.
10. For early examples of this phenomenon, see J. Godber, History of Bedfordshire (1969), 451; T. Cocking, The History of Wesleyan Methodism in Grantham and Its Vicinity (1836), 270; R. F. Skinner, Nonconformity in Shropshire (1964), 25.
11. Cf., J. D. Walsh, "The Yorkshire Evangelicals in the Eighteenth Century" (Cambridge University PhD. Thesis, 1956), 113.
12. Ibid., 331 f.
13. C. H. E. Smyth, Simeon and Church Order (1940), 250 ff.
14. J. D. Walsh, "Methodism at the End of the Eighteenth Century" in R. E. Davies and E. G. Rupp, A History of the Methodist Church in Great Britain (1965), I, 294.

15. Cited in W. Carus, Memoirs of the Life of the Rev.
     Charles Simeon (1847), 139.
16. Cf., Elisabeth Jay, The Religion of the Heart (1979),
     59 f.
17. Cf., L. Tyerman, The Life of the Rev. George White-
     field (1867) I, 534.
18. Cf., Ibid., 395 fn.
19. Whitefield had been instrumental in converting many
     Baptists and Independents. See C. E. Shipley, The
     Baptists of Yorkshire (1912); G. Hughes, With Free-
     dom Fired (1955), 10 ff.; C. E. Watson, "Whitefield
     and Congregationalism," Transactions of the Congre-
     gational Historical Society, VIII (1922), 171 ff.;
     A. H. W. Harrison, The Evangelical Revival and
     Christian Reunion (1942), 129 ff.
20. Whitefield said of Wesley's catholic spirit: "Most talk
     of a catholic spirit; but it is only till they have
     brought people into the pale of their own church.
     This is downright sectarianism, not catholicism." See
     G. Whitefield, Works (1771), I, 372.
21. Cf., M. Edwards, After Wesley (1935), 123.
22. Cf., Whitefield, Works (1771), II, 169 f.
23. See J. B. Figgis, The Countess of Huntingdon and Her
     Connexion (1891); A. C. H. Seymour, The Life and
     Times of Selina Countess of Huntingdon (1844); F. A.
     Bretherton, The Countess of Huntingdon (1940).
24. See J. Campbell, Letters on Wesleyan Methodism ...
     and a History of Whitefield's Churches (1847); T.
     Timpson, British Ecclesiastical History (1838), 456
     ff.; Edwin Welch (ed.) Two Calvinistic Methodist
     Chapels 1743-1811 (1975).
25. See Watson, op. cit., 174 f.
26. Cited in A. L. Hunt, David Simpson and the Evangel-
     ical Revival (1927), 247.
27. R. Rouse and S. Neill, eds., A History of the Ecu-
     menical Movement (1954), 315.
28. G. Redford and J. A. James, eds., The Autobiography
     of the Rev. William Jay (1855), 48; E. Sidney, The
     Life of the Rev. Rowland Hill (1834), 137; G. Weight,
     The First and Last Sermons Delivered in Surrey Chap-
     el (1833), 5 ff.
29. A. Haldane, The Lives of Robert ... and His Brother,
     James Alexander Haldane (1855), 273.
30. Cf., W. T. Owen, Edward Williams (1963).
31. T. S. Raffles, Memoirs of the Life and Ministry of the
     Rev. Thomas Raffles (1864), 2 ff.
32. T. Coleman, Memorials of the Independent Churches in

Northamptonshire (1853), 285; W. Goode, A Memoir of the Late Rev. William Goode (1828), 7 fn.

33. J. Milner, Completed Works (1794), VIII, 387.

34. J. Newton, The Works of the Rev. John Newton (2nd ed. 1816), II, 573.

35. J. D. Walsh, "The Yorkshire Evangelicals," 37.

36. L. Tyerman, The Life and Times of the Rev. John Wesley (1870), I, 375.

37. J. Milner, Selection of Tracts and Essays (1810), 417.

38. G. F. A. Best, "The Evangelicals and the Established Church in the Early Nineteenth Century," Journal of Theological Studies, X (1959), 71 f.

39. I am grateful to John Walsh for sharing with me his unpublished "Theology of the Evangelical Revival." Much of the following material is based on this article.

40. Cf., Smyth, op. cit., 185; Owen, op. cit., 142; E. F. Clipsham, "Andrew Fuller and Fullerism," The Baptist Quarterly, XX (1963), 97 ff.

41. See D. Turner, A Modest Plea for Free Communion at the Lord's Table (1772); R. Robinson, The General Doctrine of Toleration applied to the particular case of free Communion (1781); R. Hall, The Duty and Importance of Free Communion Among Real Christians of Every Denomination (n. d.).

42. W. Wilson, The History and Antiquities of the Dissenting Churches and Meeting Houses in London (1808), IV, 550.

I.

Interdenominational cooperation among evangelicals,
which found its fruition during the 1790's, owed not a little
to several previous experiments in united effort.   The first
of these was the Prayer Call of the early 1740's which,
early as it was, influenced the direction of the foreign missionary movement half a century later.   At this time a
group of Scottish ministers led by John Erskine of Edinburgh periodically met together in prayer and intercession.
Not much is known about these early prayer meetings or
even exactly why they took place, but they paralleled in a
remarkable fashion Philip Doddridge's plan of 1742 to establish quarterly prayer meetings in England as a first step
towards a foreign missionary movement. [1]   The Prayer Call
was not confined to Britain, for the correspondence of Erskine with Jonathan Edwards in New England led the Con-
necticut theologian to produce his famous tract entitled An
Humble Attempt to Promote Explicit Agreement and Visible
Union of God's People in Extraordinary Prayer.   Disturbed
by the deplorable state of religion in America, divisions
within the Church of Scotland, the Jacobite uprisings in
Northern Britain, the persecutions of Protestants in France
and increasing wickedness and luxury all over the world,
Edwards encouraged Christians of different denominations
to unite in fervent prayer in anticipation of the imminent
millennium.   Many years later, Edward's Humble Attempt
inspired Baptists in England to organize the famous Prayer
Call of 1784 which also called upon Christians of all denominations to join the Baptists in united prayer for revival
and mission. [2]   In turn, the Prayer Call movement did much,
according to the evangelical founding fathers of the London
Missionary Society, to encourage the establishment of an un-

23

denominational institution that would finally unite the evangelical denominations in foreign missions.

Already by the mid-eighteenth century, the early Prayer Call movement may possibly have inspired one or two interdenominational societies.   The first of these was perhaps the Society for Promoting Religious Knowledge Among the Poor founded in 1750.   The "Book Society" as it was better known, gave away to the poor Bibles and "other good books" in the hope that "under the divine influence, the tendencies of corrupt nature may receive a timely check, and the powerful influence of vicious examples, in these sinful times, be more effectively guarded against."[3]   It was hoped that because the Society was "wholly void of all party views" that it would "engage others of every Christian denomination among us, who truly fear GOD, love protestant religion and liberties, and wish well to immortal souls, to countenance, encourage, and promote it."[4]   Predating the pan-evangelical Religious Tract Society by almost fifty years, the Book Society numbered among its patrons evangelicals like Lady Huntingdon, Thomas Haweis, John Newton, John Ryland, Henry Venn, and many others.[5]

The formation of the Book Society was closely followed by Wesley's refounding of the Society for Reformation of Manners in 1757.   This new society attempted, like its predecessor in the late seventeenth century, to improve the manners of the lower classes by legal threat and literary encouragement and to agitate for laws that would check the profaneness of the British Sunday.   The Society was undenominational and included in 1763 fifty Wesleyans, twenty Whitefieldites, twenty Anglicans and seventy Dissenters.   By 1765, however, it was heavily in debt due in part to a verdict secured against it for using false evidence in the Court of the King's Bench and it had to be closed down one year later.[6]

The first major interdenominational society after the Calvinistic Controversy was the Naval and Military Bible Society, founded in 1779 by several Wesleyans and Anglicans. The purpose of this society, as its name implied, was to provide the British forces, both at home and abroad, with Bibles and religious tracts.   It therefore anticipated the pan-evangelical British and Foreign Bible Society by over twenty years.[7]

By the 1780's, the evangelicals had as yet not established an interdenominational missionary society.   But this did not mean that they had not tried. In 1783, Thomas Coke, the Wesleyan, proposed founding an undenominational missionary society which would embrace all evangelicals, Arminians and Calvinists alike. Though Coke's "Plan for the Establishment of Missions among the Heathen" never came to fruition, it anticipated the pan-evangelical London Missionary Society by eleven years. [8] Four years later appeared the Society for the Abolition of the Slave Trade which was an interdenominational attempt to ban slavery through Parliamentary legislation. Though not a foreign missionary society, the Abolition Society nevertheless led many evangelicals to see in the West Indies and in Africa virgin territory for a future interdenominational missionary effort. [9]

The greatest organizational response to the irenic developments that we have been discussing, however, was the Sunday School Movement of the mid 1780's. The Sunday School movement which began simultaneously in England and Wales was a voluntary affair financed largely by the middle class to supplement the inadequate number of poor schools built in the early half of the eighteenth century. [10] In this sense it was partly a revival and partly a continuation of the early Charity School movement. Unlike the Charity School movement, however, the Sunday Schools soon became to a large extent organizationally undenominational. At Stockport, for example, the local Sunday School established in 1784 was managed by a committee of gentlemen belonging to the various Nonconformist denominations and the Church of England. [11] At Manchester in the same year, a committee composed of Churchmen and Dissenters and even Roman Catholics united to form a Sunday School while in Coventry, George Burder, a local Independent minister, wrote a letter to the Mercury urging the adoption of a similar plan. [12] The Sunday School movement was so popular by 1785 that prominent religious leaders of the day including Bishop Bathurst and John Wesley gave it their unqualified support. [13]

For the first two or three years, the Sunday School movement was only loosely organized on a national level. But out of the modest Sunday School established in London by the Baptist layman William Fox, there grew up in 1785 the Society Established in London for the Support and Encouragement of Sunday Schools or, as it was better known, the Sunday School Society. [14] Directed by a committee of twenty-four laymen, half churchmen and half Dissenters, the Society gave away to its affiliated Sunday Schools spelling books, Bibles, grants of money, and timely organizational

advice. It recommended strongly that in order to avoid interdenominational conflict, students should not read denominational catechisms on the Sabbath, but instead restrict themselves to reading the Old and New Testaments.[15] It was also suggested that on Sunday, scholars should attend a place
of worship chosen by their parents. Because of its undenominational plan, the Society (in the beginning at least) was
approved by the Archbishop of Canterbury and the Bishops
of Salisbury and Llandaff, recommended by the Dean of
Lincoln in a widely publicized charge and applauded by men
as dissimilar in outlook as Robert Raikes, Thomas Charles,
and the Unitarian Joseph Priestley.[16]

It is difficult to determine to what degree the Sunday
School movement was meant to be an interdenominational,
church-oriented affair. Many, of course, saw the Sunday
Schools simply as instruments of social control to stem the
tide of vice and immorality. Viewed in this light, the
schools merit comparison with the earlier societies for the
reformation of manners. Others, however, saw the Sunday
Schools as excellent vehicles through which to inculcate undenominational Protestant Christianity. The Baptist James
Dore, for example, claimed that the Sunday School in his
London neighborhood was "animated by the very soul of Protestantism, and breathes its genuine spirit." He went on to
say that it was "pleasing to see Churchmen, and Dissenters,
Friends, Paedobaptists and Anti-paedobaptists, cordially
unite in supporting this truly Protestant cause."[17] In the
same spirit, Rowland Hill of Surrey Chapel hoped that children who were encouraged to attend in rotation Anglican
church and Nonconformist meeting house on Sunday, would
grow up to find "themselves at liberty from the narrow con-
tracted spirit of a party: so as that if they meet with a bad
minister in a meeting they may seek for a good one in a
church; and if a bad preacher be found in a church, they,
on the other hand, may seek for a good one in a meeting."[18]
So too, many evangelicals imagined that the Sunday School
movement itself would perhaps have an even more irenic effect on the adults who subscribed to it. Robert Hawker,
vicar of Charles near Plymouth, thought the plan of many
Sunday Schools "an excellent remedy to heal those needless
divisions, for it embraces in its bosom all orders, sects
and persuasions."[19] Indeed, the Sunday School Society could
congratulate itself by 1789 "that the mutual animosities which
have in former times disunited the professors of the Christian faith, have now given way to a more liberal construction
of each others motives."[20] Self congratulation, however,

was premature for, as we shall next see, the Sunday School movement received in 1789 a temporary though damaging blow from the French Revolution.

II.

The outbreak of revolution in France in 1789 affected the interdenominational movement, especially as it was institutionalized in the early interdenominational organizations, in two rather contradictory ways.   In the long run, the Revolution would unite Dissenters and Churchmen behind their government in a concerted effort to protect English liberties and religion against French radicalism and atheism.   But this unity was enjoyed only after the French Revolution veered to the left.   The immediate impact of the Revolution on an emerging pan-evangelicalism was extremely divisive.

Many Dissenters applauded the Revolution in 1789 because they believed that the new constitutional liberties given to French Protestants were a portent of the repeal of Nonconformist disabilities in their own country.   Joseph Priestley's position in this regard is well known; but even orthodox Dissenters welcomed the Revolution with enthusiasm.   In 1792, for example, David Bogue, the Independent minister at Gosport, preached a very pro-Revolutionary sermon at Salters Hall in London. [21]   Robert Haldane of Glasgow echoed Bogue's words in the north. [22]   Both of these men believed that ultimately the Revolution would not only benefit Nonconformity, but also deal a deadly blow to the Roman Church whose fall they felt to be imminent.   To many evangelical Anglicans, however, the Bogues and the Haldanes and the Dissenters they represented appeared to be "perfect democrats" set on destroying Church and State.   Thomas Robinson, vicar of St. Mary's in Leicester, wrote to William Wilberforce in 1792 regarding Nonconformist support of the Revolution:[23]

> I am sorry to observe, that among the numerous class of dissenters, whose aim is to abolish every national establishment of religion among us, there are many of real piety.   I know not how they can reconcile their conduct with the Scripture injunctions to obey magistrates & follow after peace. But, by an unhappy association of ideas, they seem to think, that while they are opposing our Church they are doing God service and promoting the cause of his truth.

John Newton, hitherto one of the most catholic-minded "regulars," believed in 1793 that "all the Dissenters, even the
orthodox not excepted, are republicans and enemies to government."[24] Even as late as 1801, John Crosse, another
"regular," told Wilberforce that political Dissent "so far as
nature prevails ... must accomplish the downfall of the Establishment."[25] Remarks like these served to promote unfounded fears that English Dissenters were agents, or at
least dupes, of the Continental Illuminati whose clandestine
conspiracy might soon subvert Church and government in
England as it had done in France.[26] Such fears did much
to hinder the emerging pan-evangelicalism of the late eighteenth century. They not only brought the interdenominational Anti-Slavery campaign to a temporary halt,[27] but also
forced many Sunday Schools into virtual dissolution.[28]

Many of the Dissenters who initially supported the
Revolution were sickened by the excesses of the Terror and
by the militarism of Napoleon.[29] There was soon a reaction to the euphoric welcome given to the Revolution in its
early stages, and Dissenters hurried to demonstrate their
loyalty to King and constitution and to dissociate themselves
from the Jacobin taint.[30] Some even refused to support the
movement for the repeal of the Test Acts because it was
largely led by "democratic" Unitarians. Despite these as-
sertions of loyalty, the Dissenters did not quickly regain the
confidence of their Anglican brethren and suspicions of Nonconformist politics still prejudiced evangelical churchmen
against the Missionary and Tract Societies when they were
founded at the close of the century.[31] Not until about 1810
did large numbers of Anglicans care to fraternize closely
with Dissenters in a joint enterprise against vice and lower-
class sedition.[32] Yet some thaw in relations was already
perceptible by the late 1790's,[33] and the tension gradually
relaxed until, after about 1810, evangelicals were drawn
closer than they had ever been before.[34]

The social dislocations produced by war, coupled with
continual excitement as regimes toppled and huge armies
marched across the continent, had yet another, more immediate impact on pan-evangelicalism. The Revolution had
done much to excite an atmosphere of millennial prophecy
and expectation unparalleled since the English Civil War.
Studying political developments in France in light of the
Book of Revelation, the evangelicals--among the most ha-
bitual students of the Bible--felt confident that they were
about to witness the dawn of a new period in Christianity

when anti-Christ would fall, civil and religious liberties
would spread, and bigotry would be suppressed forever.
Ever since the Reformation, they pointed out, the Papal
power had gradually decayed. Now its humiliation at the
hands of France confirmed that it was on the brink of total
ruin.

At first, the evangelicals believed that the French
Revolution itself was God's instrument in bringing about the
downfall of anti-Christ, but when the Revolution veered to
the left and Christian religion in France was replaced with
a form of state deism, their exegesis had to be altered. It
now became evident that France itself was the Beast prophesied in Scripture and, when war broke out between Britain
and France, that Britain would be God's agent in anti-Christ's
destruction.[35] Moreover, if anti-Christ was soon to fall in
France and Protestant religion was eventually to replace it,
there was good reason to believe that Christianity would be
brought to the heathen and the Jew and that the evangelicals
themselves would be God's chosen agents in making millennial prophecy a reality.[36] As we shall see, disagreements
over whether the Jew or the heathen should first be converted indirectly resulted in the emergence of the London
Society for Promoting Christianity Amongst the Jews in the
early nineteenth century.[37] Finally, and perhaps most significantly as far as the pan-evangelical movement was concerned, by the process of missionizing the heathen and the
Jew, the evangelicals believed that God would remove certain divisive "obstacles" within the Christian fold itself.
Thus, the Evangelical Magazine, referring to "the unhappy
contentions and divisions which subsist among Christians"
predicted that "the present diversity of opinion shall, in a
great measure, cease, and that golden age of Christianity
return, in which it shall again be said, the multitudes of
them that believed were of one heart, and of one soul."[38]

There was much debate about the date of the millennium and the form in which it would appear. Richard Brothers thought that it would take place in 1795. Thomas Coke
suggested that it would come in 1866. Andrew Fuller, who
refused to pin down a date, said cautiously that it was not
far off. David Bogue predicted after 1795 that the millennium would probably take place in the distant future.[39] But
it did not matter what the precise date was. Far more important was the general conviction shared by evangelicals of
many kinds that their own generation was either to be the
last of this world, or the first of the latter days.

There was also considerable debate on how the millennium would be ushered in. Most evangelicals expected
that Christ's advent as judge of the world and the final defeat of Satan would take place after the millennium. This
thought, as we shall see, prompted many evangelicals to
draw together in preparation for the final judgment. But
there was also a small number who believed that Christ's
Second Coming would precede the millennium. Preparation,
they believed, was useless since Christ alone, unassisted by
finite beings, would usher in the new age. The so-called
"Pre-Millennialists" grew in numbers during the nineteenth
century and proved to be a very inhibiting force in the pan-
evangelical societies they patronized, but for the time being
they were only a minority party. [40]

Most evangelicals were not only unified in their belief that they had a very important role to play in the millennium but, as we have seen, believed that the millennium
called for a united Christendom. Thomas Coke, for example,
prophesied that a "complete external union" of the Christian
church would take place during the millennium. The Baptist
Robert Hall also predicted that during the millennium, Christians would all be of one mind and one heart, though his
colleague Andrew Fuller half-jokingly remarked that they
would be of one mind and one heart as Baptists. By 1797,
the evangelical clergyman David Simpson could even see the
union predicted in millennial prophecy already beginning to
take place in the various pan-evangelical societies that had
been established. [41] To a large degree, as we shall soon
see, Simpson's observation was accurate.

                                III.

Largely as a result of the various developments we
have been describing, two basic concepts of pan-evangelicalism had emerged by the end of the eighteenth century which
shaped and molded the pan-evangelical societies we will shortly examine. [42] The first could be described as "idealistic"
since its adherents applauded the nondenominational ideas of
the early Evangelical Revival, especially as they were propagated by George Whitefield, hoping to reconstruct them in a
number of institutions open to all evangelicals. Like the
Apostle Paul, the idealists believed that while there were
many Christian communities in the world, these communities
were one in the Body of Christ. Samuel Greatheed's General
al Union Recommended to Real Christians, an early manifesto of this group, pointed out that, [43]

> The Church is one body, of which our Lord Jesus
> Christ is the Head. Whether as private Christians,
> or as distinct Societies, we are all members one
> of another; and if we neglect the duties, which, as
> such, we owe to each other, and to our exalted
> head; it must be displeasing to Him and hurtful
> to us.... The first Christian Churches were
> united. They corresponded, sympathised, and
> cooperated together. We have too long resem-
> bled the scattered bones of Ezekiel's Vision.

Because the idealists considered the Church as one
in Christ, they tended to emphasize the points on which all
Christians agreed, minimizing the points in which they dif-
fered. Greatheed wrote:[44]

> What are the points of difference between real
> Christians, compared with the greatness of those
> objects in which we all agree? ... We ask you,
> therefore, to treat your separate interests, as
> subordinate to the general cause of our Lord; to
> lay aside, so far as the occasion requires, all
> things in which we differ.

Stress, therefore, was placed on Christian experience shared
by all evangelicals. "It is an affecting consideration to them
who are brethren in Christ," Greatheed wrote, "that, amidst
all the diversity of their forms and opinions, there is a general and striking resemblance, both in their inward, and
their outward experience."[45] Therefore, by virtue of their
oneness in Christ, Christian denominations were urged not
only to cooperate with each other in a wide range of Christian activities but, indeed, to sit with each other at a common communion table. John Mitchell Mason, the American
evangelical who was also instrumental in many pan-evangelical
organizations established in Britain, wrote:[46]

> Communion is indisputably an act and expression
> of union. And it is on this very ground that the
> reciprocal communion of Christians and Christian
> churches is asserted to be their privilege and duty.
> They are united--they are one. They are one in
> interests infinitely more valuable, they are united
> in bonds infinitely more strong, than all the other
> interests which subdivide them.

The idealists did not immediately press for an organic union of the church. Rather, like Zinzendorf, whom

they greatly admired and read, they emphasized unity over
uniformity. Greatheed wrote: "We aim at Union, not uniformity; We wish to excite your zeal, not to alter your
opinions; We long to promote your love to all fellow Christians, not to lessen your attachment to those with whom you
are immediately connected."[47] Nevertheless, in the process
of cooperating with each other in various activities and sharing the same communion table, the idealists looked forward
to the day when the Church would again be organically one.
Significantly, Greatheed declared that the primary objective
of the Bedfordshire Union of Christians which he founded in
1797 was to "restore the universal Church of Christ to some
measure of its primitive harmony and unity," only secondar-
ily to spread the knowledge of the Gospel to the domestic
heathen.[48]

        The second concept of pan-evangelicalism was a more
"realistic" or pragmatic one, because its adherents realized
that a united Church in the eighteenth century was impractical and a dream only to be realized in the millennium.   In
1802, for instance, the Christian Observer, an evangelical
Anglican publication, remarked that evangelicals would "rejoice to see the Church on earth resemble that which is in
heaven, in unity as well as in holiness: but they have no
hope, at this late period of the world, of reducing all its
members to one model."[49] The realists were a denominationally diverse and unrelated group of "regular" churchmen,
Baptists, and Wesleyans. During the Revival, for reasons
we have mentioned, all three had established denominational
parameters which effectively served to insulate themselves
from other evangelical denominations.   Although they still
shared with other evangelicals common spiritual experiences
and theological beliefs, they desired to preserve their respective denominational identities.   Christian unity, therefore,
was not discussed by them in terms of intercommunion or
organic union, but rather in terms of cordiality and candor.
The Christian Observer urged that "the exercise of ... for-
bearance, candour, and brotherly love, towards those who
differ from [us], so repeatedly and so forcibly inculcated in
the New Testament" was more incumbent upon Christians of
different denominations than the sharing of the sacraments.
The magazine continued: "And with respect to such Anti-
sectarians, as belong to the Church of England, I have found
them capable of acknowledging and honouring the piety found
among Dissenters, without the least diminution of attachment
to the constitution of their own church."[50]   Unity, therefore,
was primarily a unity of spirit.   "Christian unity consists in

having one heart: renewed, guided, sanctified by the same spirit," Daniel Wilson told the Anglican-dominated Eclectic Society. But he quickly added that "uniformity is not necessary."51

Generally speaking, the realists were willing to participate with other evangelicals in a number of activities, but only if this participation did not compromise their denominational allegiances and theological beliefs. Respecting the sharing of pulpits, for example, Andrew Fuller, the Baptist closed-communionist, wrote somewhat caustically: "I have no partiality, certainly, for the Established Church. I believe it will come down, because it is inimical to the kingdom of Christ; yet I respect many Churchmen, and still shall not refuse preaching in their pulpits, provided I may go in my own way."52 Evangelical Anglicans also set limits to the degree in which they would cooperate with Dissenters and Methodists in pan-evangelical enterprises. If cooperation meant the formation of undenominational mission churches that might somehow prejudice the national establishment, they would demur and withhold their patronage. But if cooperation did not compromise church order, requiring them only to distribute Bibles without note or comment, or tracts that portrayed universal Protestant truths, they would participate in pan-evangelical activities with as much zeal as anyone else. The realists, therefore, subscribed to pan-evangelicalism as long as it did not require them to overstep denominational boundaries or compromise theological principles. How these concepts or philosophies of pan-evangelicalism worked in practice after 1790 is a matter that we must now discuss in more detail.

NOTES

1. See Evangelical Magazine, 5 (1797), 376.
2. Cf., A. Fuller, "A Few Persuasives to 'A General Union in Prayer' for the Revival of Religion," in Works (1846), XX, 926 f.; E. A. Payne, The Prayer Call of 1784 (1941).
3. An Account of the Society for Promoting Religious Knowledge Among the Poor (1769), 4.
4. Ibid., 5.
5. Cf., K. R. Manley, "John Rippon and Baptist Historiography," The Baptist Quarterly XXVII (1979), 116.
6. See J. Wesley, A Sermon Preached Before the Society for Reformation of Manners (1763), 7, 11; Cf., W. B.

Whitaker, The Eighteenth Century English Sunday
(1940), 119 f. G. V. Portus, Caritas Anglicana (1912),
243 f.

7.   See G. Cussons, Memoirs (1819), 71 f.

8.   See W. J. Townsend, et al., A New History of Methodism (1909), II, 288; G. G. Findlay and W. W. Holdsworth, The History of the Wesleyan Methodist Missionary Society (1921), I, 65; N. A. Birtwhistle,
"Founded in 1786: The Origins of the Methodist Missionary Society," Proceedings of the Wesley Historical Society, XXX (1955); J. A. Vickers, Thomas
Coke (1969), 132 f.

9.   Cf., T. Clarkson, The History ... of the Abolition of
the African Slave Trade (1808), I, 442, 569; A. Plum-
mer, The Church of England in the Eighteenth Century (1910), 206. The Sierra Leone Colony, founded
in the 1790's by Clapham Sect evangelicals, grew
directly out of the Abolition Society. It was an attempt to find a home for emancipated slaves. For
the link between the abolition movement and foreign
missions, see J. Wilks, An Apology for the Missionary Society (1799); R. G. Cowherd, The Politics of
English Dissent (1959), 46.

10. See M. G. Jones, The Charity School Movement (1938),
142 ff.

11. W. I. Wild, The History of the Stockport Sunday School
(1891), 3.

12. W. G. Robinson, William Roby (1954), 60; H. F. Burder, Memoir of the Rev. George Burder (1833), 133.

13. J. H. Overton, The English Church in the Nineteenth
Century (1894), 247.

14. J. Ivimey, Memoir of William Fox (1831); W. T.
Whitley, A History of British Baptists (1923), 260 f.
Whitaker, op.cit., 219 f.

15. Plan of a Society Established in London ... for the
Support and Encouragement of Sunday Schools (1793),
8 f.

16. Cf., W. Dealtry, A Vindication of the British and Foreign Bible Society (1810), 185; M. G. Jones, op.cit.,
152.

17. J. Dore, A Sermon Preached at Maze Pond (1789), 32.

18. R. Hill, An Apology for Sunday Schools (1801), 31.

19. R. Hawker, "Sunday Schools Recommended" in Works
(1826), II, 207.

20. Plan of a Sunday School Society Established in London
(1789), 6. For the definitive study of the Sunday
School movement, see T. W. Laqueur, Religion and

Respectability: Sunday Schools & English Working Class Culture 1780-1850 (1976).

21. D. Bogue, A Sermon Preached at Salters' Hall (1793), 46; Cf., J. Bennett, Memoir of the Life of David Bogue (1827), 240 ff.

22. See D.N.B.

23. Bodl: MSS Wilberforce, C 3, f.12: T. Robinson to W. Wilberforce, 12 December 1792.

24. Cited in J. Bull, Memorials of the Rev. William Bull (1864), 221.

25. Cited in J. D. Walsh, "The Yorkshire Evangelicals in the Eighteenth Century" (Cambridge University PhD. Thesis 1956), 313.

26. M. J. Quinlan, Victorian Prelude (1941), 90 f.

27. E. Halevy, A History of the English People in 1815 (2nd Revised Edn. 1949), 456.

28. For the dissolution of Sunday Schools during the French Revolution, see A. P. Wadsworth, "The First Manchester Sunday Schools," Bulletin of the John Rylands Library, XXXIII (1950), 315; A. T. Hart, The Eighteenth Century Parson (1955), 84; M. G. Jones, op.cit., 153; J. H. Overton, op.cit., 247 f. There were, of course, many other reasons why undenominational Sunday Schools declined at the end of the century. The Blue Coat School in Birmingham, for example, created interdenominational friction because the scholars were being apprenticed only to Anglican merchants. See A. H. Driver, Carr's Lane (1948), 28. Schools also foundered on the rocks of the Calvinistic Controversy, as did the Sunday School at Bamford in Lancashire in 1800. See B. Nightingale, Lancashire Nonconformity (1890), III, 255. Others broke up when one denomination imposed its catechism on the other. See J. W. Middleton, An Ecclesiastical Memoir (1822), 209. It must be noted, however, that many Sunday Schools weathered the Revolution and remained undenominational.

29. Cf., J. Griffin, The Encouraging Aspects of the Times (2nd ed. 1806), 27 f.

30. Cf., E. Parsons, A Vindication of the Dissenters Against Charges of Democratic Schemes (1802); R. Hawker, An Appeal to the People of England on the Subject of the French Revolution (1794); R. Haldane, Address to the Public Concerning Political Opinions (1800).

31. Cf., C. Hole, The Early History of the Church Missionary Society (1896), 54.

32. For a review of the impact of the Revolution on inter-
     denominational relations, see W. R. Ward, "The Re-
     ligion of the People and the Problem of Control" in
     C. J. Cuming and D. Baker, Popular Belief and
     Practice (1971), 237 ff; V. Kiernan, "Evangelicalism
     and the French Revolution," Past and Present, I
     (1952), 44 f. A. J. Russell, "A Sociological An-
     alysis of the Clergyman's Role with a Special Refer-
     ence to its Development in the Early Nineteenth Cen-
     tury" (Oxford University D. Phil. Thesis 1970), 35 f.,
     234 f.

33. According to Patrick Colquhoun, only nineteen societies
     were founded in the last half of the eighteenth cen-
     tury, and only five in the last quarter. The "mush-
     room" growth of these organizations came only after
     the Revolution. See F. K. Brown, Fathers of the
     Victorians (1961), 328. For a parallel development
     in religious periodicals, see F. E. Mineka, The Dis-
     sidence of Dissent (1944), 48 f.

34. Cf., D. Bogue and J. Bennett, History of the Dis-
     senters from the Revolution in 1688 to the Year 1808
     (1808), IV, 204 f.

35. J. Griffin, op. cit., 46 f.

36. Cf., D. Bogue, The Diffusion of Divine Truth (1800),
     14, 39.

37. For more on millennial prophecy and the Jews, see C.
     Jerram, An Essay tending to Shew the Grounds Con-
     tained in Scripture for a Future Restoration of the
     Jews (1796); M. Verete, "The Restoration of the Jews
     in English Protestant Thought," Middle Eastern Stud-
     ies, VIII (1972), 8 f.; J. Parkes, "Lewis Way and
     His Times," Transactions of the Jewish Historical
     Society of England, XX (1959), 190.

38. Evangelical Magazine, 1 (1793), 163.

39. Cf., Vickers, op. cit., 330; A. Fuller, Works (1846),
     XII, 572. D. Bogue, Objections Against a Mission
     to the Heathen Stated and Considered (1811), 6.

40. Cf., I. H. Murray, The Puritan Hope: A Study in Re-
     vival and Prophecy (1971), 187; D. N. Hempton, "Evan-
     gelicalism and Eschatology," Journal of Ecclesiastical
     History, XXXI, No. 2, April 1980, 179 ff.

41. Vickers, op. cit., 331; R. Hall, The Duty and Impor-
     tance of Free Communion (1820), 43; D. Simpson, A
     Plea for Religion and the Sacred Writings (5th ed.
     1808), 324 f.

42. For a similar discussion of pan-evangelicalism in Amer-
     ica, see L. A. Loetscher, "The Problem of Christian

Unity in Early Nineteenth Century America," Church History, XXXII, No. 1, March 1963, 6 f.

43. S. Greatheed, General Union Recommended to Real Christians (1798), viii f.

44. Ibid., ix.

45. Ibid., 33.

46. J. M. Mason, A Plea for Catholick Communion in the Church of God (2nd ed. 1816), 355.

47. Greatheed, op. cit., ix.

48. Ibid., xvii.

49. Christian Observer (1802), 708

50. Ibid., 709

51. Cited in J. Pratt, Eclectic Notes (1865), 352.

52. A Fuller, Works (1846), XVIII, 847 f.

PART II:

THE LONDON MISSIONARY SOCIETY

I.

It is not surprising that the feelings of evangelical
union finally took institutional form in 1795.   The time was
propitious.   The evangelical "idealists" hoped that the fears
aroused by the Jacobinical sermons of Bogue and Haldane
had died away.   On the Continent, the excesses of the Terror had come to an end and hopes were aroused that peace
might be negotiated between Britain and revolutionary France.
If fears were subsiding, hopes were mounting.   Millennial
expectation was still in the ascendant, soon to be given new
impetus by the spectacular descent of the French armies into Rome, the citadel of anti-Christ.

Nor was it surprising that the first focus for a united
evangelical front should be foreign missions.   The Revival
was nothing if not mission-minded.   There had been several
tentative attempts to further the cause of foreign as well as
home missions.   The English Moravians had long contributed
to the missionary impulse of their church, creating mission
stations as far away as Greenland.   Lady Huntingdon's Connexion had made an abortive attempt in 1772 to dispatch missionaries to the Cherokee Indians in Georgia and the Wesleyan Methodists were already active in foreign missions
as early as 1786 if not before.   During the 1780's, interest
in the conversion of the heathen had been widely aroused by
the publication of Captain James Cook's Voyages, read by a
large public including fascinated evangelicals who quickly
realized its significance for the extension of the Gospel in
foreign and exotic lands.   In America and Britain, Jonathan
Edwards' Humble Attempt encouraged evangelicals on both
sides of the Atlantic to engage in concerted prayer for revival and missions.

Hope became reality with the founding of the Baptist

Missionary Society in 1792.   The B. M. S. had in part been
inspired by the writings of Edwards and Cook.   Interestingly,
it had originally occurred to William Carey, the Society's
founder and first missionary, that missions might be inter-
denominationally organized, but as he later wrote in his
missionary manifesto An Enquiry into the Obligations of
Christians to Use Means for the Conversion of the Heathens,
"the present divided state of Christendom" has made it "more
likely for good to be done by each denomination engaging
separately in the work. "[1]   In this view, he was supported
by the Independent George Burder, spokesman for the Warwickshire Independent Association who also believed that
missions would have to be denominationally organized. [2]

It was perhaps Melville Horne who, for the first
time, openly advocated the concept of missions as a united
or cooperative effort involving all evangelicals.   Formerly
a Wesleyan itinerant preacher, Horne was ordained in 1786
to fill the curacy at Madely left vacant at the death of John
Fletcher.   He later migrated to Olney after serving a short
and rather unhappy stint in Africa as Chaplain to the Sierra
Leone Colony. [3]   While in Sierra Leone, Horne had observed
the beneficial effects of missionary cooperation.   Possibly
this experience played an important part in his decision to
write his famous Letters on Missions: Addressed to the
Protestant Ministers of the British Churches, published in
1794, fourteen months after his return to England.   In his
advice to future missionaries, Horne wrote:

> I would not have him indifferent to his own pe-
> culiarities, whether they respect the doctrines he
> receives as truth, or the points of ecclesiastical
> polity he considers as most friendly to religion;
> but I would have him thoroughly sensible, that the
> success of his ministry rests not on points of
> separation, but on those wherein all godly men
> are united.

Horne therefore believed that a missionary should be "far removed from narrow bigotry, and possess a spirit truly catholic. "   He continued:

> It is not Calvinism, it is not Arminianism, but
> Christianity that he is to teach.   It is not the
> hierarchy of the Church of England; it is not the
> principles of the Protestant Dissenters, that he
> has in view to propagate.   His object is to serve
> the Church Universal.

Horne's conclusion was quite clear: "Let liberal Churchmen and conscientious Dissenters, pious Calvinists and pious
Arminians, embrace with fraternal arms."[4]

Sometime during the spring of 1794, the founding
fathers of what was soon to become the London Missionary
Society met at the Dissenter's Library, Red Cross Street
in London to discuss missions in general and Horne's Letters in particular. These men had been called together by
the Anglican John Eyre, one of the Society's future secretaries. Like many of his type, Eyre had a varied evangelical inheritance. At first an itinerant in Tavistock in
Devon, he entered Lady Huntingdon's Connexion as a student
and minister, moved on to Anglican orders after graduating
from Emmanuel College, Cambridge, served for a time as
curate to Cecil and Cadogan, and by now was editor of the
Evangelical Magazine.[5] The Londoners who met with Eyre
included Alexander Waugh, minister of Wells Street Congregational church; James Steven, Scots Presbyterian minister
of Crown Court Chapel; John Love, also a member of the
Church of Scotland and minister of Artillery Street Chapel;
and later, Matthew Wilks, Calvinistic Methodist minister of
Whitefield's Tabernacle. During the course of the summer,
these meetings evolved into formal fortnightly discussions
which gradually grew in size and involved an even larger
number of men including Thomas Haweis, the Oxford-educated rector of All Saints, Aldwincle, whose review of
Horne's pamphlet in the Evangelical Magazine was read by
a large evangelical constituency.[6] But they had not yet
drawn in David Bogue, the prominent Independent minister
from Gosport who many historians incorrectly believe founded
the London Missionary Society on his own initiative.[7] Born
in Berwickshire and educated at the University of Edinburgh,
Bogue later came to England and eventually served as the
Independent minister at Gosport in Hampshire where, in
1780, he opened an academy for Independent ministerial candidates.[8] Bogue had also been a keen supporter of the foreign missionary cause, but apparently his interest in missions came from reading William Carey's Serampore letters
during the summer of 1794, not from reading Horne's work
like the others.[9] Agreeing with Carey that missions in
Britain should be denominationally organized, Bogue subsequently published in the Evangelical Magazine for September
1794 an article addressed "To the Evangelical Dissenters
who Practice Infant Baptism" which, as its title suggested,
called for a paedobaptist and Nonconformist society to match
the Baptist effort.[10] But by November 1794, Bogue had not

only seen the advantage to a pan-evangelical effort in missions, but he had also been invited by the founding fathers to meet with them at Baker's Coffee House in London formally to plan the new organization and form its first committee. [11] By September 1795, the London Missionary Society was a reality. [12]

The activities of the first general meeting of the London Missionary Society that September and the sermons that were preached on the occasion, have been described too often to merit repetition here. Since this was the first time in recent memory that Dissenters and Anglican churchmen had joined together in an interdenominational enterprise, the occasion seems to have been an emotional one. One historian described David Bogue and John Eyre rushing into each other's arms when they met at Spa Field's Chapel, an encounter which epitomized the reconciliation of Church and Dissent. [13] The sermons aroused deep feeling and excitement. The preachers included Thomas Haweis, Rowland Hill, David Bogue, Samuel Greatheed, and others, but Bogue's sermon was the most dramatic by far. His famous homily on the "Funeral of Bigotry" has been appreciatively remembered through the years, and its fame perhaps explains why it has so frequently been assumed, as we have mentioned, that he alone was the moving force behind the Society's formation. In a classic expression of evangelical idealism, Bogue declared that henceforth "bigotry was dead!"[14]

> We have now before us a pleasing spectacle, Christians of different denominations, although differing in points of church government, united in forming a society for propagating the Gospel among the heathen. This is a new thing in the Christian church ... Here are Episcopalians, Methodists, Presbyterians, and Independents, all united in one society, all joining to form its laws, to regulate its institutions, and manage its various concerns. Behold us here assembled with one accord to attend the funeral of bigotry: And may she be buried so deep that not a particle of her dust may ever be thrown up on the face of the earth.

The Evangelical Magazine recorded that the crowd's response to Bogue's words was "one general shout of joy." Such a scene, it reported, "was perhaps, never before beheld in our world."[15] But for the more sober minds at

this gala occasion, Samuel Greatheed's sermon was perhaps
more prophetic of the future of pan-evangelicalism in foreign
missions.   "Blessed be God for the numerous assembly present of those who preach, as well as those who hear the Gospel" Greatheed proclaimed.   "Yet, where are many others?"[16]
Conspicuously absent at the meeting were, among others, a
large number of evangelicals representing the Baptist, Wesleyan, and even the Anglican churches.   The London Missionary Society, for reasons that we shall examine, lacked
denominational comprehensiveness even at this early and
euphoric stage.

II.

The foundation of the London Missionary Society was
not always greeted with enthusiasm, not even by some of
those who professed to share the Reformed "doctrines of
grace" which it propagated.   The Protestant Dissenters Magazine which largely reflected conservative and anti-evangelical
Nonconformist opinion, treated the Society circumspectly
and even critically.   One correspondent called for great
"caution and prudence" in dealings with this new and "unnatural coalition of parties."[17]   The Hypercalvinists, who
objected to "indiscriminate" offers of grace, believed that
God would convert the heathen by his own sovereign authority and that the London Missionary Society, as a merely
human contrivance, lacked the "miraculous power" which
was indispensable for the conversion of the heathen.[18]   But
far more dampening than criticisms from those who did not
share the evangelical assumptions was the lack of interest
shown by some fellow evangelicals.   As we have pointed out,
the Particular Baptists, Wesleyan Methodists, and the "regular" evangelical Anglicans were notably absent from the
meetings which founded the Society.   But was this the intention of the founding fathers?   There is a good deal of
evidence--which we shall now examine--that it was not and
that a number of the founding fathers of what was to become
the London Missionary Society expected their society to com-
prehend and unite evangelicals of all kinds of denominational
and theological allegiances.   Since the London Missionary
Society was the first of the four great pan-evangelical societies to be examined in this study, and since its creation
deeply influenced the outlook of its successors, this question
needs some discussion.

It has traditionally been assumed that the founding

fathers (themselves Calvinists and paedobaptists) never hoped
to win over Arminians like the followers of Wesley or the
Particular Baptists even though they anticipated heavy support from Anglican evangelicals, the great majority of whom
shared the theological assumptions of the founders. [19]   Perhaps hopes somewhat outran expectations.   It may well be
that the fathers of the London Missionary Society were less
optimistic about support from the Baptists and the Wesleyans
than they were from the Anglicans.   Nevertheless, they
pitched their aspirations higher than has generally been realized, and the customary view of the London Missionary
Society as an organization designed merely for Calvinistic
and paedobaptist Nonconformists needs some qualification.

Though it is extremely difficult to determine exactly
how catholic the founding fathers initially intended their society to be, clues might be found in the Society's so-called
"Fundamental Principle," and, indeed, in what the fathers
themselves said about their new organization.   The Fundamental Principle of the London Missionary Society was added
to the Society's by-laws in 1796.   It was an irenic statement which set out to define the kind of mission that the
Society would establish in foreign lands.   It said:[20]

> As the union of Christians of various denomina-
> tions in carrying on this great work is a most
> desirable object, so, to prevent, if possible, any
> cause of future dissension, it is declared to be a
> fundamental principle of The Missionary Society,
> that its design is not to send Presbyterianism,
> Independency, Episcopacy, or any other form of
> Church Order and Government, about which there
> may be difference of opinion among serious per-
> sons, but the glorious Gospel of the Blessed God,
> to the heathen; and that it shall be left (as it ought
> to be left) to the minds of the persons whom God
> may call into the fellowship of His Son from among
> them to assume for themselves such form of Church
> Government as to them shall appear most agree-
> able to the Word of God.

It is quite clear from this statement that on points
of ecclesiastical order and church government, the directors were open-minded.   Thus Presbyterians, Independents,
and Episcopalians would be sent into the mission field to
establish whatever form of church government or ecclesiastical polity that appeared to them and their converts most

agreeable to the word of God. No doubt the founders assumed rather naively perhaps that once in the mission field,
surrounded by a great multitude of heathens, such diversi-
ties of polity and church government would seem irrelevant
and insignificant. But were the directors also open-minded
on the question of theological diversity? Did they also mean
to send out Arminians as well as Calvinists and Baptists as
well as paedobaptists to preach the word of God in what ever way they thought best? Indeed, did they intend the governing body of the Society in England also to include representatives from these various theological camps? Three
days after the Fundamental Principle was voted on, a group
of directors attempted to press on missionary candidates a
confession of faith or a theological test. Significantly, this
motion was vetoed by the majority of directors present.[21]
This would seem to indicate that missionary candidates holding theological views at variance with the majority would not
be barred, at least in general principle, from serving the
Society. What the founding fathers themselves said about
the catholicity of their society possibly supports this suggestion.

Few of the founding fathers ever declared, for example, that the London Missionary Society was exclusively
designed to send out Calvinistic and paedobaptist missionaries. It is true, of course, that David Bogue had called
for a rather denominational response to the challenge of
the Baptist Missionary Society in his September 1794 Evangelical Magazine article mentioned above. But Bogue was
neither present at the earliest of the London Missionary Society's founding meetings in the Spring of 1794, nor was his
article the inspirational force that some historians have
made it out to be.[22] Indeed, the original founding fathers,
several months before Bogue had joined their ranks, had
been inspired by Melville Horne's Letters on Missions which
they had read and discussed together at these early meetings. As we have seen, Horne, unlike Bogue, called for
a missionary response that would include Arminians as well
as Calvinists, Churchmen as well as Dissenters, and, by
implication, Baptists as well as paedobaptists. It was
Horne's pamphlet and not Bogue's article, it must again
be stressed, that was first read by the founding fathers,
and it was Horne's vision of a mission embodying all denominational and theological persuasions, not Bogue's call
for a mission sponsored solely by paedobaptists and Dissenters, that was the primary stimulus in leading these
men to found the London Missionary Society in 1795.[23]

Moreover, Horne's ecumenical vision was shared by almost all of the early directors. In his review of Horne's Letters, Thomas Haweis hoped that individuals would be "united
together, without respect to different denominations of Christians, or repulsive distance arising from the points in dispute between Calvinists and Arminians."[24] After reading
Horne's Letters and Thomas Haweis' review, John Townsend,
another founding father and minister of the Independent church
at Bermondsey, said that he was "powerfully stimulated to
desire that some measure might be adopted to procure a
simultaneous movement of British Christians in this honour-
able service." In this statement, Townsend did not exclude
Wesleyans or Baptists.[25] Nor did John Love, the Scots
Presbyterian minister at Artillery Street in London.   Possibly as a corrective to David Bogue's call for a paedobaptist and Nonconformist missionary society, Love echoed
Melville Horne in 1795 when he hoped that "not only Evangelical Dissenters and Methodists will be found generally
disposed to unite in instituting a society ... but that many
members of the established church, of evangelical sentiments ... will also favour us with their kind cooperation."[26]
Three years after the London Missionary Society was established, one of its more active directors, Christopher
Sundius of London, wrote a letter to the evangelical brethren in Sweden proclaiming the hope for a general reconciliation between evangelical denominations in Britain and pray-
ing that the organization he directed would be instrumental
in that realization.[27] This letter underlines what many of
Sundius' colleagues were writing and saying at this time.
But what makes this particular letter especially significant
is the fact that its author was not only a prominent member of the Wesleyan Connexion, but a relative, through mar-
riage, of John Wesley himself.[28] That such a prominent
Wesleyan personage was also a director of the London Missionary Society would seem to indicate that the governance
of the new mission would not be restricted to Calvinists.

The same was true of its missionaries. Many historians have long assumed that the London Missionary Society would not accept Baptist, Wesleyan or even Anglican
missionary candidates. There is evidence, however, to the
contrary. It would be misleading to suggest that representatives from these evangelical groups applied to the Society
in large numbers; but prior to the second decade of the
nineteenth century they were not discouraged, especially
if they could satisfy the directors that denominational or
theological partisanship would not be the object of their

missionary activities.   George Vason, a member of the
Park Street Particular Baptist Chapel in Nottingham, was
an early lay missionary of the Society.[29]   Samuel Greatheed, Independent minister at Newport Pagnell and an early
director, in countering a charge that the Society discrim-
inated against Wesleyan missionary applicants, pointed out
quite clearly that most of the directors were willing to consider applicants recommended by the leading members of
the Wesleyan Connexion.[30]   And there were several Anglicans, such as Orlando Dobbin of Armagh and Henry Beidenback of Islington, who served the Society as missionaries
even after the Church Missionary Society, an Anglican organization, was founded in 1799.[31]   Though the number of
Baptist, Wesleyan and Anglican missionaries serving the
London Missionary Society during these years was negligible,
the fact that they were represented at all is of some significance.[32]

     But perhaps the strongest evidence that the London
Missionary Society was originally designed to encompass all
evangelicals can be found in the Society's first name which
was, simply, "The Missionary Society."   It was not until
1818, that the Society, largely in recognition of the existence
of other missionary societies, changed its title to the less
sweeping and inclusive "The London Missionary Society."
If the founding fathers had intended to found a society in
1795 only for Calvinists and paedobaptist Dissenters, they
would probably have called their new organization the "Calvinistic Missionary Society" or, following David Bogue's
early suggestion, "The Missionary Society for Dissenters
who Practice Infant Baptism."   But since there was little
reason to believe in 1795, at least from the viewpoint of
most of the founding fathers, that their organization was
anything but the missionary society for all evangelicals who
wished to serve it as patrons of missionaries, "The Missionary Society" was deemed an appropriate title.   For all this,
if the invitation was freely given to all evangelicals to join,
there were reasons why many would not accept.

                                    III.

     The Particular Baptists were the least likely to pa-
tronize the London Missionary Society.   By 1799, the Baptist Missionary Society was firmly entrenched in Serampore,
India with several missionaries now in service in addition
to the original four and the mission was beginning to bear

fruit. At home, the Baptist society was no longer burdened by the debt that early on had threatened its existence. This was due, no doubt, to the wise administration of Andrew Fuller, the Society's first Secretary. Consequently there was little reason why most Baptists would have wanted to patronize the London Missionary Society. Still, some Baptists showed a great deal of interest in the L.M.S. when it was founded in 1795. Samuel Pearce, the catholic-minded open communionist, attended the first general meeting of the Society where he heard David Bogue preach his famous sermon on the "Funeral of Bigotry" and he wrote back to his wife several days later that "you my love, will join me in a hearty amen to so evangelical a wish."[33]

As praise was given, so praise was received, and one year later Pearce could tell William Carey that "the London [Missionary] Society publicly owned that our zeal kindled theirs and that it was God who first touched your heart with the fire from His holy altar."[34] Unfortunately, much of this Baptist good-will was later misinterpreted by the directors of the L.M.S. Encouraged by open communionists like Pearce who shared with them some of their aspirations, many London Missionary Society directors hoped in 1795 to draw Baptists into Society affairs. Referring, for example, to instances in which paedobaptist denominations had supported the Baptist Missionary Society even after the L.M.S. was founded, Samuel Greatheed wrote to the Baptist John Sutcliffe in November 1795 a letter which hinted that there would surely be "some among your congregations who have the ability and disposition to help us..."[35] But most Baptists had meant their friendship to be a simple demonstration of Christian good-will, not an encouragement for London Missionary Society agents to raise money in Baptist chapels as they would later do.

Wesleyan involvement in the London Missionary Society, on the other hand, was much more within the realm of possibility. The Wesleyan missionary organization (if it could even be called that) was still pitifully weak. It suffered not only from lack of Connexional interest, but also from Thomas Coke's administrative inexperience. Furthermore, by 1795 most evangelicals wanted to extinguish forever the last flickerings of the Calvinist Controversy. For several years now, Calvinists and Arminians alike had seen the controversy as an extremely unfortunate chapter in the history of the evangelical movement not only because it had almost destroyed the evangelical cause itself, but also be-

cause, as they now realized, it had been based on faulty
theological premises.[36] Moderate Calvinism, of course,
had already done much to pave the way for reconciliation;
there were now many indications that this would be finally
achieved.

Perhaps the most significant development in this direction was the invitation to the Calvinist Rowland Hill, John
Eyre, and Samuel Greatheed, all directors of the L.M.S.,
to preach at Wesley's City Road Chapel in 1798. This was
indeed a most remarkable invitation. Not a few of the City
Road trustees would have remembered Rowland Hill's slan-
derous attacks on John Wesley during the Calvinist Controversy not many years before, yet Hill was one of the men
invited to preach. Of John Eyre's invitation, William Jay,
the Independent minister from Bath, commented several
years later "how it was wondered at, when Mr. Eyre of
Homerton, of Calvinistical sentiments, was asked to preach
at Mr. Wesley's Chapel, in Moorfields, and preached without giving offence."[37] But it was not offense that Eyre and
the others meant to give. His sermon on that occasion, entitled Union and friendly intercourse Recommended among
such of the various denominations of Calvinists and Members
of the late Mr. Wesley's Societies as agree on the essential
truths of the Gospel, provides us with a good indication of
the distance which Moderate Calvinism had come since the
1780's and how far the Calvinists were willing to go in
achieving reconciliation with their former enemies. Eyre
not only suggested in his sermon that both parties could
unite around the "grand essential truths of the Gospel," but
even remarked that the Wesleyans were really "practical
Calvinists!" But it is the preface to Eyre's sermon that
interests us the most. In it Eyre prophesied that both
parties could look forward to a new era of interdenominational cooperation in spreading the Gospel and thought "that
the period for accomplishing it is not far distant."[38] Reaction to the City Road sermons was interesting. They led
the Wesleyan John Pawson, for example, to believe that
after almost a half century of controversy, the Calvinists
were now willing "to acknowledge us as brothers, to love
and esteem us, and to strengthen not weaken our hands."[39]
For Pawson and most other Wesleyans, however, a "union
of brotherly affection" meant only the occasional sharing of
pulpits, certainly not an open license for London Missionary
fundraisers to take collections in their chapels.[40]

The London Missionary Society's greatest disappoint-

ment, however, came when regular Evangelical Anglicans
failed to give it their patronage. Unlike the case of the
Particular Baptists and the Wesleyans, there was now really no theological barrier to evangelical Anglican participation. Evangelical Churchmen, of course, practiced infant
baptism, and, with several important exceptions, almost all
of them were Calvinists. Moreover, in 1795 they did not
have their own missionary society. It was therefore difficult for the founding fathers of the London Missionary Society to understand why so many of their evangelical brethren in the Church of England resisted repeated invitations
to join their society.

Of course, there had been from the beginning, and
would continue to be, a small number of "irregular" evangelical churchmen who patronized the Society, but their influence and prestige in the Anglican world was not very extensive. Rowland Hill, for instance, belonged really more
to a denomination of his own than to the Anglican church in
which he had been ordained a deacon. Educated at St. John's
College, Cambridge, from which he graduated in 1769, Hill
was refused ordination by six bishops in succession because
of his irregular activities while a student. Not until 1773
did he receive ordination to the diaconate by Dr. Wills, the
Bishop of Bath and Wells, and he never proceeded to the
priesthood. In 1773 he was curate in a Somerset village
though he spent most of his time itinerating, and in 1783
the proprietary Surrey Chapel was erected for him, where
he remained the rest of his life as a prominent, though eccentric, London preacher. [41] Thomas Haweis was almost
as irregular. A Cornish convert of Walker of Truro, Haweis had been a successful though controversial curate at
St. Mary Magdalen in Oxford and thereafter occupied an
anomalous position as both Rector of Aldwincle and chief
trustee of the Countess of Huntingdon's Connexion which
brought down on his head the censure of many Anglican
evangelicals. [42]

Apart from these two men and John Eyre with whom
we have already met, there was little firm Anglican support. Men like George West, Rector of Stoke-next-Guild-
ford, and William Winkworth, Chaplain at St. Saviours in
London, both Anglican priests, only played peripheral roles
in the Society's early development. Melville Horne was a
director for one year (1797) and preached an occasional sermon for the Society, but his efforts were re-directed to the
Church Missionary Society when that organization was founded

in 1799. [43] So, from the very beginning, the L. M. S. fought
an uphill battle to win evangelical Anglican support for the
pan-evangelical cause in foreign missions.   The battle was
largely lost by the turn of the century.

Several reasons may be suggested why evangelical
churchmen were reluctant to patronize the London Missionary Society.   As we have noted, early support of the French
Revolution by many evangelical Dissenters had convinced
several churchmen that the Society contained far too many
"republicans" bent on destroying Church and State.   Other
churchmen questioned the propriety of assisting in the establishment of undenominational mission churches.   Some
feared that Nonconformist control of the Society would ultimately prejudice mission churches in favor of a congregational form of church government.   Others again feared that
the Society's undenominational principle, by its vagueness,
would encourage a disintegration of church order and lead
to anarchy and indiscipline. [44] But there was a far more
immediate reason for the unwillingness of evangelical Anglicans to be drawn into the affairs of the London Missionary
Society in 1795.   In that year, Joseph Jane, the evangelical
Vicar of St. Mary Magdalen in Oxford gave £4000 toward
the founding of an evangelical Anglican missionary society.
Subsequently a group of evangelical churchmen, including
Jane himself, met at Rauceby to lay the foundations for
what would later become the Church Missionary Society.
Though it was not until 1799, when the project was passed
on to the Eclectic Society in London, that Jane's dream
became a reality, many evangelical churchmen were no
doubt aware of the Rauceby meetings in 1795 and preferred
to defer their work for foreign missions until their own
Church society was in being. [45]

Though several London Missionary Society Anglicans
participated in the Eclectic Society discussions which ultimately led to the founding of the C. M. S. , they did so largely in order to protest against a fresh organization which
would rival their own.   Thomas Haweis, at one Eclectic
Society meeting, said that though a loyal Anglican, he feared
that the formation of an Anglican missionary society would
diminish any chance that the Bishops would bestow patronage
on his own society. [46] He later lamented bitterly to Thomas
Scott, the famous Bible commentator and Chaplain of the
Lock Hospital in London, that "all Christians, foreign as
well as my countrymen, cannot unite in one great object." [47]
Rowland Hill, voicing a similar opinion, could not understand

why his Church friends wished to form a new missionary society when one already existed, and asked his Anglican brethren: "Ours is a missionary society for all: why leave us?"[48]

It must have been lamented by some of the more
idealistic exponents of evangelical union that their great
plan for a pan-evangelical foreign missionary society would
never be as comprehensive in membership as it set out to
be. Baptists and Wesleyans and now even "regular" churchmen had gone their separate ways, leaving the L.M.S. in-
complete in its denominational representation. The first
three decades of the Society's history, therefore, were to
be years of a half-realized ideal, but the story of the pan-
evangelical impulse in foreign missions, as we shall see,
was not yet over.

IV.

Even though the London Missionary Society was never
able successfully to establish a comprehensive evangelical
union in foreign missions, its success as a missionary organization in its own right and its influence over future pan-
evangelical operations, must not be underestimated. The
size of the Society and the scope of its activities made it
one of the largest missionary enterprises in Britain. Do-
mestically, it attracted the support of a high proportion of
the important paedobaptist and Calvinistic Dissenters in the
Kingdom. No fewer than 850 prominent evangelical ministers and laymen served as directors of the Society between
1795 and 1830. These men built up a network of auxiliary
missionary societies which, by 1830, linked evangelicals
together from Scotland to Cornwall. In Europe, the Society's example inspired similar organizations which maintained strong ties with London. The first Continental societies were the Netherlands and Swedish Missionary Societies founded shortly after the London Missionary Society,
and they were followed by others in Basel, Berlin, and Par-
is. The movement spread to the United States in 1796 with
the creation of the New York Missionary Society. In the
mission field itself, the L.M.S. by 1820 had established fifty
stations manned by 140 missionaries.[49] By 1830, Society
missionaries had brought Christianity to every continent on
the globe--to Capetown in South Africa and Travancore in
India as well as to obscure and little known places like Eimeo
in the Society Islands and Great Namaqualand in Africa.

The influence of the London Missionary Society on

the pan-evangelical ideal was important. It was the first
major attempt at evangelical union on a large scale in Britain and it therefore set the pace and example for similar
associations. Indeed, the Religious Tract Society and the
London Society for Promoting Christianity Amongst the Jews
directly owed their foundations to the L. M. S. ; the British
and Foreign Bible Society indirectly. Its network of auxiliary societies, constantly in contact with each other and
with the parent society in London, brought thousands of
Christians into practical and spiritual harmony. Unity was
also nurtured in London each year when Society directors
and patrons from all over the country attended its anniversaries in May. Unfortunately, not much is recorded of the
spirit of fraternity within the domestic operations of the
L. M. S. As is so often the case, when a movement flour-
ishes, its successes and achievements are taken for granted.
Only when it faces controversy are its failures examined in
detail. Nevertheless, there are several instances on record
which demonstrate how pan-evangelicalism in the London Missionary Society reached out to the larger church.

In the early years of the Society, for example, its
directors frequently participated in the ordinations of Society missionaries. In the case of the missionaries John
Jefferson and John Eyre (no relation to the Anglican Secretary), the Evangelical Magazine reported that "two such ordinations have seldom occurred, in which Episcopalians, Seceders, Antiburghers, Presbyterians, Independents and Methodists all united."[50] At the Society's anniversary in June
1799, the directors took a critical step and initiated a communion service at the end of Missionary Week, perhaps the
first time in recent memory that Anglicans and Dissenters
had sat at the same communion table. The service at Haberdasher's Hall in London--performed by twelve ministers--
included the Anglicans Thomas Haweis, William Cooper, and
George Hamilton, together with an interdenominational group
of Dissenters. The Evangelical Magazine reported this memorable event in the following way:[51]

> About fifty ministers were among the communicants.
> Such a solemn, delightful season, has seldom been
> known ... It was highly gratifying, to behold
> ministers and brethren of the Episcopal, Presby-
> terian, Independent, and Methodist, denominations,
> uniting as one in the body of Christ, to eat of the
> same bread, and drink of the same cup.... May
> we not hope that this example of liberality will

excite multitudes at home and abroad to unite in
the same manner, and that members of the whole
church of Christ on earth, thus living in peace,
shall enjoy the presence of the God of Peace among
them.

It was perhaps in its foreign operations that the
L. M. S. contributed most to Christian union.   Since it is
not within the scope of this book to discuss at length pan-
evangelicalism outside Britain, we have not been able to
do justice to the creative impact of the Society in this field.
But others have.   As Norman Goodall points out, the London Missionary Society, through its Fundamental Principle,
did much to provide an environment in which the great union
churches of North and South India, China, and Malagasy
could later develop and flourish. [52]   But it was the individual efforts of the missionaries themselves that deserve special praise and recognition here.   Isolated from Britain, often in foreign lands hostile to their ministries, the missionaries from virtually all of the societies found a very real
and vital Christian union in their common successes and
failures, joys and sorrows.   The stories of interdenominational fellowship in the mission stations that dotted the world,
some of which we will allude to in the next chapter, are
touching and place in proper perspective the relative unim-
portance of subsequent interdenominational strife at home.
Nevertheless, though the achievements of the London Missionary Society were inestimable, the Society faced many
formidable problems in its relationship with other societies.
It is to these that we must now turn.

NOTES

1. W. Carey, An Enquiry (1792), 84. Interestingly, sev-
    eral years later, Carey proposed a "federation" of
    missionaries to meet every ten years at the Cape of
    Good Hope. See R. Rouse, "William Carey's Pleas-
    ing Dream," International Review of Missions, XXXVIII
    (1949), 181 ff.
2. Cf., I. Fletcher, "The Fundamental Principle of the
    London Missionary Society," Transactions of the Con-
    gregational Historical Society, XIX (1963), 224.
3. For Horne's biography, see C. Hole, The Early History
    of the Church Missionary Society (1896), 632.
4. M. Horne, Letters on Missions: Addressed to the Pro-
    testant Ministers of the British Churches (1794), 60,
    21.

5. For Eyre's biography, see Evangelical Magazine,
    11 (1803), 225 ff. A prominent place in the early
    pan-evangelical movement should be given to the
    Evangelical Magazine. It was founded in 1793 and
    included among its contributors evangelicals from all
    camps of the Revival with the possible exception of
    the Wesleyans. The impact of this publication on
    subsequent pan-evangelical enterprises including the
    London Missionary Society has often been noted. See
    R. Lovett, The History of the London Missionary
    Society (1899), I, 10.; F. E. Mineka, The Dissidence
    of Dissent (1944).
6. See Evangelical Magazine, 2 (1794), 476 f.; A. S.
    Wood, Thomas Haweis (1957), 191 f.
7. Cf., J. Bennett, Memoir of the Life of David Bogue
    (1827), 170; W. Brown, The History of the Propaga-
    tion of Christianity Among the Heathen Since the Re-
    formation (1854), II, 98 fn.; N. Goodall, A History
    of the London Missionary Society (1954), 2 f.; G. G.
    Cameron, The Scots Kirk in London (1979), 94.
8. For Bogue's unpublished biography, see C. Terpstra,
    "David Bogue 1750-1825: Pioneer and Missionary
    Educator," (Edinburgh University Phd Thesis 1959).
9. For an account of Bogue's visit to Bristol and John
    Ryland Jr.'s chapel where he read Carey's letters,
    see W. Ellis, The History of the London Missionary
    Society (1844), 16; W. C. Northcott, Glorious Com-
    pany (1945), 16 f. Ryland's involvement in this meet-
    ing has led at least two historians wrongly to assume
    that as a Baptist, he was instrumental in the found-
    ing of the L.M.S. See J. T. Godfrey and J. Ward,
    The History of Friar Lane Baptist Church (1903),
    217 f.
10. Evangelical Magazine, 2 (1794), 378 f. Terpstra points
    out that when Bogue wrote his article, he had in
    mind a society primarily for Independents. See Terp-
    stra, op.cit., 157 f.
11. Besides the men already mentioned, the key ministers
    involved in planning the Society from January to Sep-
    tember 1795 included William Francis Platt, Inde-
    pendent minister at Holywell Mount Chapel; John Tow-
    ers, Independent minister at the Barbican; Joel Abra-
    ham Knight, Connexion minister as Spa Field's Chap-
    el; Thomas Williams, one-time Wesleyan but now an
    episcopally-ordained member of Lady Huntingdon's
    Connexion; James Knight, son of Titus Knight and
    Independent minister at Collier's Rent (Southwark);

Joseph Brooksbank, Independent minister at Haberdasher's Hall; George Townsend, former member of
Lady Huntingdon's Connexion but now pastor of the
Independent chapel in Ramsgate; and Thomas Haweis,
Rector of Aldwincle in Northamptonshire but also a
resident in London.   Prominent evangelicals like William Roby, Independent minister at Canon Street chapel in Manchester and Edward Williams, then minister
at Carr's Lane, Birmingham, were two of the more
enthusiastic provincial patrons.   The inclusion of
these men is based on attendance records (nine meetings or more) between January 8 and September 8,
1795, as recorded in the L.M.S. Minutes.

12. Cf., I. Fletcher, "The Formative Years of the London
Missionary Society," unpublished MS in the L.M.S.
archives (1961).

13. Ellis, op.cit., 25.

14. Sermons Preached in London at the Formation of the
London Missionary Society (1795), 425.

15. Evangelical Magazine, 3 (1795), 425.

16. Sermons, op.cit., 64 f.

17. Protestant Dissenters Magazine, (1795), 518 f.

18. Cf., J. Stoughton, Religion in England Under Queen
Anne and the Georges (1878), II, 346 fn.; J. R.
Leifchild, John Leifchild (1863), 24.

19. Cf., Missionary Magazine (1797), 448 where the Scottish Presbyterian George Cowie (a director of the
L.M.S.) told his countrymen that the Wesleyans would
be excluded from the Society.   See also J. C. Marshman, The Life and Times of Carey, Marshman and
Ward (1859), I, 395, where the same was said of
the Baptists.

20. L.M.S. Minutes, May 9, 1796; Cf., N. Goodall, The
Fundamental Principle of the London Missionary Society (1945); I. Fletcher, "The Fundamental Principle of the London Missionary Society," Transactions of the Congregational Historical Society, XIX
(1963).

21. L.M.S. Minutes, May 11, 1796.

22. Apparently, some of the London ministers wanted Bogue
to be excluded from the meetings at which the Society was planned because they considered him to be
"a high and overbearing man."   See Fletcher, op.cit.,
225.

23. The seminal importance of Horne's Letters at these
early meetings is made very clear by Matthew Wilks
in a letter he wrote many years later to the historian

James Bennett. The MS letter, postmarked 22 August 1827, is in the possession of Irene Fletcher,
Librarian Emeritus of the L. M. S. who kindly brought
it to my attention.

24.   Evangelical Magazine, 2 (1794), 478.
25.   J. Townsend, Memoirs (1828), 55.
26.   Evangelical Magazine, 3 (1795), 11 f.
27.   L. M. S. Home Correspondence (1.5.A): C. Sundius to
the Swedish Brethren, April 1798.
28.   See Wesleyan Methodist Magazine (1904), 215 f.; J. H.
Rigg, Jabez Bunting (1906), 61.
29.   See S. Pigott, ed. , An Authentic Narrative of Four
Years Residence at Tongataboo (By Geo. V.) (1815).
Vason writes: "... the Directors of the London Mission[ary Society], after examining my religious principles, and my motives for accompanying the Missionaries [on the Duff], wished me to become one of
their number." It should be pointed out that Vason
served the Society as a bricklayer, not as a preacher,
although he is listed as a missionary. See Ibid. , 19.
Cf. , J. Orange, Narrative of the Late George Vason
(1840), 216 f.; Godfrey and Ward, op. cit. , 227, 233.
30.   J. Campbell, Maritime Discovery and Christian Mission (1840), 280 f.
31.   See L. M. S. Minutes, March 30, September 14, 21, 1829.
32.   I can find no evidence that Baptist missionaries were
involved in the L. M. S. at the level of director although Joseph Reyner, identified by Ford K. Brown
as a Baptist layman, was a director between 1796
and 1827. See F. K. Brown, Fathers of the Victorians (1961), 245, 352.
33.   Angus. Pearce Letters: S. Pearce to Wife, September
20, 1795.
34.   Cited in S. P. Carey, Samuel Pearce: The Baptist
Brainerd (3rd ed. , n. d.), 179.
35.   L. M. S. Autograph Book: S. Greatheed to J. Sutcliffe,
November 3, 1795. Enclosed with this letter was a
"Plan" of the L. M. S. which Greatheed hoped Sutcliffe would circulate among the Baptist churches.
For an early attempt at cooperation in missions between Baptists and the Independents in Worcestershire in 1794, see S. Pearce, Missionary Correspondence (1814), 3 f. After 1795, missionary prayer
meetings involving L. M. S. directors and their Baptist counterparts were frequent. See J. Rippon, The
Baptist Annual Register, 3(1801), 39. On at least
one occasion, Pearce contemplated preaching a fund-

raising sermon for the L.M.S.   See Angus.   Pearce
Letters: S. Pearce to Wife, January 29, 1798.

36.   Cf., W. R. Ward, Religion and Society in England
(1972), 17; D. Bogue and J. Bennett, History of the
Dissenters (1808), IV, 237 f.; J. D. Walsh, "Meth-
odism at the End of the Eighteenth Century," in
E. G. Rupp and R. E. Davies, A History of the
Methodist Church in Great Britain (1965), I, 297.

37.   Cited in G. Redford and J. A. James, eds., The Autobiography of the Rev. William Jay (1855), 173.   Cf.,
Evangelical Magazine, 6 (1798), 161.

38.   J. Eyre, Union and Friendly Intercourse Recommended
(1798), 5, 24.   In reference to the founding of the
L.M.S., Eyre alludes to Wesleyans who "mingled
with us in our assemblies, assisted us in our de-
liberations, adopted our plans, and cooperated in
accomplishing them with the utmost vigour." Ibid.,
10.   Is Eyre referring to Wesleyan participation or
at least support in the founding of the London Missionary Society?   Eyre's counterpart in the Wesleyan
camp could have been Thomas Taylor.   See T. Taylor,
The Reconciler; or an Humble Attempt to ...
reconcile the Experimental Calvinists with the
Experimental Arminians (1806), v-vi.   In the preface of this book, Taylor wrote: "I apprehend,
the two parties I wish to be united, namely,
[those] who are called Arminians and Calvinists,
are the only sects who are labouring to spread
vital and practical godliness throughout the world.
... And these having all the world against them,
it is highly necessary they should be united among
themselves."

39.   M.C.A. Pawson Papers: J. Pawson to J. Benson,
April 9, 1798.

40.   If there was an ecumenical thrust within Wesleyan
Methodism at this time, it was directed not toward
the Calvinistic Dissenters but toward the Church of
England.   In 1798, Thomas Coke was secretly ne-
gotiating with William Wilberforce for a reunion of
the Wesleyan Connexion with the Church of England.
See Bod. MSS Wilberforce, d 17, f. 129; c 3, Fols.
39 and 43:   T. Coke to W. Wilberforce, March 1798,
March 26, November 3, 1798.   Cf., J. A. Vickers,
Thomas Coke (1969), 202 f.

41.   For Hill's biography, see P. E. Sangster, "The Life
of Rowland Hill," (Oxford University D. Phil. Thesis
1965).

42. For Haweis' biography, see A. S. Wood, Thomas
     Haweis (1957).
43. Other clerical directors of the L. M. S. between 1795
     and 1800 were George Campbell Brodbelt, incumbent
     of Loudwater in Buckinghamshire who served the So-
     ciety between 1799 and 1800, David Jones, rector of
     Llangen in Wales (1797-1799), and John Walker, Fel-
     low of Trinity College, Dublin and founder in 1804
     of the Walkerites, an extreme Calvinistic sect. This
     list may be extended to include Thomas Pentycross,
     rector of St. Mary's Wallingford and Thomas Wills,
     one-time chaplain to Lady Huntingdon and an itinerant
     Anglican. Neither of these men was a director, but
     both played a very influential role in the Society's
     early development. Some historians have mistakenly
     believed that Church evangelicals withdrew in force
     from the L. M. S. to form the Church Missionary So-
     ciety in 1799. See C. I. Foster, An Errand of Mer-
     cy (1960), 66. Until the founding of the C. M. S.,
     most evangelical clergymen, with the exception of
     those mentioned above, remained uninvolved in for-
     eign missions except for occasional contributions to the
     Society for the Propagation of the Gospel and the various
     Methodist and Nonconformist missions then in existence.
44. Cf., C. Hole, The Early History of the Church Mis-
     sionary Society (1896), 156; Congregational Magazine
     (1831), 212; Goodall, op. cit., 3 ff.; M. M. Hennell,
     John Venn and the Clapham Sect (1958), 235; W.
     Goode, A Memoir of the Late William Goode (2nd ed.
     1828), 60; C. H. E. Smyth, Simeon and Church Or-
     der (1940), 294.
45. For the founding of the Church Missionary Society, see
     C. Hole, op. cit.; E. Stock, The History of the Church
     Missionary Society (1899), I, 68 ff.
46. Hennell, op. cit., 234.
47. C. M. S. General Correspondence (G. AC. 3. 1) f. 39:
     T. Haweis to T. Scott, November 15, 1800.
48. Cited in E. Sidney, The Life of the Rev. Rowland Hill
     (1834), 177.
49. See Lovett, op. cit., I, 110.
50. Evangelical Magazine, 4 (1796), 385. Cf., Evangelical
     Magazine, 5 (1797), 516.
51. Evangelical Magazine, 7 (1799), 252.
52. Goodall, op. cit., passim.

Though the London Missionary Society was never able
to fulfill within itself the dream of pan-evangelical unity, it
still acted as if it were an organization for all evangelicals.
This not unnaturally produced considerable conflict with denominations that had their own missionary societies and
were not willing to share with the London Missionary Society the largesse and the manpower of their own members.
Consequently, part of the history of the attempted movement
towards evangelical unity must necessarily concern itself
with the inter-societal relations that existed between the
L. M. S. and its "competitors." This competition had two
important effects on the London Missionary Society's internal development. First it demonstrated to the Society's directors that their organization was not, after all, the only
missionary society in existence and that, indeed, other missionary societies had an equal if not more legitimate claim
on the support of their denominational brethren. Secondly,
because of a metamorphosis within the Society by which the
Congregationalists took an increasingly disproportionate share
in the Society's governance, it soon became apparent that
the London Missionary Society, if not in name, was in fact
becoming a denominational organization like its neighbors.
In this chapter we will first examine the London Missionary
Society's continuing attempt to establish a relationship--
ineffectively as it turned out--with its denominational neighbors, and then consider the way in which the Society's failure
to win a wider pan-evangelical following assisted its internal
development into a denominational organization dominated by
the Congregationalists.

Relations between the London Missionary Society and
the Baptist Missionary Society during the first decade of the
nineteenth century were cordial. Since William Carey and
his colleagues were well established in India by 1800, their

information and encouragement at the time in which the London Missionary Society planned its own Indian mission, was gratefully received. In 1801, for example, William Carey told the directors of the London Missionary Society that he was very busy in the Baptist mission and that there was work "for a thousand more."[1] When the L. M. S. missionaries George Cran and August Des Granges arrived in India four years later, Carey expressed hope that "no difference of opinion respecting any of the ordinances of the gospel will be permitted to interrupt our Christian union and fellowship," and urged "that you will write in the most frank and unreserved manner, and permit us to participate in your joys and your sorrows, that by mutual sympathy and mutual counsel we may animate each other in the work of the Lord."[2] Cooperation on the home front was equally cordial. Baptists frequently appeared at London Missionary Society anniversaries as official representatives of the Baptist Missionary Society and the L. M. S. reciprocated.[3] Literature freely flowed back and forth between the two societies. The London Missionary Society sent all their general circulars to the Baptist Missionary Society and its missionaries and the Baptists did likewise.

The end of the first decade of the nineteenth century, however, witnessed some deterioration in Baptist-paedobaptist relations and this in turn damaged goodwill between the two societies. In 1810, Thomas Haweis, a London Missionary Society director, made some serious accusations about Baptist "sheep-stealing" in an Evangelical Magazine article, and this led to an indignant walk-out by the magazine's Baptist contributors and the subsequent re-founding of the Baptist Magazine.[4] Since most of the contributors of the Evangelical Magazine were also London Missionary Society directors, the affair had an adverse effect on relations between the Baptist Missionary Society and the L. M. S. It was now that Andrew Fuller who for years had been agitating for a return to a closed communion table finally got his way, and from 1812 on, most Particular Baptists in Britain as well as in the mission field, ceased sharing their communion table with non-Baptists.[5] Robert Hall, himself a Particular Baptist and an advocate of open communion, lamented this decision and said that though he had the highest esteem for the Baptist mission in India, he could not "but feel some alarm for the consequences of the fact being known to the heathen world, that they form a separate caste from their fellow Christians."[6]

Two other irritating problems further exacerbated an

already fragile relationship between the two societies.   First there was the question, already alluded to in the last chapter, of missionary collections being taken by London Missionary Society fundraisers from among Baptist congregations.   During the first decade of the century, the London Missionary Society had been very careful not to do this.   When, for example, the London Missionary Society's first ship, the Duff, was captured by French privateers in 1799, and the Society launched a massive fundraising campaign to recover the financial loss, George Lambert the Independent minister from Hull and L. M. S. director, checked himself from calling for a collection at an interdenominational prayer meeting he was attending because he was on Baptist premises and realized that the Baptists were understandably "rather inclined to support their own [mission]."[7]   After 1810, however, London Missionary Society collectors were not so reluctant to go after Baptist money.   Whether or not the London Missionary Society thought that previous paedobaptist support for the Baptist Missionary Society justified this practice is uncertain, but it nevertheless provoked the wrath of Andrew Fuller who complained that the directors of the London Missionary Society were "greatly driven for money, and betake themselves to strange means to obtain it.   We have never pushed collections; but they have increased of their own accord, and go on to increase, especially in our own denomination."[8]

    The second problem of this period involved what we shall call "the problem of the missionary convert to adult baptism."   A number of L. M. S. missionaries, after baptizing countless numbers of adult native converts, announced their own conversion to the doctrine of adult baptism and then migrated to the Baptist Missionary Society.   Though this naturally delighted the B. M. S. which gained seasoned missionaries at the expense of its rival, it distressed the London Missionary Society greatly.   The problem of the missionary convert commenced early in the century and continued to plague relations between the two societies long after.[9]

    Partly as a result of these frictions, the societies avoided each other's anniversaries throughout most of the second decade of the century and had as few dealings with each other as possible.   However, this was followed by a thaw. In 1820, the London Missionary Society asked William Ward, on leave from the Baptist mission at Serampore, to preach at their annual meeting.[10]   The Baptist Missionary Society reciprocated two years later by inviting William Jay, the

famous Independent minister of Argyle Chapel in Bath and a
director of the London Missionary Society, to preach at their
anniversary, thus recommencing a pattern of reciprocal invitations that continued beyond our period.[11] This was indeed a surprising turn of events, but occurrences which had
taken place as early as 1818 had begun to pave the way for
reconciliation. In that year, as we shall see, the Missionary Society decided to change its title to the less presumptuous "London Missionary Society." Andrew Fuller had always disliked the arrogance of the Society's original title;
now his animus was somewhat abated.[12]

        One year later, the London Secretaries Association
was founded. This organization brought the various missionary society secretaries together for monthly discussions
on mission-related topics and provided a much needed channel of communication denied them in previous years.[13] Finally, and perhaps most significantly, a gradual change had
taken place within the London Missionary Society itself.
Dominated primarily by Congregationalists by 1820, the Society began to see itself as a denominational organization.
A second generation of directors had by now replaced most
of the founding fathers who, because of death and retirement, no longer managed the Society's affairs. As a result, much of the pan-evangelical idealism of the 1790's had
retired with them.

                                    II.

        Wesleyan relations with the London Missionary Society
had at first also been warm. The tone had been set in 1795
when the L.M.S. assured Thomas Coke that its intention was
"to act as Brethren toward missionaries from other denominations."[14] In the mission field, fraternal relations continued, for the most part, throughout our period and were
little affected by subsequent events in Britain. In 1816, for
example, one Wesleyan missionary reported that he had been
graciously received by a colleague associated with the London Missionary Society who "very kindly offered to assist
me in every possible way, assuring me, that if I should ac-
company him to Nemacqua Land, he would make me welcome to part of his house, where after remaining with him
a sufficient length of time to speak their language, he would
introduce me to other tribes, where I might form a settle-
ment on what plan so-ever I thought proper."[15] The Wesleyans reciprocated. When the L.M.S. missionary Richard

Knill arrived in Colombo, Ceylon in 1819, he was openly
received by the Wesleyans with "kindness & attention" and
for this act of Christian friendship, the London Missionary
Society voted the Wesleyans a set of the Society's transactions and their annual report. [16] On the home front, initial
dealings were equally friendly.   Representatives from the
Wesleyan Connexion regularly attended London Missionary
Society anniversaries as late as 1808 and the L.M.S. reciprocated. [17]   Christopher Sundius, a wealthy London merchant and, as we have mentioned, a prominent member of
the Wesleyan Connexion, was also a director of the London
Missionary Society between 1797 and 1802, and seems to
have acted as a liaison between the two groups.   In the
provinces, where L.M.S. and Wesleyan fundraisers often
met each other, there was also much fraternization.   For
example, one Wesleyan fundraiser told Thomas Coke that
while on a collection tour at Stamford, he "very unexpected-
ly ... met Mr. Berry from Bath, & Mr. Greatheed of Newport Pagnell, who lent us their assistance on the Lord's
day ..."[18]

     By the second decade of the century, however, rela-
tions had deteriorated substantially.   This was primarily due
to two factors.   In the first place, the West Indies had always been a bone of contention between the London Missionary Society and the Wesleyan Connexion.   As early as 1798,
Thomas Coke begged the L.M.S. not to compete with the
Wesleyans in Jamaica when he heard that they were planning
to establish their own mission in this part of the world.
Nevertheless, the London Missionary Society decided "on
account of the great extent of the unoccupied field in that
Island ... to go forward immediately to bring into effect
the mission already determined ..."[19] At first this proved
to be only a minor point of irritation between the two societies, but when the London Missionary Society, with its
superior financial and organizational strength, began to expand the West Indian mission, the traditional Wesleyan predominance in the area was threatened seriously, for the
Wesleyans had neither the money nor the manpower to compete.   Consequently, in 1809 Coke warned Robert Johnson,
a fellow Wesleyan, that "we must endeavour to supply the
West Indies well, or we shall lose them ... [The L.M.S.
does] not preach where we have preachers, but watch every
opportunity to seize on a vacancy."[20]   Early the next year,
the threat apparently still existed, because Coke again wrote
Johnson that "It is a melancholy observation, that for many
years (I believe, for five or six) the work in the West Indies

has been losing ground, and I ascribe this in great manner
to the want of a full supply of missionaries. If we do not
keep up a full supply of missionaries God will give up that
great work to the Calvinists."[21] Even on the home front,
Coke was anxious lest his Connexion's plan to send a mission to France be eclipsed by the London Missionary Society
which had recently introduced French into the curriculum of
its missionary academy at Gosport, run by David Bogue.
"Oh let us send Christianity in the form of Methodism, to
France," Coke wrote George Highfield in 1811 because
"Bogue's youngsters will supplant us, if we do not make
haste."[22]

Secondly, relations had deteriorated over the problem of missionary collections. As in the Baptist case, London Missionary Society fundraisers had no qualms after 1800
about asking Wesleyan Methodists for money. It should
again be pointed out that the London Missionary Society saw
nothing wrong in this activity. The name of their society,
as we have mentioned before, was simply "The Missionary
Society" and most of its directors believed that their organization was indeed the missionary society for all evangelicals, the Wesleyans included.[23] Consequently, by the
second decade of the nineteenth century, the Wesleyans
faced the danger of losing financial support to the Calvinists at a time when their own mission needed every penny
it could scrape together to survive. Writing in 1810, two
Wesleyan itinerants on a fundraising tour for the Connexion
complained to Robert Smith, Secretary of the Connexion's
missionary committee in London, that "the Calvinists dog
us from place to place and they aim to lead astray all they
can."[24] Two years later, Coke reported to Smith:[25]

> The London Missionary Society are forming com-
> mittees of two or three of our friends, to raise
> annual subscriptions among our societies and hear-
> ers for the support of their mission. This they
> have been doing for some time by the means of
> their friends only ... But they now are endeavour-
> ing to enlist our friends in the work ... A Rev.
> Mr. Collinson [sic] has already been here and at
> Newcastle, and I believe, at Bristol, and all over
> the Kingdom, to preach in our Chapels as well as
> other places for the Calvinist missions.

And in 1813, George Banwell of Chichester was writing to
Smith about John Hunt, the Congregationalist brother of Legh

Hunt and a director of the L.M.S. who, for the purposes of
fundraising "went and hired one of the houses which was offered us." Banwell went on to complain that Hunt "is a
powerful and bitter enemy to the cause of Methodism [and]
in this mission, he watches us as narrowly as a cat does a
mouse and says he'll oppose us wherever we go."[26] In-
trusions like this provoked the wrath of not a few Wesleyan
leaders.   Thomas Coke, for instance, told Smith in 1813:[27]

> It is impossible for me to tell you the strong sen-
> sations that some of us felt when we read, in the
> last Evangelical Magazine, that the Dissenters had
> recently preached and made collections in one of
> our chapels in Leeds for their Missions, at a
> time when our missionary affairs are so awfully
> embarrassed.

London Missionary Society encroachments played a
part, albeit a minor one, in the establishment in 1818 of
the Wesleyan Methodist Missionary Society.   The founding
of a mission patronized by the Wesleyans, of course, was
a dream that well predated the second decade of the nineteenth century.   Thomas Coke had long wanted Conference
to give more recognition to foreign missionary concerns and
establish them on a sounder basis, but John Wesley had felt
that Conference should give home missions priority.   In the
troubled days that beset the Connexion immediately after
Wesley's death in 1791, Conference had been compelled to
turn its attention to more pressing domestic concerns.   Until 1813 therefore, the Wesleyan foreign missionary effort
was left largely to the supervision of Thomas Coke and one
or two associates.   Once the Connexion had attained a certain degree of internal stability, however, it was able to
pay closer attention to its foreign missionary concerns.
Yet this attention may well have been given special urgency
by Conference's realization, that unless their foreign mission was consolidated and better funded, the mission field
would fall into Calvinist hands by default.

It is perhaps one of the ironies of the history of foreign missions that in its quest to be a "catholic" society,
the London Missionary Society almost forced the Wesleyans
into the position of having to found their own missionary organization in self defense.   Indeed, when the Wesleyans announced to the world the birth in Leeds of what would eventually become the Wesleyan Methodist Missionary Society,
many L.M.S. directors were both surprised and hurt.   But

when, at the founding meeting of the Leeds society, William
Eccles, Independent minister of the city's Old White Chapel
and a prominent director of the London Missionary Society
suggested to the assembled Wesleyans that "the missionary
cause is but one, and that in which all denominations of
Christians are united," Jabez Bunting, who was presiding
over the meeting, pointedly corrected any misconceptions
that might have arisen from Eccles' proclamation by instructing his colleagues that "there is no common fund in
existence, out of which all Missionary establishments may
claim and receive pecuniary assistance. The cause is one,
but it is promoted by several distinct societies, each of
which has its distinct and separate fund."28 Bunting was
discreetly telling the London Missionary Society to keep its
hands off Wesleyan money!

Like the Baptists, the Wesleyans avoided London Missionary Society anniversaries during the second decade of
the nineteenth century. But by 1818, for reasons we have
already mentioned in the Baptist connection, relations between the two societies greatly improved. Jabez Bunting
was present at the 1818 general meeting of the London Missionary Society when it altered its name.29 One year later,
through a generous offer from Joseph Butterworth, the Wesleyan M. P., the London Missionary Society held one of its
anniversary sermons at the Wesleyan Chapel at Queen Street
in London.30 It was not, however, until 1823, that a director of the London Missionary Society preached at the
Wesleyan Missionary Society anniversary, thus re-commenc-
ing a regular pattern of mutual invitations.31 So, too, the
founding of the London Secretaries Association in 1819 and
the change of outlook that had taken place within the London
Missionary Society itself, all contributed to the easing of
former animosities and a resumption of peace and cordiality.

III.

Relations between the London Missionary Society and
the Church Missionary Society were able to weather the vi-
cissitudes of the first three decades of the nineteenth century and beyond for a number of reasons. In the first place,
because the evangelical patrons of both societies shared similar theological beliefs, doctrinal controversy did not stand
in the way of cooperation to the same degree that it had
done for the Baptist and Wesleyan societies. Moreover, a
small number of "regular" Anglican churchmen who were

directors of the Church Missionary Society also served token
appointments on the directorship of the London Missionary
Society thus opening channels of communication hitherto not
enjoyed by either the Baptists or the Wesleyans until the
founding of the London Secretaries Association in 1819. The
threat of misunderstanding, therefore, was greatly minimized.

The hard feelings harbored by some L. M. S. Anglican
patrons against colleagues who had decided to patronize the
Church Missionary Society when it was founded in 1799, were
mitigated somewhat by the attitudes of the Church society itself. When the Duff was captured by French privateers in
the summer of 1799, the Church Missionary Society sent to
the L. M. S. a contribution together with several letters of
condolence from prominent directors assuring the London
Missionary Society that the C. M. S. was its coadjutor and
not its rival. [32] Even Charles Simeon, who by this time
was very careful about his dealings with irregular Anglicans
and Dissenters, dashed off a quick letter to the London Missionary Society encouraging the directors to "persevere in
their efforts."[33] Needless to say, the London Missionary
Society was grateful for this help and encouragement.

Relations between both societies were perhaps most
cordial in the mission field. The Church Missionary Society was very slow in getting its first missionaries off,
but when they finally succeeded, the missionaries sent out
by them were Lutherans whom C. F. Steinkopf, Lutheran
pastor of the Savoy in London and Foreign Secretary of the
London Missionary Society, had helped the directors of the
C. M. S. to find. The Church Missionary Society reciprocated. In New South Wales, for example, the great Anglican missionary Samuel Marsden, a director of the C. M. S.
offered in 1802, to act as a liaison between the two societies
in this area, and even to visit the L. M. S. station at Otaheite
"in order to inspect the mission, and promote as much as
possible the designs of the [London Missionary] Society."[34]
Consequently, it was men like Marsden and Steinkopf who
set the pace for continued cooperation between the two societies.

Relations, at least during the first decade of the century, were as cordial at home as they were in the mission
field. Unlike the Baptists and Wesleyans, "regular" Anglicans affiliated with the Church Missionary Society participated in L. M. S. anniversaries almost without interruption
from 1799 until 1830 and beyond. [35] The London Missionary

Society reciprocated.   It was also a normal occurrence that
Church Missionary Society strongholds in London like St.
Saviours, St. Brides, St. Leonards and St. Andrews, would
throw their doors open to at least one missionary sermon
during London Missionary Society anniversaries.   So, too,
there was a regular sharing of missionary literature between the two societies throughout the first thirty years of
the century and beyond.

     While relations between the two societies remained
relatively fraternal through the years, we must stress that
it was a fraternity initially qualified by two Anglican suspicions that we have discussed in another context--namely
the long-term belief that the London Missionary Society was
in part patronized by enemies of the Church of England who
had irresponsibly supported the French Revolution and a continuing fear that the undenominational mission churches which
the L. M. S. hoped to establish were in some way irregular
and ultimately prejudicial to the establishment.   These suspicions largely explain why the Church Missionary Society
was established in the first place, and, as the Evangelical
party within the Church of England grew in size, importance
and respectability, why its members were even more cir-
cumspect than before, in avoiding unnecessary associations
with individuals or organizations which might give evangelical Anglicanism a bad name.   Consequently, "regular" Anglican churchmen, who before 1800 had avoided the London
Missionary Society, continued to do so after 1800 even when
they had securely established their own missionary organization and no longer believed as intensely that the Dissenters
were republicans bent on undermining Church and State.

     If anything disrupted inter-societal relations during
our period, it was again the difficult problem of missionary
collections.   Like the Baptists and the Wesleyans, the Church
Missionary Society also objected to L. M. S. fundraising in-
cursions into Anglican parishes.   In 1814, for example, the
Church Missionary Society complained of an L. M. S. circular entitled "To Friends of Missionary Societies."   It was
designed, they claimed, to convince Anglicans that churchmen were among the London Missionary Society's strongest
advocates, so that they could gain "a footing (an intrusion,
some thought) in Church of England congregations."[36]   This
complaint was not unfounded.   James Vaughan and Thomas
Biddulph, two Church Missionary Society directors from
Bristol, had complained two years before that they "had no
atom of jealousy of the missionary success of Dissenters on

their own ground; but to see Dissenters who had a broad
area of their own, coming to gather a harvest out of Church
fields," made them "extremely uneasy."[37] There was a
similar situation in Liverpool where, in 1813, Richard Blacow, Vicar of St. Mark's, protested that "scarcely a finger
is moved among us, while the whole body ... of ... Calvinist Dissenters are pushing forward with a vast momentum" and warned that if nothing was done about the situation,
"we shall soon have an episcopal Establishment with a dissenting population."[38]

The arrogant sounding title of "The Missionary Society" also created a great deal of mischief. In 1813, Basil Woodd, then Rector of Drayton Beauchamp, complained
that the clergy perpetually confounded the London Missionary
Society with the Church Missionary Society and suggested
that "this circumstance, on the occasion of future sermons,
ought to be very distinctly stated, as the interests of the
Church Missionary Society are very materially injured by
the confusion."[39] The degree to which this confusion ir-
ritated Church Missionary Society officials in London can
be gauged by a letter that Josiah Pratt, the C.M.S. Secretary, wrote to the Cork Auxiliary in 1814. In it, he expressed "regret ... that the Missionary Society is putting
forth pretensions to the support of the Church" when the
Church Missionary Society had existed in Ireland for several years. The effect of this situation, Pratt continued,
was seriously to cut into his society's collections.[40] One
enterprising patron of the C.M.S. even suggested turning
the tables on the London Missionary Society by omitting the
word "Church" from Church Missionary Society circulars
thereby leading the Dissenters to believe that the C.M.S.
was their society also![41] But after the change in name
and composition of the London Missionary Society, even
these irritations had vanished by 1820.

IV.

Harried by conflict with denominations they had initially hoped to win to the cause of pan-evangelicalism, the
directors of "The Missionary Society" slowly came to realize that their organization was in fact but one missionary
society among many. This acceptance of reality was perhaps symbolized by the Society's change of title in 1818.
At that year's anniversary, Robert Steven, an Independent
lay director of the L.M.S. proposed that the name of the

Society be changed from "The Missionary Society" to the
less presumptuous "London Missionary Society." In this
proposal, Steven pointed out that as several other missionary societies had been formed since the institution of the
L. M. S. in 1795 "some confusion had arisen for want of a
title more distinctive than that which was then adopted."
And since other societies had, for a number of years, re-
ferred to The Missionary Society as the London Missionary
Society, Steven proposed (and it was unanimously agreed)
"that hereafter in all publications of the Society, its Title
shall be thus expressed:--'The Missionary Society, instituted in the year 1795, usually called The London Missionary Society.'"[42] At the same meeting, David Bogue, by now
an old man, had to admit that when the L. M. S. "was instituted, it stood nearly alone--it was a General Society,
and the name was by no means improper: but other Societies have arisen. It is now highly proper that we should
take a name that may not be thought assuming or improper."[43]

    This change in title, however, only reflected a
more basic change in the Society's internal composition by
1818. By that time the Society was dominated by the Congregationalists and therefore was no longer interested in
recruiting Baptist, Wesleyan or even Anglican assistance
in the form of money or missionaries. In part, the evolution of the London Missionary Society into a Congregational
organization was assisted by the migration of many Calvinistic Methodists, English Presbyterians and ministers of
Lady Huntingdon's Connexion into Independency.[44] Converse-
ly, as the other missionary societies gained in strength and
prominence, they attracted away from the London Missionary Society what little Baptist, Wesleyan and Anglican patronage it initially possessed. But the development of the
London Missionary Society into a Congregational institution
reflected even broader changes within Nonconformity itself.

    There had always been prior to 1818 a small anti-
pan-evangelical faction within the evangelical movement.
Proud to be called Congregationalists or Baptists, these
men had no desire to sacrifice denominational identities at
the altar of pan-evangelicalism. The centrifugal force of
denominationalism within the evangelical movement was not
very strong in the early years, but by the second decade of
the nineteenth century, it had become an increasingly powerful force, and gave birth to several attempts to group like-
minded chapels into a coherent union.[45] Ironically, the

London Missionary Society itself had done much to nurture
the hardening of denominational consciousness within the
Congregational camp. Independents who had previously been
unified only in regional associations and county unions began to find a national identity in London when they came
each May from all parts of the country to attend the Society's anniversary. [46] Indeed, it was during the Society's
Annual Meeting in 1806, that a group of Independents formed
the first Congregational Union. [47] Because the leading Independents of the day did not support this early scheme, the
Union dissolved after only three years, but the relative successes of the Welsh Calvinistic Methodists in 1811 and the
Particular Baptists in 1812 in forming their respective unions
encouraged the unionless Independents into making the London Missionary Society a kind of surrogate union for their
denomination until a more permanent union could be established in 1832. [48]

The parent society in London, however, did everything it could to preserve the semblance of evangelical unity
especially since demands from provincial directors that the
Society be brought more in line with denominational policy
portended serious conflict between the still interdenominational parent society in London and the Congregationally-
dominated auxiliaries in the provinces. In 1814, for example, John Angell James of Birmingham complained to
George Burder that the parent society's plan to establish
an interdenominational auxiliary in his area was wishful
thinking since most of Birmingham's evangelicals were already engaged in their own denominational societies. [49] Soon
a Congregational pressure group representing several provincial auxiliaries suggested that it would perhaps be better
if the Independents formed a missionary society of their own
which made no pretence to being pan-evangelical. John Griffin, the Congregational minister in Portsea represented this
group well when he wrote William Alers-Hankey in 1818:
"[Our] denomination has now a magazine, it is said, of rising influence ... and some think that it should [now] have
a distinct Society for missionary and general objects ... in
order to counteract the avowed principles of some other societies."[50]

Though a Congregational schism never took place, a
compromise was worked out to make the L. M. S. more responsive to the wishes of its chief denominational sponsors.
Constitutional modifications within the London Missionary Society reflected this compromise. The Society, for instance,

no longer encouraged Anglicans to apply as missionaries,
apparently in an effort not to offend the Church Missionary
Society.[51] By 1823, the Society's Fundamental Principle
was modified to preclude Baptists from being accepted as
missionaries, a far cry from the early ideals of the founding fathers most of whom would have permitted Baptists to
serve the Society alongside non-Baptists.[52] About the same
time, missionary candidates holding Arminian theological
views were similarly discouraged from applying to the Society even though in the early years they too could probably
have served the Society as missionaries.[53]

          These decisions probably served to placate the more
militant Congregationalists while maintaining the semblance
of interdenominational cooperation at least among the paedobaptist and Calvinistic denominations.   But from 1820 on,
the Society moved organizationally further into Congregationalism.   In 1819, the London Missionary Society auxiliary in
Sheffield founded the Home Missionary Society for the West
Riding of Yorkshire, the purpose of which was to encourage
the establishment of Congregational churches.[54] In earlier
years, this kind of extracurricular activity would probably
have been considered out of step with the Society's professed
aim.   By 1828, the monthly meetings of the London Board
of Congregational Ministers was being held on London Missionary Society premises.[55]   Indeed, a year later the Society's evolution into a Congregational missionary organization was so complete that Isaac Mann, a Baptist historian,
believed it to have been established in 1795 by the Independents.[56] In later years, the name of the Society was again
changed to better reflect its denominational affiliation: it
was now called the "Congregational Council for World Missions." Yet for all its failures, an ecumenical seed had
been sown by the founding fathers of the London Missionary
Society which, in a more auspicious climate, would ultimately bear fruit.

                                NOTES

1.   L. M. S. Minutes, August 10, 1801.
2.   Cited in W. Innes, Remarks on Christian Union (1811),
        37.
3.   As did Joseph Hughes in 1798 and 1810, John Rippon
        in 1798 and 1801, John Ryland Jr. in 1803 and An-
        drew Fuller also in 1803.   These visits are record-
        ed in the Evangelical Magazine.

4.   For Haweis' article entitled "The Present State of Evan-
     gelical Religion" see Evangelical Magazine, 18 (1810),
     506, wherein he wrote: "The Particular Baptists
     have greatly enlarged their numbers, not perhaps so
     much from the world, by awakenings of conscience
     in new converts, as from the different congregations
     of Dissenters and Methodists." Cf., R. H. Martin,
     "English Particular Baptists and Interdenominational
     Cooperation," Foundations: The Baptist Journal of
     History, Theology and Ministry, XXII (1979), 233 ff.

5.   Cf., Angus. Fuller Typescripts: A. Fuller to W.
     Ward, November 17, 1812. E. D. Potts, "A Note
     on the Serampore Trio," The Baptist Quarterly,
     XX (1963-4), 115 f.; Ed. D. Potts, British Baptist
     Missionaries in India (1967), 49 f., 117.

6.   R. Hall, The Duty and Importance of Free Communion
     (1820), 42.

7.   L. M. S. Home Correspondence (1.7.A): G. Lambert
     to J. Eyre, August 6, 1799.

8.   Angus. Fuller Typescripts: A. Fuller to W. Carey,
     July 15, 1812.

9.   Cf., Angus. Fuller Typescripts: A. Fuller to W.
     Ward, September 21, 1800; Baptist Magazine, 6 (1814),
     82; L. M. S. Minutes, November 11, 18, 1816. De-
     cember 16, 1816; B. M. S. Minutes, December 31,
     1816.

10. Baptist Magazine, 14 (1822), 305 fn.

11. B. M. S. Minutes, June 21, 1822.

12. Writing about the L. M. S., J. C. Marshman said: "The
     Society took the designation of The Missionary Soci-
     ety, and Mr. Fuller was accustomed, when alluding
     to it, to write the word THE in capital letters, and
     many facetious remarks did he make, in his letters
     to Serampore, on the pride which 'lurked under the
     definite article.'" J. C. Marshman, The Life and
     Times of Carey, Marshman, and Ward (1859), I,
     395.

13. Minutes of the London Secretaries Association are de-
     posited in the archives of the British and Foreign
     Bible Society. Unfortunately, only the topics dis-
     cussed have been recorded for the early years and
     not the substance of what was said. See J. H. Rit-
     son, Records of Missionary Secretaries: An Account
     of the Celebration of the Centenary of the London
     Secretaries Association (1920).

14. L. M. S. Minutes, September 29, 1795.

15. Missionary Notices of the Wesleyan Methodists (1816),
     92.

16. L. M. S. Minutes, December 13, 1819.

17. For example, Thomas Coke in 1798 and 1808, John
    Pawson and Thomas Rankin in 1799 and Jabez Bunting
    in 1805. These visits are recorded in the Evangel-
    ical Magazine.

18. M. M. S. Home Correspondence Box 1: R. Brackenbury
    to T. Coke, August 19, 1806. The "Mr. Berry" re-
    ferred to was probably Joseph Berry, the Independent
    minister at Warminster and not Bath. Berry was a
    director of the L. M. S. from 1812.

19. L. M. S. Minutes, February 26, 1798. For Coke's in-
    itial protest, see L. M. S. Home Correspondence Ex-
    tra (1.1.D.): T. Coke to L. M. S., February 26,
    1798. Cf., J. A. Vickers, Thomas Coke (1969),
    301 f.

20. M. M. S. Home Correspondence Box 1: T. Coke to R.
    Johnson, November 15, 1809.

21. M. M. S. Home Correspondence Box 1: T. Coke to R.
    Johnson, January 1, 1810.

22. M. M. S. Home Correspondence Box 1: T. Coke to G.
    Highfield, December 26, 1811.

23. The Missionary Society's name bothered a number of
    Wesleyans, including Richard Watson who complained
    about it to Bunting. Apparently Methodists often sup-
    ported the L. M. S. thinking that its fundraisers repre-
    sented the Wesleyan mission. See G. G. Findlay and
    W. W. Holdworth, The History of the Wesleyan Meth-
    odist Missionary Society (1921), I, 43 fn.

24. M. M. S. Home Correspondence Box 1: J. Alexander
    and J. Eddy to R. Smith, June 22, 1810.

25. M. M. S. Home Correspondence Box 1: T. Coke to R.
    Smith, October 29, 1812. The "Mr. Collinson" re-
    ferred to was George Collison, divinity tutor at Hack-
    ney College and an L. M. S. director from 1803.

26. M. M. S. Home Correspondence Box 1: G. Banwell to
    R. Smith, December 1, 1813.

27. Cited in Findlay and Holdsworth, op. cit., 43 f.

28. Cited in T. P. Bunting, The Life of Jabez Bunting
    (1887), II, 50 f. (italics in text). Cf., G. Smith,
    The History of Wesleyan Methodism, II (2nd ed. 1862),
    545. R. H. Martin, "Missionary Competition between
    Evangelical Dissenters and Wesleyan Methodists in the
    early nineteenth century: A Footnote to the Founding
    of the Methodist Missionary Society," Proceedings of
    the Wesley Historical Society, Vol. XLII, Part 3
    (1979), 81ff.

29. Evangelical Magazine, 26 (1818), 268 f.

30. L. M. S. Minutes, March 15, March 22, 1819. Attending the L. M. S. anniversary in 1820, Butterworth observed that prejudices which had previously prevented this kind of cooperation had greatly subsided. Evangelical Magazine, 28 (1820), 263.
31. C. Jay, Recollections of William Jay (1859), 191 f. G. J. Stevenson, City Road Chapel London and Its Associations (1837), 302.
32. J. Pratt, Eclectic Notes (2nd ed. 1865), 131.
33. L. M. S. Minutes, September 9, 1799.
34. L. M. S. Minutes, March 29, 1802.
35. For a list of Anglican clergymen affiliated with the C. M. S. who attended L. M. S. anniversaries, see Evangelical Magazine, 14 n. s. (1841), 493.
36. C. Hole, The Early History of the Church Missionary Society (1896), 409.
37. Ibid., 233. Vaughan and Biddulph subsequently established a C. M. S. auxiliary in Bristol.
38. Ibid., 307.
39. Ibid., 329.
40. C. M. S. Home Correspondence: J. Pratt to H. Irwin, March 9, 1814.
41. Hole, op. cit., 284.
42. Evangelical Magazine, 26 (1818), 263 f.
43. Ibid., 265.
44. Cf., T. Timpson, British Ecclesiastical History (1838), 552; L. E. Elliot-Binns, The Early Evangelicals (1953), 218.
45. See A. Peel, These Hundred Years: A History of the Congregational Union of England and Wales (1931), 12 ff.
46. Ibid., 10, 58.
47. See W. G. Robinson, A History of the Lancashire Congregational Union (1955), 27; B. Nightingale, The Story of the Lancashire Congregational Union (1906), 24 f.
48. Congregational Magazine (1831), 127 f.
49. L. M. S. Home Correspondence (3. 1. C): J. A. James to G. Burder, June 18, 1814. Cf., L. M. S. Home Correspondence (2. 7. A): H. O. Wills to G. Burder, August 27, 1812.
50. L. M. S. Home Correspondence (2. 6. A); J. Griffin to W. Alers-Hankey, July 10, 1818.
51. L. M. S. Minutes, February 14, 1814; October 28, November 25, 1822.
52. L. M. S. Minutes, March 24, 1823 wherein it is stated "That whilst it has been ever since the foundation of the Missionary Society, a principle regarded as fun-

damental, that a difference of sentiment relating to
ecclesiastical polity should not form an impediment
to Christian ministerial cooperation in carrying on
its labours, it has been the opinion of the board, not
less uniformly admitted, that the missionaries employed in its service, should practice infant baptism."
Only five years earlier, in 1818, the Society had
recommended "That in conformity with the fundamental principles of the Society, the administration of the
ordinances of Baptism and the Lord's Supper be left
entirely to the discretion of the missionaries." L.M.S.
Minutes, November 9, 1818.

53.   Cf., L.M.S. Minutes, December 27, 1824; L.M.S. Com-
      mittee of Examination Minutes, December 27, 1824.

54.   J. G. Miall, Congregationalism in Yorkshire (1868),
      178.   Cf., Evangelical Magazine, 27 (1819), 336.

55.   L.M.S. Minutes, December 22, 1828.

56.   I. Mann, Twelve Lectures on Ecclesiastical History
      and Nonconformity (1829), 478.

PART III:

THE BRITISH AND FOREIGN BIBLE SOCIETY

I.

Not very long ago, almost any British child brought
up in an evangelical home could recite the well-known story
of the Welsh girl Mary Jones and her part in the founding
of the British and Foreign Bible Society. This story is
worth a brief retelling since it illustrates the dramatic way
in which many evangelicals rather naively believed that their
society came into existence. [1]

Mary Jones lived in the rural Welsh village of Llanfihangel y Pennant at the turn of the nineteenth century near
one of the famous Circulating Schools established by Thomas
Charles, the prominent Anglican evangelical. Her greatest
dream was to possess a Bible of her own for which she had
industriously saved her pennies. When she asked her tutor
where she could purchase a Bible in her native language, she
was told that she must go to Bala, some twenty-eight miles
away and see Thomas Charles himself. Though the distance
was great, "she walked it cheerily, her young heart sustained by the hope of finding at the end of her journey the
long-yearned-for-treasure." At first it seemed that her
journey had been in vain, for Charles and his colleague
David Edward told Mary that Welsh Bibles were very scarce,
and that they could not afford to sell her even one of the
few they possessed. Mary "wept as if she would break her
heart." The kindhearted Thomas Charles finally relented and
sold her one of his own valuable Welsh Bibles. We are told
that after the transaction was made, in a characteristically
Welsh response to the situation, Mary Jones with her bene-
factors stood with

> tears streaming from their eyes; the girl now
> weeping sweet tears of unutterable joy: Mr.

> Charles shedding tears of mingled sorrow for his
> country's famine for the Word of God, and of holy
> sympathy with that young disciple who so rejoiced
> in the possession of the great treasure; while good
> David Edward was overpowered with the scene be-
> fore him, and he also wept like a child.

Then Charles told Edward,

> Well, David Edward, is not this very sad, that
> there should be such a scarcity of Bibles in the
> country, and that this poor girl should thus have
> walked some twenty-eight or thirty miles to get
> a copy? If something can be done to alter this
> state of things, I will not rest till it is accom-
> plished.

With this solemn vow, Charles then set out on his famous
quest to supply Bibles for his countrymen, and the result
was the founding of the British and Foreign Bible Society.

The importance of the Mary Jones story lies more
in the realm of myth and symbol than of history.   Though
Mary Jones really existed, her influence over Thomas
Charles in the founding of the Bible Society was more leg-
endary than real.   Nevertheless, the national dilemma that
the legend has come to symbolize had a profound impact on
future pan-evangelical developments.

From the very year that the London Missionary Society was founded, pan-evangelicalism in foreign missions
had faced insurmountable barriers.   There was, indeed,
only one missionary society that claimed to represent all
evangelical denominations, but its claim, as we have seen,
was contested by the existence of Baptist, Wesleyan, and
Anglican organizations.   Nevertheless, there were other
causes around which evangelical denominations could unite.
Soon after the L. M. S. was founded, the evangelicals became interested in interdenominational cooperation locally,
and a number of interdenominational itinerant societies and
evangelical county unions were established throughout the
Kingdom.   But like the Religious Tract Society, founded in
1799 to provide itinerant home missionaries with religious
literature, the itinerant societies and county unions were
only slightly more pan-evangelical than the London Missionary Society out of which they had evolved.   As we shall
see in a subsequent chapter, the Particular Baptists had

joined the Calvinistic Nonconformists in the Religious Tract
Society, but the Wesleyans and the "regular" evangelical Anglicans as yet had not.

It was probably the emergence of new home missionary enterprises together with the dearth of Bibles in Wales
which directed evangelical attention to the Bible as a focal
point for interdenominational cooperation. The Bible was
so obviously suited for this role that it is surprising that
a society far larger than the small, regional Naval and Military Bible Society had not been founded before. The pri-
macy of the Biblical word in evangelical theology was paramount: Here was the oracle of religious truth. The Bible,
moreover, was not only the medium of a past revelation of
the Divine Will, but it was also the medium through which
the Holy Spirit continued to awaken and regenerate sinners.
It was the most potent of all forces for the conversion of
mankind. How many evangelicals themselves had been converted while studying its pages! Even without commentaries
and glosses, the Word of God was capable, when illuminated
by the light of the Spirit, of transforming men by its own
self-evidencing truth. It seemed therefore axiomatic that
since all evangelicals recognized the unique value of the
Scriptures, none could refuse to cooperate in a united campaign for its distribution. In the Bible, therefore, the evangelicals found what they thought to be the most powerful
(and inexpensive) instrument of conversion ever known. And
in the Bible Society when it was founded, they found the perfect institutional embodiment of the pan-evangelical impulse.

Historians of the Bible Society have always held that
it was the spiritual famine in Wales which led to the discussion of a possible Bible society at meetings of the Religious Tract Society in the winter of 1802. This is largely correct, for it was a Welshman, Thomas Charles of Bala mentioned above in the Mary Jones story, who brought
the Welsh Bible crisis to the attention of the Tract Society
directors. Charles, a leader of Welsh Calvinistic Methodism and an unbeneficed "irregular" Anglican, had long been
concerned about the spiritual education of his fellow countrymen having organized Circulating Schools since 1785 and establishing a publishing house to supply these schools with
textbooks.[2] As early as 1787, Charles had discussed the
shortage of Welsh Bibles with Thomas Scott, the Anglican
Bible commentator who was then chaplain at the Lock Hospital in London. Scott and his friend John Thornton, the
evangelical merchant, informed Charles that they had been

given twenty-five Welsh Bibles by the Naval and Military Bible Society which they would dispatch to Bala, and that they would apply to the Society for Promoting Christian Knowledge for more. But their application was turned down. The S. P. C. K., which alone was responsible for publishing Welsh Bibles, had not printed an edition since 1769 and their stocks were diminishing rapidly. Nor was the Society particularly responsive to evangelical pleas, dominated as it still was by High Churchmen.

A second attempt to meet the growing crisis was engineered in 1791 by Thomas Jones, another Welsh evangelical who was curate of Creaton in Northamptonshire. Jones urged the S. P. C. K. to mass-produce Welsh Bibles so that they could be sold to his countrymen at reduced prices, and even promised to give the S. P. C. K. a substantial advance raised from among evangelical churchmen in England. But in spite of the help and advice received from William Wilberforce, then a member of the S. P. C. K., Jones' scheme ended in failure. This time the S. P. C. K. complained that the evangelicals had exaggerated the need for Welsh Bibles even though the need had been well-documented by Jones.

The S. P. C. K. finally printed 10,000 Welsh Bibles in 1799, but when they were distributed, the evangelical strongholds in Montgomery, Cardigan, and Carmarthen were notably neglected. In 1802, therefore, Jones proposed a second scheme, or what he called his "Plan." He now aimed to circumvent the S. P. C. K. by funding and printing his own Bibles. Jones' "Plan" was significant because unlike the previous proposals, it was to be completely interdenominational. [3] When, however, Jones was informed that it was illegal to print Welsh Bibles without the approval of the Welsh Bishops, he became discouraged and abandoned his scheme. But his friend Thomas Charles was not as easily put off. While in London in December 1802 to preach at Rowland Hill's Spa Fields Chapel and to find funds and a printer for the Bible scheme which had now become his own, Charles had the excellent idea of asking the Religious Tract Society to sponsor his project. Edward Morgan, Charles' biographer, tells us in the true evangelical anecdotal tradition that Charles' inspiration came one morning while in London lying in bed. "He was so pleased with it," Morgan retells, "that he instantly arose, dressed himself, and went out to consult with some friends on the subject." [4] This in turn led to formal discussions on the topic at the Tract Society later that month.

II.

At what most historians consider to have been the first of a series of early Tract Society meetings which led to the founding of the British and Foreign Bible Society in 1804, it is recorded in the Minute Book for December 7, 1802, that Thomas Charles introduced the subject of Welsh Bibles whereupon the Tract Society directors present decided that it would be highly desirable "to stir up the public mind to the dispersion of Bibles generally."[5] Intermittently between 1802 and 1804, the Tract Society met to plan the new Bible Society. Their task had been greatly simplified by lessons learned from previous pan-evangelical experiments. The new society was to be a united enterprise like its predecessors, but by avoiding their mistakes and miscalculations, it was hoped that much greater denominational and national support could be gained. Pan-evangelicalism in the London Missionary Society, they had learned, failed to mature because of the Society's ecclesiastically-oriented "fundamental principle"--Churchmen could not participate in the establishment of undenominational mission churches which they considered to be highly irregular. Pan-evangelicalism in the Tract Society, as we shall see, was often encumbered by the complexity of its objectives. It was unrealistic, for instance, to expect a great deal of unanimity in an interdenominational reviewing committee before which passed an interminable number of different tracts and pamphlets on sundry theological topics. The architects of the new Society realized, therefore, that only by avoiding ecclesiastically-oriented issues, and by restricting their objectives to one simple goal that was acceptable to all, could their new organization ever hope to achieve pan-evangelical accord on a grand scale. That goal, later also to be known as the "fundamental principle," was to be found in the simple distribution of the Bible without note or comment.

Several important decisions were made at the Religious Tract Society between December 1802 and March 1804 which significantly contributed to the Bible Society's future design. On February 8, 1803, it was decided by the directors of the Tract Society "that the translation of the Scripture established by Public Authority, be the only one in the English language to be accepted by the Society."[6] By limiting translations to those established by public authority, the founders hoped to avoid accusations that the new society was circulating Bibles translated from "Popish" or heretical texts. It was also decided on February 8, that the com-

mittee of the new society should be composed of an equal
number of churchmen and Dissenters.   For some unrecord-
ed reason, the minute was immediately altered to a more
ambiguous formula, viz. that the committee simply consist
of twenty-four directors whose denominational affiliation was
unspecified.   But when the Society was finally established in
1804, the control was again divided equally between Church
and Dissent.

The outcome of these resolutions was to encourage
the participation of "regular" evangelical churchmen like
William Wilberforce and Wesleyan Methodists like Adam
Clarke.   As we have seen, "regular" Anglicans and Wesleyan Methodists had hitherto preferred not to patronize pan-
evangelical organizations in force.   Wilberforce began attending Tract Society meetings as early as 1803 and chaired
a committee that unsuccessfully approached the King for his
patronage, but his participation was significant for another
reason. [7] By 1803 many "regulars" were more ready to
acknowledge that orthodox Nonconformists were not seditious
"republicans" but loyal Englishmen who supported the British
constitution as they themselves did.   As suspicions faded,
the barriers to cooperation so evident in the history of the
London Missionary Society were largely removed.

There is no doubt that Wilberforce's name attracted
many Anglican patrons who otherwise would have been reluctant to join the new society.   Still, as the inaugural meeting of the Bible Society approached, there were many who
hesitated to support it.   One such was Charles Simeon, the
Rector of Holy Trinity, Cambridge and doyen of the "regular" evangelical Anglicans. [8]   Another was John Owen who
would soon become the Society's Anglican secretary.   Because he was a "regular" clergyman, Owen initially regarded the combination of churchmen and Dissenters in a pan-
evangelical institution as "utterly chimerical" and therefore
took "little pains either to understand or recommend it." [9]
Other clergymen probably shared his doubts.   Owen finally
decided to attend the Society's inaugural meeting on March
7, 1804, only because he noticed the name of his friend,
Granville Sharp, among the signatures on a Society circular.
But at the inaugural meeting, Owen quickly gave up his skep-
ticism.   He saw gathered before him "respectable" men of
different denominations--even Quakers--and when C. F.
Steinkopf, the Lutheran Pastor of the Savoy in London gave
a passionate address on the Society's behalf, Owen found
himself standing up "by an impulse which he had neither

the inclination nor the power to disobey," and adding his
testimony to those which exulted in the spectacle of so many
people of different denominations gathered together for the
purpose of circulating the Gospel.[10] By March 1804, the
Society had a sufficient number of prominent names on its
subscription lists to prove its strength and seriousness of
purpose.

Several other important resolutions were passed in
the spring of 1804 which developed the Society's design.   At
the inaugural meeting itself, the new society adopted the
R. T. S. resolution of February 8, 1803, which laid down
that the committee should consist of thirty-six (increased
from twenty-four) members.   Josiah Pratt, Lecturer at St.
Mary Woolnoth, feared that the ambiguity of the Society's
directorial composition might cause an imbalance in denominational representation, opening it to charges from churchmen or Dissenters that the other controlled the affairs of
the Society.   Consequently, it was decided in May that the
committee would consist of thirty-six laymen: fifteen to be
Anglicans, fifteen to be Dissenters, and the remaining six
to be foreigners resident in London.[11]   Significantly, the
committee was to be composed entirely of laymen, although
every clergyman or minister who subscribed one guinea or
more each year would be entitled to vote at committee meetings.

A second important resolution involving the Society's
secretaries was passed on March 12, 1804.   The most likely candidate for the position seemed to be Joseph Hughes,
the Baptist who chaired many of the early Tract Society
meetings at which the Bible Society was discussed.   Educated at Aberdeen University where he founded one of the
first Sunday Schools in Scotland, Hughes had for a time
been a professor at the Baptist College in Bristol, but eventually moved to Battersea in 1787.   Because of his proxim-
ity to Clapham, Hughes was on friendly terms with the evangelical Anglicans of the Clapham Sect.   In 1799, he became
the first Secretary of the Religious Tract Society.[12]

When Hughes' name was put up for nomination, his
friend John Owen objected, feeling that it would be impolitic
to elect "a Dissenting Minister, however highly respectable
and meritorious, the Secretary of an institution which was
designed to unite the whole body of Christians, and for which
its directors had evinced so laudable an anxiety to obtain the
patronage and cooperation of the Established Church."[13]   Con-

sequently, the office of Secretary was split in three ways.
Josiah Pratt, Secretary of the Church Missionary Society,
was initially appointed the Anglican Secretary, Joseph Hughes
the Nonconformist Secretary, and C. F. Steinkopf the Secretary for the foreign churches.[14] A final important decision was the appointment of John Shore, Lord Teignmouth,
former Governor-General in India, as the Society's first
President.[15] Shore was an excellent choice, not only because of his prominence in public affairs, but also because
he was an able linguist who later contributed to the Society's
first translations.

As things stood by the end of 1804, the British and
Foreign Bible Society was a well-balanced institution. Though
clergymen and ministers possessed a vote in committee, the
Society's directors were all laymen, and equally divided between Church and Dissent and the Foreign churches as were
the Society's three secretaries. The architects of the Society intended to attract no criticisms on the ground that
they favored a particular party. Oddly enough, however,
the new society seemed to have forgotten its most important
rule. At the Tract Society meeting of February 8, 1803, as
we have seen, it had been decided that the Bible Society
would only circulate the authorized version of the Bible.
But for some strange reason, this resolution was not included in the legislation of 1804.[16] Only with the onslaught
of controversy with the S. P. C. K. did the directors realize
the implications of this omission and quickly added to the
Society's constitution the "fundamental principle" that only
Bibles authorized by public authority, without note or comment, would be circulated by it.

III.

The strength of the Bible Society rested in the simplicity of its design and objective, a fact which it relentless-
ly tried to communicate to friends and enemies alike. When,
for example, Thomas Twining, in a letter to the chairman
of the East India Company in 1807, accused the Society of
inflaming the delicate religious situation in India by the "universal dissemination of the Christian faith," Lord Teignmouth was quick to assure him that the "ultimate point, in
the case of the Society ... is ... not 'the Dissemination of
the Christian faith,' but THE CIRCULATION OF THE SCRIP-
TURES" and furthermore added in case the point was missed
that the Bible Society could "support no Missionaries, erect

no Churches, endow no schools, disseminate no Tracts; it
cannot issue even a Dissertation to recommend the Bible,
nor annex a single Note to explain it."[17]

The identification of the Bible Society with foreign
missions was only natural.   Bible Society directors sat simultaneously on the boards of most of the evangelical foreign missionary societies.   The fact that it had foreign
agents only confirmed this association of ideas in the minds
of many people.[18]   The Society, however, went out of its
way to deny this link.   To a correspondent who thought that
the Bible Society was but another foreign missionary organization, Joseph Tarn, the Society's assistant secretary,
wrote: "Allow me to assure you that the British & Foreign Bible Society never sent out missionaries or had such
a measure in contemplation; their sole object being the more
extensive circulation of the Holy Scripture, to which they
have most scrupulously adhered ..."[19]   In fact, the image
that the Society wanted to create was not that of some kind
of sectarian organization noisily propagating a disruptive
brand of religion, but that of a respectable business institution which simply published and disseminated Bibles.   John
Owen even liked to compare the Bible Society with Lloyds,
the insurance company.   "The line of business is, with few
exceptions," he wrote, "as direct at the Bible Committee
as it is at Lloyds; and there is little reason to expect the
peculiar tenets of Calvin or Socinus to enter into a debate
for dispersing an edition of the Scripture, as there would
be if the same men met to underwrite a policy of insurance."[20]   Consequently, in order to avoid being identified
by critics with any church or conventicle, it was rigid policy that the general meetings of the Society should be held
in secular places like the London Tavern.   Religious activities such as prayers and sermons were carefully avoided
at Society meetings.   Proceedings were so businesslike, that
one clergyman could tell his Bishop,[21]

> On going to the committee room, or to the hall,
> I make no compromise of principle, even in ap-
> pearance, in any way.   I offend not, either in
> letter or in spirit, against any one article of my
> Church.   I break no law, or canon which I have
> subscribed.   I violate no duty which I owe to my
> ecclesiastical rulers.   I am countenanced by many
> of my superiors, by some of the highest authority
> in my Church.   And when I have transacted the
> business on which I have attended, I leave the

assembly, I trust, uncontaminated by the work in
which I have been engaged, or by the persons with
whom I have associated.

The very make-up of the Society's committee and the
business it transacted at least prevented the Society from
gaining too clerical an appearance. As the governing body
was composed entirely of laymen, laymen predominated in
committee meetings and as the directors were mostly prominent businessmen and politicians, the meetings were carried on in a very business-like and parliamentary fashion.
In fact, the Society's minutes and correspondence are, for
the most part, singularly monotonous, for they deal almost
exclusively with business transactions including orders for
Bibles, payments and receipts. [22] Yet the businesslike image
the Society tried to project was not always accepted even by
Society patrons. As we shall see in the Test Controversy
of 1830, there were indeed many people who believed the
Society to be a religious institution that dispersed more than
just Bibles.

As a business institution which only circulated Bibles
and did not interfere with denominational autonomy, the Bible Society was a very attractive proposition to pan-evangelical "realists" who had previously refused to patronize
the L.M.S. and the Tract Society. Regular clergymen like
Thomas Biddulph, Richard Cecil, William Dealtry, Thomas
Scott, Basil Woodd, Thomas Gisborne, and, later, even
Charles Simeon became among the Society's warmest advocates. Among prominent evangelical Anglican laymen, the
Society numbered William Wilberforce, Zachary Macaulay,
Henry Thornton, Charles Grant, Granville Sharp, and, of
course, Lord Teignmouth, the Society's first President.
Virtually all of the evangelical Dissenters who patronized
the various missionary societies, also supported the Bible
Society. The Wesleyans valued their connection with the
Society so highly, that they took the unprecedented step of
allowing Adam Clarke to remain permanently in London so
that he could continue to assist the Bible Society with its
foreign translations. [23] A Baptist, as we have noted, was
was the Society's Nonconformist Secretary.

Although the Bible Society was predominantly patronized by evangelicals, it attracted a number of non-evangelical subscribers. In the Anglican camp, Bishops Beilby
Porteus of London, John Fisher of Exeter and Thomas Burgess of St. David immediately accepted Vice-Presidencies.

By 1810, eleven Bishops and two Irish Archbishops patronized the Society.[24] Two years later, William Otter, a future bishop, claimed that of the forty-eight bishops in Great
Britain, twenty openly supported the Society.[25] Not a few
non-evangelical Anglican clergymen and laymen also patronized the Bible Society. At Cambridge University, Edward
Daniel Clarke, the professor of mineralogy, though no evangelical, rallied to the support of the Society when the Cambridge auxiliary was founded. At Oxford University, the
Principal of Jesus College, David Hughes (also no evangelical), gave his patronage to the Society. In government
circles, not only did the evangelical Spencer Perceval back
it, but also Lord Liverpool and Robert Peel who could not
be numbered among the Parliamentary "Saints."[26]

Dissenters not usually associated with pan-evangelical
enterprises also found their way to the Bible Society in surprising numbers. We have already noted the Quaker's contribution to the founding of the Society; they continued to support it through the years as did many General Baptists.[27]
There were also an embarrassing number of Unitarian patrons. When the Society was criticized for this fact in 1810,
William Dealtry claimed that there were only one or two,
but upon further investigation he had to admit that the number was larger than he had originally imagined.[28] As we
shall see, Unitarian patronage was to cause much controversy.

Those least expected to patronize the Society were
the Roman Catholics. Late in 1804, Johann Gossner, a
Roman Catholic priest from Swabia asked C. F. Steinkopf
for Bibles with which to supply his people.[29] Later, Gossner negotiated directly with the German Bible Society at Nuremberg and became a regular agent of the Society. Contact with Roman Catholics existed at home also. In 1805,
Robert Shaw, the rector of Kilkenny in Ireland, reported
that he had written to the "Popish" Bishop of the Diocese
of Waterford and Lismore to enquire "whether he has any
objection to the Testament being introduced into schools as
a school book," and was pleased to report that the Bishop
had responded favorably to his letter. Shaw cautioned London, however, that if this news were to be made public, it
would be prudent to avoid publishing his name lest the good
Bishop be censured by his superiors.[30] Instances of cooperation between British Roman Catholics and the Bible Society continued through our period even when the Pope condemned Bible societies in 1816.[31]

The soliciting of patronage in the early years was rather unsystematic. In the autumn of 1804 a number of prominent provincial evangelicals were asked by the directors in London to submit a list of the people in their areas most likely to support the new society. This procedure caused some confusion at first because many of the evangelicals approached for lists were not sure what type of supporters the directors had in mind. One Nonconformist minister, for example, assumed that Anglicans were not intended and therefore sent back his list with only Dissenters listed.[32] It was soon clear to all, however, that Church patronage was crucial to the Society's success. Thomas Richardson of Bristol told Joseph Tarn that "whenever the effort is made, in order to succeed, it appears to me requisite that the scheme originate with the Establishment" and doubted whether recruitment would meet with much success if launched only by Nonconformists.[33]

At first the Society's search for patrons met with scant success, but with the introduction of the Auxiliary system in 1809 and its ancillary fundraising and Bible distribution operations, membership increased rapidly. Though the auxiliary system found its genesis in London, Birmingham, and Glasgow between 1805 and 1806, the first "official" auxiliary was established in Reading in 1809. From now on the number of auxiliaries established each year increased rapidly. In 1809 alone, auxiliaries were established in Nottingham, Newcastle, Exeter, East Lothian and Edinburgh. By 1811, their number had increased so phenomenally that the parent society in London faced a crisis of control. Too many auxiliaries, as we shall see later, had diverged from the simple principle of the Society and did much more than just distribute Bibles. Consequently, by 1811 the parent society saw a need to regulate and codify the constitutions of its provincial auxiliaries by publishing a small pamphlet of rules to which they were required to adhere.[34]

IV.

The Bible Society was by far the largest and most ambitious of the great pan-evangelical organizations examined in this study. It can safely be said that most prominent and active evangelicals in Britain subscribed to and patronized its activities. Membership statistics put the size of the Society in perspective. Baptist Noel estimated in 1832 that there were over 37,000 committee members.[35]

Joseph John Gurney claimed in the same year that there
were over 100,000 subscribers.[36] By 1814 the Society had
auxiliaries in almost every English county. Ten years later, according to one estimate, there were over 859 Bible
Society auxiliaries, 2,000 Bible Associations and 500 Ladies
organizations dotting the nation.[37] On the Continent and in
America, Bible societies in close association with London
mushroomed between 1804 and 1830: In Russia alone, there
were over 300 Bible societies by 1824. With a growth rate
like this, we should not be surprised to find that the Bible
Society in the first five years of its life, distributed over
150,000 Bibles and 800,000 in the second five years. Indeed, by 1825 the Society had spent well over £1,165,000
printing and issuing 4,252,000 Bibles in 140 languages and
dialects including fifty-five languages in which it had never
before been printed.[38]

        Statistics alone, however, do not really indicate the
importance of the Bible Society both as an agency of religious revival and as perhaps the most important institutional
embodiment of the pan-evangelical urge. The importance of
the Bible Society as an agency of reformation cannot be dis-
puted. As Ford K. Brown somewhat humorously suggested:
"If every one of the 4,252,000 Bibles issued by 1825 had
been printed in the language of the Esquimaux and piled up
on the frozen tundra the Bible Society would still have been
next to Abolition the most powerful agency of Evangelical
reform."[39] Not only did Society Bibles by themselves convert abject sinners, dangerous convicts and seditious radicals, but the group activities of the auxiliaries that distributed them throughout Britain seemed to promote revival and
a general increase in church attendance.[40] One correspondent from Tavistock, for example, claimed that "since the
establishment of the auxiliary Society in this town there has
been an increased attendance, at the Established Church,
and in other places of public worship."[41] Another reported
that because of the distribution of Bibles in Ireland, "the
Sabbath Day now becomes a truly delightful scene."[42] The
Anglican Charles Jerram said that Bible Society meetings
in his neighborhood brought clergymen together from different parishes to ascertain by what means their respective
parishioners might be supplied with Bibles. As a result,
the clergy "became better acquainted with each other [and]
were led to consider the religious state of their people, and
to concert the best means of promoting their spiritual interests."[43]

        The Bible Society also had a profound impact on the

spirit of church union.   Bearing in mind the obstacles that
the Society had to overcome when it was first established
including the Anglican fears of Nonconformity and the Nonconformist suspicions of establishments, its progress in
bringing Christians of various churches and denominations
together was quite remarkable.   Writing in 1816, an editor
of the Christian Observer only exaggerated a little when he
said the "Prejudice, selfishness, indolence, covetousness,
the spirit of nationality, of monopoly ... had, up to this
period, proved to be principles of tough, unbending, unac-
commodating texture ... But now, except in a committee
room or two, or in the shady purlieu of a professor's soli-
tary study, or in the chilling corner of a few quadrangles,
where the spirit of Popery is not cast out, these once formidable enemies have, like the army of Sennacherib, melted
away."[44]   Alexander Knox paid tribute to the Bible Society
when he described it as an incubator of Christian goodwill
and understanding, in which Arminians rubbed shoulders with
Calvinists, Baptists with paedobaptists, and Churchmen with
Dissenters.[45]   One enthusiastic evangelical Anglican proudly
claimed that the Bible Society had the honor of commencing
a "new era in the Christian world."   "They have roused the
torpor of other religious institutions: they have thrown down
the barriers which separated man from his brother, and
united in one body the energies of the pious and the wise."[46]

     That the next two chapters concentrate less on the
enormous achievements of the Bible Society, and more on
the controversies that troubled it, is due to an insuperable
deficiency in source materials.   Though the Society's minutes
and correspondence are voluminous, they deal mainly with
the routine of administration and hardly even do they record
the instances of interdenominational cooperation which continually took place.   But then the Bible Society, as we have
mentioned, was never meant to be a "religious" institution.
Sermons and prayers, as we have seen, were forbidden at
Society meetings, and so we find no instances of Bible Society officials taking part at ordinations or communion services as did those at the London Missionary Society.   Printed sources provide surprisingly little help in gauging the influence of the Bible Society as an agency of interdenominational union.   The biographies of Bible Society directors and
patrons, for instance, were mostly written in the 1840's and
1850's when the Oxford Movement had hardened Anglican and
Nonconformist relations, and their authors were too prone to
dismiss the pan-evangelical movement as a relatively unim-
portant force in the lives of the men they wrote about.[47]
Nevertheless, we get occasional glimpses of the kind of

fraternization that flowed directly from the activities of the
Bible Society and its interlocking chain of auxiliaries.   In
August Hare's The Gurney's of Earlham, for example, Joseph
John Gurney, the great Quaker reformer and patron of the
Bible Society, reminisced about the founding of the Norwich
Auxiliary Bible Society which was attended by a concourse
of Quakers, Anglicans, Lutherans, Congregationalists, Presbyterians, and Baptists.   "We had a vast party at Earlham,"
Gurney wrote, "and a remarkable day, a perfectly harmonious mixture of High Church, Low Church, Lutheran, Baptist, Quaker!   It was a time which seemed to pull down all
barriers of distinction, and melt us into one common Christianity.   Such a beginning warrants us to expect much."[48]
Joseph Hughes, the Baptist Secretary of the Bible Society,
who was also present, caught something of the deep emotion
and comradeship which an occasion like this could inspire,
when he wrote: "We seemed generally to feel like the disciples whose hearts burned within them as they walked to
Emmaus."[49]   The bristling barriers, social as well as doctrinal, which set Christian apart from Christian, fell as
committee members sat round tables or on platforms, discussing how best to propagate the Word which was the symbol and vehicle of their common spiritual life.   If the meetings of the Society precluded communal worship or doctrinal
discussion, they could easily lead to further, less inhibited
associations elsewhere.   Thus John Leifchild, the Independent, told of frequent walks with Joseph Hughes, perhaps after a Bible Society meeting, from Hughes' house at Battersea to Mrs. Rebecca Wilkinson's at Clapham "where we met
a select party of clerical brethren, and discussed with them
the texts we had preached from, and other subjects of a
theological nature."[50]   In a period when religious controversies ran high, and the social gap between Churchman
and Dissenter yawned increasingly wide, the continued association of evangelical men of good will in innumerable
Bible Society auxiliaries was a force for charitableness even
more than for charity, a quiet but incalculably important
agency for the integration of Christians into a common fellowship and shared purpose, however limited it might be.
Indeed, we may conjecture with Elie Halevy, that the shared
ideology of evangelicalism, which brought peers, merchants,
shopkeepers and workmen into a common constituency of
the spirit, was one of the most important stabilizing factors
in English society in this period of acute social tension.[51]
The association of different classes and denominations in
philanthropic causes like the Anti-Slavery movement or, on
a far larger and longer basis, in the Bible Society, was a

force for unity in many directions.   These achievements
must be kept firmly in mind as we turn to the tensions both
within the Society and its external relations which it had to
struggle to overcome.

NOTES

1. See W. Canton, A History of the British and Foreign
   Bible Society (1904), I, 456.   The following quotations
   are drawn from this source.
2. For Charles biography, see D. E. Jenkins, The Life
   of the Rev. Thomas Charles (1908).   The following
   material is taken largely from Jenkins, op.cit., I
   567 ff.; II, 107 ff., 248 ff.
3. Ibid., II, 496.; Canton, op.cit., I, 468.
4. E. Morgan, A Brief History of the Life and Labours of
   the Rev. Thomas Charles (1828), 286, 292.
5. R.T.S. Minutes, December 7, 1802.   Cf., H. Morris,
   A Memorable Room: The Story of the Inception and
   Foundation of the British and Foreign Bible Society
   (1898), 12.
6. R.T.S. Minutes, February 8, 1803.   Cf., Morris,
   op.cit., 13 ff.
7. R.T.S. Minutes, April 21, 1803; Morris, op.cit., 15.
   Wilberforce's sons have created the myth that he was
   one of the initiators of the Bible Society, but this is
   largely incorrect.   See R.I. and S. Wilberforce, The
   Life of William Wilberforce (1838), III, 91.
8. Even after the Bible Society was founded, Simeon was
   hesitant actively to solicit patronage.   In a letter to
   Joseph Tarn, he expressed relief that he would not
   personally have to circulate the Society's plan in
   Cambridge.   He did, however, include a list of clergymen to whom Tarn himself might write.   B. S.
   Home Correspondence: C. Simeon to J. Tarn, August 14, 1804.
9. J. Owen, The History of the Origin and First Ten
   Years of the British and Foreign Bible Society (1816),
   I, 37.
10. Ibid., 38, 44.
11. B.S. Minutes of General Meetings, May 2, 1804.
12. For Hughes' biography, see J. Leifchild, Memoir of
    the Late Rev. J. Hughes (1835).
13. Owen, op.cit., I, 53.
14. Pratt was Secretary for one month, but because of re-
    sponsibilities as Secretary of the Church Missionary
    Society, he handed the post over to John Owen.

15. For Teignmouth's biography, see C. J. Shore, Memoir
     of the Life and Correspondence of John Lord Teign-
     mouth (1843).
16. Cf., B.S. Minutes of General Meetings, March 7, 1804,
     May 2, 1804.
17. Owen, op.cit., I, 325, 332 f.
18. See for example, B.S. Home Correspondence: T. Hawk-
     ins to J. Tarn, July 1805; Miss Cottrell to Bible So-
     ciety, July 30, 1810.
19. B.S. Home Correspondence: J. Tarn to Miss Cottrell,
     August 2, 1810 (Copy). Cf., C. J. Shore, op.cit.,
     II, 131; J. Poynder, Reasons Why I Am a Member of
     the Bible Society (1830), 32.
20. J. Owen, A Letter to a Country Clergyman (1805), 50.
21. Poynder, op.cit., 69 f. Cited from an address by Ed-
     ward Cooper, Rector of Yoxall.
22. John Owen wrote in the preface to the third volume of
     his history: "To the charge of monotony it will not
     be perhaps quite so easy to reply. Such a quality is,
     to a certain degree, inherent in the very nature of
     the Bible Society; and cannot be wholly avoided, by
     any contrivance, however artificial and ingenious with
     which its transactions may be related." Owen, Bible
     Society Origins, III, viii.
23. See G. Smith, History of Wesleyan Methodism (1863),
     II, 447 f.
24. W. Dealtry, A Vindication of the British and Foreign
     Bible Society (1810), 170.
25. W. Otter, A Vindication of Churchmen Who Become
     Members of the British and Foreign Bible Society
     (1812), 22 fn. Ford K. Brown's estimate that four
     fifths of the Bench and nine tenths of the clergy op-
     posed the Bible Society is highly inaccurate. See
     F. K. Brown, Fathers of the Victorians (1961), 257.
26. For Peel, see B.S. Home Correspondence: T. Motter-
     shaw to J. Owen, February 12, 1812, where it is
     said that the proposed auxiliary at Stafford enjoyed
     his support.
27. The colorful story of the Gurney family's involvement
     in the founding of the Norwich Auxiliary Bible Society
     can be found in A. J. C. Hare, The Gurneys of Earl-
     ham (1895), I, 229. For the General Baptists, see
     B.S. Home Correspondence: J. Pritt to J. Tarn,
     January 1, 1810.
28. Dealtry, op.cit., 83 f.
29. B.S. Miscellaneous Book, I, 33 f: J. Gossner to
     C. F. Steinkopf, October 18, 1804.

30. B.S. Miscellaneous Book, II, 2: R. Shaw to Bible
     Society, December 18, 1805.
31. One correspondent reported that he had received the
     following letter from a Quaker in Dublin: "Thou
     wilt rejoice to hear that a Roman Bishop has en-
     listed himself in our cause & has already given
     proof of his attachment to the principles of the so-
     ciety.   Thou wilt be surprised to hear that this lib-
     eral minded Bishop gave me his decided opinion--
     'That the Scriptures should be distributed without
     note or comment'--and that he had advocated the
     measure in a synod of the Bishops of his own com-
     munity." B.S. Home Correspondence: R. Sainthill
     to J. Tarn, March 26, 1818. For the Pope's po-
     sition on the Bible Society, see Anti Biblion, or the
     Papal Tocsin ... The Present Pope's Bull Against
     Bible Societies (2nd ed. 1817).
32. B.S. Home Correspondence: T. Kidd to J. Tarn,
     April 5, 1805.
33. B.S. Home Correspondence: T. Richardson to J. Tarn,
     February 13, 1809.
34. See Owen, Bible Society Origins, II, 537 f.
35. B. W. Noel, An Appeal on Behalf of the British and
     Foreign Bible Society (1832), 13 f.
36. J. J. Gurney, Terms of Union (1832), 23 f.
37. F. K. Brown, op.cit., 250 f.
38. Ibid., 249 f.
39. Ibid., 261.
40. Robert Steven told of a radical in Ireland who, after
     reading the Bible exclaimed: "If this be Christianity
     no Christian can be a rebel." B.S. Paterson Letters,
     Book I, f. 123: R. Steven to J. Paterson, October 1815.
41. B.S. Home Correspondence: J. Rundle to J. Tarn,
     October 19, 1815.
42. B.S. Home Correspondence: J. Hawksly to A. Blest,
     June 22, 1818.
43. J. Jerram, ed., The Memoirs ... of the Late Rev.
     Charles Jerram (1855), 280.
44. Christian Observer, 15 (1816), 728.
45. A. Knox, Remains (1834), III, 180.
46. Christian Observer, 15 (1816), 539.
47. Wilberforce's biography is perhaps the best example
     of this problem. In 1827, William Jay lamented:
     "Mr. Wilberforce's life is forthcoming, but I expect
     it will be a very partial representation of him, es-
     pecially on the score of his liberality. It is written
     by his two clerical sons, who are so high, that one

of them has published a tract [which] calls upon members of the Church to have 'no social or friendly intercourse with any Dissenters' ... Yet their honoured
father used to say,--'Though I am an Episcopalian, I
should like to commune once every year with every
Christian church that holds the Head.'" See G. Redford and J. A. James, eds., The Autobiography of
the Rev. William Jay (1855), 311 fn.

48. Hare, op.cit., I, 230.
49. Ibid., 232.
50. J. R. Leifchild, John Leifchild (1863), 70.
51. Cf., E. Halevy, A History of the English People (1927),
    166.

I.

With an aim that could unite all evangelicals and a
constitution that was designed to minimize internal friction,
the Bible Society got on with the seemingly uncontroversial
business of publishing and distributing Bibles. The Society
was soon to learn, however, that even this simple task would
excite the opposition of many fellow Christians, especially
High Church Anglicans. Indeed, High Churchmen considered
the Bible Society as an enemy from the start. Not only did
it challenge the authority of the S. P. C. K. , but it threatened
to draw unsuspecting clergymen into an organization that was
professedly the agent of no particular party or sect, but in
reality a front for the recruitment of evangelicals, even Nonconformists. High Churchmen felt far more embattled towards the Bible Society than to comparable evangelical institutions because a steady trickle of High Church clergymen
were joining it. Even before the Bible Society had issued
its first Bible, therefore, it reeled under a swift and unexpected attack from High Church writers. As a result, much
of the early energy of the Society was directed to defending
itself on this flank rather than with the task of promoting
general evangelical union.

It was the printing of the Welsh Bible that brought
the Bible Society into collision with the S. P. C. K. , setting
off a long and protracted controversy between High Churchmen and evangelicals that continued on and off for eighteen
years and ultimately shook the foundations of the Bible Society. [1] In April 1804, the Society appointed a subcommittee
to investigate the possibility of publishing Bibles in English,
Welsh, and Irish, and by the end of the summer, it was decided to print 20, 000 Welsh Bibles and 5, 000 Welsh Testaments. Thomas Charles was then commissioned to work

from the 1799 Oxford Welsh edition of the Bible originally
published by the S. P. C. K. , making necessary corrections
in the text and sending these corrections back to London for
the subcommittee's approval.   Charles' proposal to alter
only the orthography of the text was agreed to by the Syndics
of the Cambridge University Press, and work commenced.

But by December 1804, the S. P. C. K. had lodged a
complaint against Charles' work even before it was completed.   The initiator was John Roberts, vicar of Tremeir-
chion, who had himself edited the 1799 Oxford edition of the
Welsh Bible for the S. P. C. K.   Roberts complained in a letter to George Gaskin, the General Secretary of the S. P. C. K. ,
that unwarranted "innovations" were being introduced into
Charles' text which, he felt, would be detrimental to the
interests of the Church of England. [2] He also protested that
the care of editing the Bible Society's Welsh edition had
been "committed to two leading characters among the Methodists. "[3] Without officially notifying the Bible Society of
these accusations, Gaskin sent copies of Roberts' letter to
all of the Bible Society Vice-Presidents.   This action upset
several influential patrons and caused a great deal of anxiety to Bishop Porteus who had cautiously supported the Society from its inception.   On Porteus' suggestion, the Bible
Society announced that it would formally investigate the allegations brought forward by Roberts.

Nobody at the Bible Society itself really took Roberts
seriously, and after a formal investigation, Charles was
completely exonerated.   But matters did not rest here.
Soon the S. P. C. K. began to question the authenticity of
the 1799 Welsh edition which Charles was editing and announced that they had decided to print 20, 000 Welsh Bibles
of their own from the edition of 1746.   This prompted the
Bible Society, after conferring with the Cambridge University Press, to conform to the S. P. C. K. decision, but within a matter of days, the S. P. C. K. had changed its mind
once again.   Now it was determined that the 1752 edition
of the Welsh Bible was even more accurate than the one
for 1746.   Tired perhaps of the S. P. C. K. 's fickleness in
the matter, Lord Teignmouth finally sought the advice of
Thomas Burgess, Bishop of St. David's who, after convening a
conference of his fellow Welsh Bishops, counseled the Bible
Society that the 1752 edition would meet with their approval. [4] Here matters finally rested.

The controversy obviously had some unfortunate ef-

fects on the Bible Society. Letters poured in from the
provinces prompted by rumors, largely spread by the news-
papers, that the Bible Society was publishing its Welsh Bible from an irregular text. To answer these queries, the
Society had to assure its patrons "that the liberties supposed to have been taken, were with the orthography of the
text, & not with the text itself."[5] The controversy had one
beneficial effect, however, because it forced the Society to
make a very important addition to its constitution. Sometime before March 1805, Thomas Sikes, the High Church
vicar of Guilsborough, published a very acrimonious attack
on the Bible Society which questioned whether the purity of
the Society's translations could be maintained when entrusted
to "sectaries" like Thomas Charles.[6] John Owen responded
to this accusation by pointing out to Sikes that "it has already been stated that the Society is restrained to editing
and distributing the versions, printed by authority," and
was therefore protected against irregular or heretical translations.[7] Owen had forgotten, however, that the original
principle of the Society, drawn up in 1803, and insisting
that translations could only be based on those established
by public authority had inadvertently been left out of the Society's constitution in 1804. If Owen was not aware of this
oversight, another High Church critic, William Van Mildert,
the future Bishop of Durham, brought it to the attention of
Bishop Porteus who immediately asked Owen for a clarifica-
tion of the Society's fundamental principle.[8] As a result,
the Society's constitution was revised to read:[9]

> The designation of this Society whall be "The Bri-
> tish and Foreign Bible Society"; the sole object of
> which shall be, to encourage a wider circulation of
> the Holy Scriptures: The only copies in the lan-
> guages of the United Kingdom to be circulated by
> the Society, shall be the authorised version, with-
> out note or comment.

Armed with a revised constitution and a "fundamental
principle" which now seemed finally impregnable to further
criticism, the Bible Society felt secure in its position. The
Welsh Bible problem and the attacks that flowed from it,
however, were only a foretaste of what was soon to come.
In fact it mattered little how simple and pure its motives
were. High Churchmen felt threatened by the mere fact
that the Bible Society was evangelical and interdenominational and, worst of all, successful. As the Bible Society
expanded in size and in the scope of its activities, it in-
evitably faced even more serious criticisms from its enemies.

II.

The early controversy with the S. P. C. K. over Welsh
Bibles only lasted one year, but it portended future conflict.
Most High Churchmen hoped that the Bible Society was a
feeble body which would soon collapse, but with the advent
of the auxiliary system in 1809 and the successful recruitment of evangelical and non-evangelical churchmen alike,
they began to fear that perhaps the Bible Society was a more
formidable enemy than they had originally thought.

The controversy that we shall examine now represented a struggle between two conflicting philosophies.   The
evangelicals held that the responsibility for the conversion
of sinners was so paramount that it dwarfed in comparison
all considerations of church polity.   They believed that in
the great mission to bring the Gospel to all people, churchmen and Dissenters should fight side by side in the common
cause.   By contrast, High Churchmen sensed that such cooperation implied an abandonment of any distinctive Anglican ecclesiology, impugning the claim of the Church of England to be a true branch of the historic catholic Church by
virtue of its episcopal order, apostolic succession, and
valid sacraments.   The very existence of the Bible Society,
with its promiscuous association of Anglicans and Dissenters
seemed to impugn the idea of a single national, established
church, an idea long held on grounds of utility but, thanks
to laymen like Burke and churchmen like Daubeny, now
pressed strongly again on grounds of high ecclesiological
principle.   It was a constant nightmare of High Churchmen
that the Evangelical Party in the Church of England was a
"Trojan Horse" within the citadel of the establishment.   It
was feared that Church Evangelicals, despite their protes-
tations of Anglican loyalty, were Dissenters in disguise, or
at least were unconsciously helping Nonconformity by breaking down the distinctive doctrines and order of the Church.
High Churchmen were determined to warn unwary Anglican
members of the Bible Society that, whether they knew it or
not, they were encouraging the dissidence of Dissent and
wounding the "Mother Church" in the process.   If they could
succeed in inducing Anglicans to withdraw their patronage
from the Society, its future would be bleak.

At each thrust from the High Churchmen in the controversy that we shall examine, the Bible Society recoiled,
tightened its constitution and ordered its more zealous advocates in far way auxiliaries to insure that its original and

official aims were still being pursued. Then it counter-
attacked. In the long run, of course, the High Churchmen
were not successful for the Bible Society weathered adver-
sity and still exists today. But indirectly, the continual re-
examination of its aims, the process of institutional intro-
spection, and the tightening of internal controls necessitated
by incessant harassment, caused a great deal of internal
damage to the Society. The internal controversies that we
shall examine in the next chapter were the indirect result
of seventeen years of controversy with High Churchmen.

         After the Welsh Bible controversy there was an un-
comfortable peace between High Churchmen and the Bible
Society which lasted only four years. A plan to found an
auxiliary at Colchester in 1810, however, unloosed a new
spate of controversy that lasted many years. The Colchester branch was perhaps singled out by the High Churchmen
for three reasons. In the first place, by 1810 the Bible Society had nine large auxiliaries and six more were being
planned. It was obviously growing faster than its enemies
had expected and would continue to do so unless stopped.
Secondly, the architects of the Colchester auxiliary were
not merely interested in recruiting evangelicals. Indeed,
they had the audacity to ask John Randolph, Bishop of London (Porteus had died in 1808) and a known High Churchman,
to become their patron as bishop of the diocese. [10]

         There was a third reason for a fresh attack on the
Bible Society, especially after 1811. That year had seen
the defeat of Lord Sidmouth's bill in Parliament which, had
it been successful, would have restricted Nonconformist
itinerant preaching. Since the Bill had been defeated by a
coalition of Nonconformists and Evangelical Anglican M. P.'s,
High Churchmen saw propaganda value in the affair and
turned it against the Bible Society. It was suggested that
this successful "sectarian" controversy in Parliament was
linked to the formation of Bible Society auxiliaries throughout Britain. [11] The High Church champions at Colchester
were Thomas Sikes (with whom we have already met) and
Christopher Wordsworth, then domestic chaplain to the Archbishop of Canterbury. Their invective against the formation
of an auxiliary drew replies from Lord Teignmouth, William
Ward, the rector of Myland, and William Dealtry, then professor of mathematics at the East India College in Haileybury.

         The Colchester fracas was only the excuse for re-

newed controversy elsewhere. High Churchmen had made
serious accusations against the Bible Society which far transcended the immediate danger at Colchester. The question
was not whether the auxiliary at Colchester would survive,
or even whether the auxiliary system would continue to make
inroads all over Britain, but whether the pan-evangelical
spirit itself would survive the attacks of its adversaries.

Cambridge was destined to be the next battlefield.
The University was important to both groups not only because the formation of its auxiliary followed close on the
heels of Colchester, but because Cambridge, especially before the building of Anglican theological colleges, was cru-
cially important as an Anglican seminary. If Cambridge
could spawn a Bible Society auxiliary, then Oxford could
also. And if evangelical "enthusiasm" could gain ground
among the ordinands at the Universities, there was no telling what parish would be safe.

For the confrontation at Cambridge, evangelicals and
High Churchmen brought out their heavy artillery. No less
a person than Herbert Marsh, the Lady Margaret Professor
of Divinity and future Bishop of Llandaff, led the High Church
cause, supported by Edward Maltby the future Bishop of Durham. As champions of the Bible Society cause came William
Dealtry of Colchester fame, Nicholas Vansittart, M. P. for
East Grinsland in 1812, William Otter, rector of Chetwynd
in Shropshire, John William Cunningham, vicar of Harrow,
Edward Daniel Clarke, professor of Mineralogy, Isaac Milner, President of Queens College, and Charles Simeon of
Holy Trinity Church. The epic story of the battle for Cambridge has been told elsewhere and does not need repetition
here, but the victory clearly went to the evangelicals.[12]
Inundated by pamphlet after pamphlet from Bible Society advocates, Herbert Marsh gave up the fight complaining in
1813 that "when an institution is supported with all the fer-
vour of religious enthusiasm ... an attempt to oppose it, is
like attempting to oppose a torrent of burning lava that issues from Etna or Vesuvius."[13]

After the decisive Bible Society victory at Cambridge,
the High Churchmen faced the prospect of fighting a losing
battle. As a result, their pamphlets became more desper-
ate, also more voluminous, running sometimes into hundreds
of pages. As predicted, an auxiliary was formed in Oxford
in 1812, but without the fracas experienced at Cambridge.
In 1814, the formation of an auxiliary at Hackney introduced

the bitter pen of Henry Handley Norris, the curate of St.
John's Chapel and Chaplain to the Earl of Shaftsbury. Norris inherited Marsh's role as the High Churchman's major
advocate. By 1815, even two Bishops, George Pretyman-
Tomline of Lincoln and George Henry Law of Chester, had
publicly taken a stand against the Bible Society.[14] By 1816
the controversy had spread to Ireland, creating a major dilemma for the Hibernian Bible Society. It would be unnecessary to record the publications between 1816 and 1822 when
the controversy unofficially ended with Norris' A Respectable
Letter to the Earl of Liverpool, because the charges brought
against the Bible Society were simply variations on old themes
written at greater length and in much more detail. In all,
over 170 pamphlets and books were contributed to the controversy between 1805 and 1822. This number would probably
double if we could examine the materials that flowed from
provincial areas.

III.

The controversy was fought over three principle issues, all of them interrelated. The first involved the immediate clash between the S. P. C. K. and the Bible Society.
The second centered on the Society's interdenominational
constitution which allegedly forced churchmen to cooperate
with "notorious" sectaries bent on undermining Church and
State. And the final issue touched on the sensitive and recurring problem of church order. All three issues seriously undermined the Society's ability to achieve its stated objective which was simply to distribute the Bible in its purest
form.

The first issue bears mentioning only briefly because
it has already been alluded to. As the S. P. C. K. was the
first organization in the Bible-distributing field, it not unnaturally considered itself the official Bible outlet for Anglican parishes all over Britain and therefore strongly resented a competitor. This resentment was expressed in
several ways. It was feared, for example, that the Bible
Society would attract subscriptions away from the S. P. C. K.[15]
High Churchmen also claimed that since the formation of the
Bible Society, the number of Prayer Books published by the
Cambridge University Press had been severely reduced in
order to fill Bible Society orders for Testaments.[16] The
inference was that the S. P. C. K. was thereby unable to supply the growing demand for Anglican Prayer Books requested

by loyal churchmen.   Members of the Bible Society leveled
their own complaints against the S. P. C. K.   For one thing,
the S. P. C. K. was a closed society by the end of the eighteenth century and it was apparently very difficult for evangelical churchmen to gain admission into it. [17]   For another,
it was well known that the S. P. C. K., through its lethargy,
had failed to supply many Anglican parishes, especially in
Wales, with Bibles.   Many Anglicans did not even know that
the S. P. C. K. existed! [18]

A second issue over which the Bible Society was compelled to defend itself involved its status as a pan-evangelical
institution.   It seemed only too obvious to many High Churchmen that the "unnatural coalition" of churchmen and Dissenters would soon give way to a sectarian predominance on the
Society's board of directors.   When this happened, many
feared that churchmen might unwittingly be used to under-
mine their own establishment.   For this reason they saw in
the Bible Society an incipient sectarian "conspiracy" against
the alliance of Church and State and arguments were marshalled to discredit not only the "promiscuous" relationship
between churchmen and Dissenters in the Bible Society, but
also in the whole pan-evangelical movement itself.

As an organization in which churchmen and Dissenters
fraternized, the Bible Society was a natural lightning-con-
ductor for such fears.   In the first place, it conjured up
frightening images of the Commonwealth and the Puritan
"rape" of the established church. [19]   Thomas Sikes, who
thanked heaven in 1805 that "the gates of nonconformity have
never, since the grand rebellion, prevailed against the Church,"
nevertheless feared that if churchmen like Lord Teignmouth
gave their "unexampled zeal and exertion" to the Dissenters
of the present day, they would "raise their memory to their
halcyon days of 1648[sic], and fill their beating bosoms, with
well-grounded hopes of once more realising those scenes,
which ... they little expected to see." [20]   Indeed, the very
organization of the Bible Society conjured up images of a
seditious institution planning to overthrow the establishment.
Even though the Society's direction was evenly distributed
between Anglicans and Dissenters, the fact that any minister or clergyman who contributed a guinea or more each
year to the Society would be entitled to vote, convinced critics that the Dissenters would pack the Bible Society en bloc. [21]
Great fear was therefore expressed that "the common room,
of this Society will be the theater of perpetual squabbles for
the pre-eminence ... until one had fairly beaten the other

out of the field, and the vanquished minority finds, that it has nothing to do with the Society, but to sanction its proceedings, and contribute to the support of its funds."[22] This point created concern that Society Anglicans would be outnumbered and outvoted by "coal-heaving ministers, bird-catching ministers, Baptist ministers of all trades, those of the Roman Catholic communion, together with the green-aproned female ministers of the friends."[23] High Churchmen like Van Mildert saw in the patrons of the Bible Society many who were "notoriously hostile both to the doctrine and discipline of the Church, and abetting with all their might, the cause of Heterodoxy and Schism."[24] Because these "secret foes" and "treacherous familiar friends" would predominate over the Anglican directors, the Society would naturally promote the cause of the establishment's adversaries.[25]

Soon, the time-honored cry of "Church in Danger" induced some High Churchmen to use cruder propaganda appeals. "Nation in Danger" was now the cry. Complaining about the ease by which admission was gained into the Society, Thomas Sikes told Lord Teignmouth that "T. Paine might (for aught I can perceive) as easily have been admitted into your Lordship's society as any of the Bench of Bishops."[26] This soon led to charges of Jacobinism. In 1818, for example, one pamphleteer pointed an accusing finger at the Bible Society's Southwark Auxiliary which had subdivided its territory into districts for the purpose of "gaining converts, and obtaining pecuniary aid." If the Southwark system spread, he feared that the country might be divided into departments in which houses would be numbered and inhabitants registered, a blueprint for systematic subversive propaganda on the lines of the radical Corresponding Societies.[27] The methods of Charles Dudley, the former Quaker (now Anglican) organizer of the Southwark system were even compared to those of the Illuminati on the Continent.[28] The coordinated and centralized nature of the Bible Society which cut across the Church's parochial system frightened clergymen, the more so since the Church of England was at present blatantly decentralized, without synods or Convocation.

Concomitant with the fears of Jacobinism was a more local fear of sectaries and heretics who would use the Bible Society for political and religious purposes. One such anxiety, which would have serious implications, as we shall see, for the Tests Controversy of 1830, involved Socinian membership in the Bible Society. In 1805, Sikes and Van Mildert

touched on this very sensitive subject by hinting that Socinian members of the Bible Society were set on destroying the
Church of England.[29]   John Owen, however, claimed that the
Socinian danger was overstated since it was questionable
whether even half a dozen of them patronized the Society.[30]
William Dealtry followed up Owen's claim five years later
by asserting, after making a diligent inquiry into the matter,
that he could count only one or two Socinians though, as we
have seen, he had to enlarge his estimate in the second edition of his Vindication, published in 1811.   Henry Handley
Norris did not let Dealtry forget this miscalculation, however, and as late as 1822, pointed to the Bible Society auxiliary at Harleston in Norfolk where the Secretary and two
committeemen were Unitarians as an embarrassing indication of the growing Socinian danger.[31]

          The final area of controversy raged around the sen-
sitive issue of church order.   If it could be shown to Bible
Society Anglicans that by associating with the Dissenters in
a conventicle atmosphere, they had abrogated their sacred
responsibility to Church and State, then the Anglican base
of the Society would be seriously weakened.   If this argument wore thin over the years, there were others to take
its place.   For example, did a clergyman not seriously
compromise his sacred trust as a member of the National
Establishment by neglecting to circulate the Prayer Book
with the Bible?

          The High Church charge that support of the Bible
Society constituted a breach of Anglican order was developed
on three grounds.   First, it was argued that the Society was
irregular because it had not received the sanction of a majority of the Bishops.[32]   Although the Bible Society tried to
counter this argument by demonstrating that it was a relatively new organization and therefore could not expect the
immediate approval of the entire bench of Bishops, the objection was not easily silenced.[33]   Secondly, many questioned
the propriety of churchmen associating with Dissenters in an
organization which, they alleged, encouraged the communal
worship of both groups.   Thomas Sikes asked Lord Teignmouth, for example, "how a clergyman of the Church, can
attend the meeting-house, without danger to his principles,
or gross indecorum towards the Church, and its spiritual
superior?"[34]   Charles Daubeny told the clergy in his diocese of Sarum in 1814 that "as members of the Church of
Christ, we have been cautioned by an apostle against being
'unequally yoked together with unbelievers'" and then pro-

ceeded to demonstrate all the disadvantages of associating with Dissenters in the Bible Society.[35] Finally, it was held that the failure to circulate Anglican Prayer Books together with Bibles represented an indirect attack on the Church of England. "When Churchmen, who have a liturgy," Herbert Marsh wrote in 1812, "and Dissenters who have none, agree in forming a Society, which by its constitution excludes the distribution of the Liturgy, the whole Society conforms to the principle of the Dissenters."[36] To insure that the Bible Society would not be charged with further irregularity on this point, the Prayer Book and Homily Society was founded in 1812 by Lord Teignmouth, Lord Gambier, William Wilberforce, and other Bible Society Anglicans, as a separate though complementary agency of the Bible Society.[37] But even this did not satisfy the critics who now asked why two separate organizations had to exist when the S.P.C.K. already performed both functions under the same roof.[38]

Seventeen years of controversy were bound to affect the Bible Society in one way or another. The Society, of course, wanted its patrons to believe that through the din of controversy it had emerged stronger than before. Thomas Gisborne, Perpetual Curate of Barton-under-Needwood, reported in 1815 that with every High Church attack on the Society, its revenues had increased dramatically.[39] Yet an examination of the Society's correspondence for these years leaves us with a rather different impression. Perhaps revenues did increase as Gisborne reported, but morale within the Society itself was often low, especially near the end of the second decade of the century. An indication of this was the alarming increase in the number of Anglican resignations during this period, traceable directly to the controversy with High Churchmen and the threat of more in the future. As the controversy escalated and strident High Church tracts continued to warn fellow Anglicans in increasingly exaggerated terms of the dangers inherent in their irregular collusion with sectaries, heretics and even Jacobins, not a few clergymen began to have second thoughts about their involvement in the Society's activities especially when some of the High Church accusations proved to be true.

But there was perhaps more immediate reasons for the decline in Anglican patronage at this time. Many of the more timid Evangelical clergymen were afraid that continued involvement in the Bible Society might provoke the displeasure of their Bishop, especially if he happened to be a High Churchman. Charles Mules of Marwood in Devonshire,

for example, the only clergyman in his neighborhood to patronize the Barnstable Auxiliary when it was founded, was
alarmed that the Bishop of Ely, a professed enemy of the
Bible Society would get wind of his activities and in consequence, force him to reside upon his living in Stapleford in
far away Cambridgeshire. His friends feared that this would
"in all probability shorten his days as he is quite an inva-
lid."[40]   Fears of this kind were not unfounded. John Owen
found himself dismissed from the curacy at Fulham because
Bishop Randolph disapproved of his activities as the Bible
Society's Secretary.[41]   Many Bible Society Anglicans began
to feel pangs of guilt about neglecting the S. P. C. K. and consequently rejoined it. Defections of this kind had devastating
effects on rural auxiliaries where there was often only one
clergyman in residence. In 1815, for example, the Branch
Society at Walsall had to dissolve because its Anglican patrons all decided to join the S. P. C. K. instead.[42]   The background of radical agitation from the Luddite Riots onwards
no doubt exacerbated the tensions in the minds of evangelical
Anglicans who wished to be friendly to Nonconformists. In
this period, when Ultra Toryism was on the ascendant, it
seemed proper that all friends of national establishments
should rally to their cause, dissociating themselves from
their critics.

Though the High Church party lost almost every battle
in its attempt to crush the auxiliary system, the long-term
effects of the controversy, coupled with the fears generated
by radical political movements, began to wear away the Society's internal cohesion. John Noble Coleman of Holwell
near Sherborne and future Perpetual Curate of Ventnor, the
Isle of Wight, told John Owen in 1818 that at the Yeovil Auxiliary anniversary, there had been unhappy dissensions between Dissenters and clergymen which he feared had greatly
weakened the Bible cause in his area.[43]   In the same year,
Thomas Jones of Denbigh claimed that in Wales the decline
of his auxiliary had been caused not only by economic depression but far more by "the desertion of a few of our Gen-
try and Clergy, who had once put their hands to the work."[44]
Two years later, Roger Carus Wilson, the vicar of Preston,
threatened to resign because of the "violent party feelings ...
even where both sides approve of the cause of the British and
Foreign Bible Society."[45]   It was not surprising that in some
areas, totally Nonconformist auxiliaries were prevalent: Often Anglican supporters were nonexistent. Under such circumstances it was impossible to carry through the expectation that auxiliary committees should be evenly divided between Church and Dissent.[46]

IV.

If most of the High Church accusations against the
Bible Society were not true, some were, and these disturbed Anglican patrons who could justify their continued
patronage of the Society only as long as it strictly maintained the purity of its original purpose which was to circulate the Bible without note or comment. It was extremely embarrassing to them when stories leaked out about auxiliaries engaged in activities of a partisan or irregular nature.

Before the auxiliaries existed, Society policy on matters relating to the "fundamental principle" was virtually
dictated by an interdenominational group of prominent laymen, ministers and clergymen centered in London. Anglican directors in particular jealously guarded the Society's
constitution and if it was in any way violated, offenders
were immediately disciplined and order restored. Paradox-
ically, the evolution of auxiliaries after 1809 created somewhat of a dilemma for these men. The existence of auxiliaries entailed some decentralization of decision making from
London to the provinces where each auxiliary was more or
less responsible for its own affairs. Consequently several
auxiliaries, controlled as they were by Dissenters, did not
always interpret the Society's laws in the same way as the
Anglican-dominated parent society, and in an age of increasing denominational consciousness, exemplified by the Baptist
and Congregational Unions, party concerns were often con-
fused with Bible Society activities. Needless to say, irregularities, when they occurred, were well publicized by the
Society's critics.

To counter violations of the Society's laws, and to
bring erring auxiliaries back into line with Society policy
as it was understood in London, the parent committee began to assert control over auxiliary affairs. But this action had two undesirable effects. In Scotland, many people
resented the authoritarian way in which the parent society
in London seemed to dictate auxiliary policy without con-
sulting those concerned. Resentment was further exacerbated when London often failed to adhere to its own decisions. As discussed in the next chapter, this resentment
did much to precipitate the Apocrypha Controversy of 1825
which brought about the Society's first schism. In other
parts of Britain, on the other hand, the inability of the
parent society to purge its more zealous auxiliaries of "irregularities" led many Anglican churchmen to believe High

Church accusations and consequently to try to purge the Society themselves.   As we shall see in the Test Controversy,
the result of this unilateral action was to pit churchmen
against Dissenters, leading to a second schism in 1832.
How these matters could precipitate internal controversy can
best be illustrated by examining three separate instances in
which the parent society and its auxiliaries or patrons dif-
ferently interpreted the Society's laws and principal objectives.

        The first involved the recurring task of interpreting
the Society's "fundamental principle" which only permitted
the circulation of the Authorized Version without note or
comment.   By this rule, it would have appeared that the
Society explicitly forbade extraneous matters such as notes,
prefaces, or tracts from being introduced or circulated with
Bibles.   But there were difficult borderline cases such as
Bibles that had traditionally been published either with marginal references or with metrical Psalms.   For example, in
1804 Granville Sharp felt that the addition of marginal cross-
references would not be "deemed a breach of the limitation
fixed by our society for the publishing of Bibles only," because the English authorized version had always included
them. 47   Besides, the demand for Marginal Reference Bibles by Anglican clergymen was too great to be disregarded.
So on February 5, 1810, the parent society decided to print
its first Bible with marginal readings and references. 48
Such also was the case of metrical Psalms which were considered a proper addendum in Scotland and Ireland.   Although
there had been a long-standing feud between the Edinburgh
printers and the English Universities over the legality of the
Scots printing Bibles with Metrical Psalms for circulation in
England, the Bible Society had almost certainly provided its
Scottish auxiliaries with these Bibles prior to 1811.

        By 1811, however, the parent society's position on
metrical Psalms had apparently changed.   In the previous
year, the Bristol auxiliary discovered that the German Bible Society in Nuremberg, to the complete ignorance of the
parent society, had printed a New Testament with explana-
tory notes attached.   Fearing protests from its own patrons
and High Church critics, the parent society quickly altered
the "fundamental principle" in 1811 by transferring the phrase
"without note or comment" to the first clause of the Society's
constitution "with a view to render it more perspicuous and
explicit."   This had broad and rather contradictory implications.   It meant a reaffirmation of the law which ruled that

matters of an extraneous nature like notes, introductions and, as far as Scotland was concerned, metrical Psalms, were to be eliminated completely from all Bibles published by the Society. Marginal references, on the other hand, were still permitted since they were considered (in England at least) as part of the Authorized Version. We have no evidence to suggest that metrical Psalms were officially banned by the Society at this time; but if we compare the number of Scottish requests for metrical Psalm Bibles that were never filled, with the number of English requests for Marginal Reference Bibles that were filled after 1811, we can only assume that the parent society was no longer supplying Scotland with the kind of Bible its countrymen wanted. [49]

By 1818, tensions between London and Edinburgh had reached a crisis over this apparent inconsistency. Though the parent society had commissioned a Marginal Reference Bible in 1810 for general distribution in England, it had never made too much of the matter, especially in its correspondence with the Scottish auxiliaries. However, in 1818 George Burder passed on to the parent society a letter from William Milne of Malacca who was preparing the Chinese version of the Bible for the Society under the auspices of the L. M. S. Milne wished the Bible Society to clarify what it meant by "note or comment" since he had to prepare his edition from scratch. Specifically, Milne inquired whether he could include in his edition items such as marginal references, explanations of difficult Western concepts and chapter contents. [50] The General Committee gave him a carte blanche to do whatever "may be deemed necessary to render the version of the Sacred Original intelligible and perspicuous." Furthermore, he was told to use as a model for his Chinese edition none other than the English Authorized Version with marginal references because it afforded "a correct example of that sort and degree of explanation which it may be permitted to introduce into the Bible."[51] But when this advice was made public in the Monthly Extracts for February 1818, the Edinburgh Bible Society registered a vigorous protest. Having been told several years before that metrical Psalms were to be banned from Scottish Testaments, the Edinburgh Bible Society angrily passed a resolution on March 16, 1818, condemning the parent society for hypocritically violating its own fundamental principle by allowing Milne to "tamper" with the text in whatsoever way he saw fit. If the parent society did not retract its instructions to Milne, the Scottish auxiliary warned, it could only fear for the "prosperity, the harmony, and even the existence" of the Bible Society. [52] When

a similar protest was registered by the Birmingham Auxiliary, the General Committee finally decided to retract its
instructions. [53] This would hardly be the last time that the
Edinburgh Bible Society would threaten dire consequences if
London did not mend its ways, but the tensions created pre-
figured the confrontation of 1825 over Apocryphal Bibles which
had much more serious consequences.

Another problem that created acute internal tensions
involved collateral society activities in England, especially
as these, in turn, involved women. It was not surprising
that the parent society became interested in women's Bible
associations in about 1817.   These had existed in one form
or another as early as 1811, but they did not attract much
attention until later.   After ten years of controversy, however, and faced with a period of financial depression, the
Bible Society needed to exploit all its resources and was
glad to avail itself of willing female support.   The women
felt that their associations, given the chance to expand,
could save the Society from possible financial ruin.   So to
C. S. Dudley of Southwark fame, was given the task of organizing women's associations on a national scale. [54]   By the
end of 1817, twenty-eight women's associations were established followed by seventy new ones in the following year.

Female emancipation was never a popular ideal in the
early nineteenth century.   The women's place was at home,
and even in religious activities she generally took a second
place to the male.   When the Bible Society saw need to exploit the energies of its evangelical women and permit near
equal participation with the men in fundraising and Bible distribution activities, there was some vigorous protest.   One
writer reported that some ladies associated with a Bible association in his neighborhood threatened that they would separate from their husbands rather than leave their Bible association.   He feared that "with the zeal and spirit, the for-
wardness and intrusive boldness of an active member of a
Ladies' Bible Association, how is it possible to retain the
softened diffidence and virgin modesty which form the great
charm of the female bosom [sic]." [55] More prurient minds
saw perverted, surrogate sexuality behind this enterprise.
A London newspaper claimed that Olinthus Gregory, Baptist
layman and mathematical master at the Royal Military Academy, once told the Women's Bible Association at Hertford
"that God would be their lover" if they distributed Bibles for
the Society! [56]

The major complaint against women's associations,

however, did not involve the issue of women's rights. Charles
Dudley already had a reputation among High Churchmen for
organizing the Southwark Auxiliary along potentially seditious
lines.   There was, therefore, grave speculation that Dudley's women might clandestinely infiltrate neighborhoods and
report back to Jacobin conspirators everything they had seen.

The women's associations by their zeal brought this
kind of speculation on themselves because they were engaged
in far more than Bible distribution.   Some bold spirits itinerated without invitation in the parishes of the very clergymen who opposed the Society, distributed their Bibles with
a short sermon, and then made inquiry into the spiritual
state of the recipients.   From a modern perspective, we
can understand that the women's associations provided one
of the few outlets through which middle class nineteenth century women could direct their creative energies. Their
over-enthusiasm was a sad commentary on the colorless and
restricted lives they otherwise led.   To Bible Society Anglicans, however, their zeal appeared extremely irregular.   To
High Churchmen, it bordered on sedition.   The fervor of
these women often did more harm than good.   William Conybeare complained that one group of zealots forced their way
into the kitchen of a conscientious clergyman, and prosely-
tized so vigorously among his household that they awakened
prejudices against the evangelical cause which might otherwise have faded away. [57]

The Ladies Association at Henley aroused especial
anxiety.   In 1817, R. B. Fisher, the Evangelical vicar of
Basildon and Secretary of the Wallingford Auxiliary Bible
Society, complained that Dudley's zealous women in Henley
were handing out moral instruction as well as Bibles and
questioning the recipients about their spiritual state.   This
might seem unexceptionable, but what was to prevent non-
evangelicals or Jacobins from similar tactics?   Perhaps,
he wrote, "some Socinian or antinomian agents may have
been propagating the peculiarities of their respective creeds?
In short, what security can you give the friends of the society that it will not be the instrument of errors?   What
security can you give the Government that it will not be
perverted to political purposes?"[58]

Under the threat of several clerical resignations over
this matter, [59] the issue was discussed by the parent committee in May and June of 1817 and proposals were passed
prohibiting the delivery of public addresses directed at Bible recipients. [60]   In November, further steps were taken

not only to purge the women's associations of irregularities,
but also to prohibit the use of devotional exercises at the
opening and conclusion of their business meetings.[61]   But
enforcement was not always easy.   Dudley and his women
unabashedly continued to itinerate on behalf of the Society,
evoking the displeasure of not a few clergymen, one of whom
complained indignantly that Dudley, an intruder into his parish and a layman at that, had preached in the local Lancastrian School during church hours, and had brazenly invited
his own Sunday School teachers to attend the lectures without previous approval.   Is it, this clergyman angrily asked,
"of no consequence whether a person hear the Gospel in a
Church or a barn, from the lips of a clergyman or an itinerant layman?"[62]   The inability of the parent society to control some of its own agents raised suspicions in the minds
of not a few Bible Society Anglicans that sectarianism had
penetrated the very leadership of the Society.

Finally, the Society faced a recurring problem involving the issue of church order, for it seemed that some
auxiliaries acted as though they were agencies of the local
denomination which happened to control a lion's share of the
membership.   Cavalierly, they encouraged prayers and sermons at business and anniversary meetings, and indulged in
discussions of religious topics unconnected with the simple
business of Bible distribution.   Joseph John Gurney, upset
by the lack of "sufficient simplicity" in many of the auxiliary
meetings he had visited, warned the parent society that American Quakers had been reluctant to support the Bible Society
largely because its meetings had developed into "opportun-
ities for religious services, I mean for prayer & preaching."
Gurney implied that if such practices continued in England,
the Society might well find itself without Quaker patronage.[63]
So, too, John Langley of Shrewsbury complained to the parent society that after a meeting of his auxiliary, several
preachers present gave notice that a revival meeting would
be held immediately afterwards in the committee room.   Lang-
ly was not opposed to revivals, but he felt that since there
was an "absolute necessity of adhering most rigidly to the
simple principle of the Bible Society," the local churches
would perhaps have been a more appropriate place for religious meetings.[64]   The age of denominational competition
was beginning to gain momentum after 1810 and it was scarcely surprising that many auxiliary societies often subordinated
the fundamental principle of the Bible Society to their own
denominational concerns.

A related problem which particularly irked the Anglican patrons of the Society, was the practice of holding meetings in religious buildings, especially Nonconformist chapels. Robert Gray, rector of Sunderland, complained to Lord Teignmouth in 1818 of a plan to move the annual meeting of the Sunderland Auxiliary Bible Society from the public assembly room where it had always been held, either to an Anglican church or a Nonconformist meeting house. To each place he, like his diocesan bishop, had "insuperable objections" since such business use of a religious place of worship diminished the veneration for a "House of God," and gave the society which assembled there an undesirable denominational appearance.65 George White, a Dissenter, expressed apprehension that if his auxiliary at Chatham met at Ebenezer Chapel, the Anglican patrons might walk out in force.66

The Society was also plagued by meetings which did not always adhere to the simple business of Bible distribution. One High Church critic told of the "orators" and the "advocates" of the Society, who "hurried from one quarter of the kingdom to the other, and with the same speeches in their mouths, à la mode of the itinerant preachers of the day, astonish the minds of their hearers with an enthusiastic burst, inflame them with spiritual raptures, and leave them in the enjoyment of Emanuel Swedenborg's invisible world; until, evaporation gradually taking place, a few days calm their sensibilities, and restore them to their sober senses."67 Under pressure of such criticisms, John Owen counseled auxiliary secretaries: "Recommend to your speakers to be brief, to speak to the question and to spurn controversy."68 But this advice was not always followed. Edward Burn, curate of St. Mary's Chapel in Birmingham told Joseph Hughes that at an auxiliary meeting in Workington, the chairman of the meeting, the Independent Spedding Curwen, in an effusion which lasted over three quarters of an hour, brought up "the Catholic Question, the mischief of religious establishments; the example of America, that does so well without them etc.," and did not stop until Burn "touched him gently on the irrelevancy of such matters."69 However hard it tried, the parent society could not always control these irregularities.

In the long run, this problem had a far-reaching effect on the Bible Society for there soon came into being a very vocal minority of dissident Anglicans within the Society whose protests over these irregularities portended even more serious confrontation in the future. In 1822, William Carus Wilson, rector of Tunstall in Lancashire complained of the "methodistical ranting" that took place at auxiliary meetings

and which upset the Quakers as much as the Anglicans.[70]
In 1825, Thomas Tyndale, the rector of Holton, complained
that he had just heard "a Dissenting minister make a most
injudicious attack on the speech of a pious clergyman ...
and detain the company for half an hour on purpose to support the dissenting interest."[71] If we remember that the
repeal of the Test and Corporation Acts was only three years
away, and that the issue of disestablishment was much discussed by the Dissenters at this time, we can well understand why these irregularities at Bible Society meetings ir-
ritated the Anglicans. John Dale Wawm, an Anglican from
Derby, informed John Owen that a joint stock company, composed almost exclusively of Dissenters, had offered to build
a new meeting room for his auxiliary, but that he had objected to this proposal because, by mutual agreement, the
building would also have been used for "political meetings"
by "our dissenting friends [who] are very violent in Derby."[72]
If these political meetings involved either the Dissenting Deputies or the Protestant Society, two Nonconformist organizations agitating for Repeal at this time, we can well understand why Bible Society Anglicans were becoming increasingly suspicious of their Nonconformist colleagues and why perhaps, a "test" was proposed in 1831 to exclude the more
threatening and radical elements like the Unitarians from
Society membership. For the time being, however, it is
important to understand that there was a growing Anglican
dissatisfaction with the ability of the parent society to regulate and control the heterodox activities of some of its more
irregular auxiliaries.

NOTES

1. The following account is based primarily on William
    Dealtry's excellently documented summary of the
    Welsh Bible controversy, published in 1810. See
    W. Dealtry, A Vindication of the British and For-
    eign Bible Society in a Letter to the Rev. Dr. Words-
    worth (1810).
2. Cf., B.S. Home Correspondence: J. Roberts to J.
    Tarn, March 18, 1805.
3. B.S. Home Correspondence: J. Roberts to G. Gaskin
    (copy), December 31, 1804.
4. B.S. Minutes of Subcommittees (1804-1810), December
    9, 1805.
5. B.S. Home Correspondence: J. Hughes to G. Simcox,
    May 14, 1806.

6. T. Sikes, An Address to Lord Teignmouth (1805), 32 f.
7. J. Owen, A Letter to a Country Clergyman Occasioned by His Address to Lord Teignmouth (1805), 55.
8. W. Van Mildert, A Letter to the Society for Promoting Christian Knowledge (1805), 42; J. Owen, The History of the Origin and First Ten Years of the British and Foreign Bible Society (1816), I, 72.
9. B.S. Minutes of General Meetings, May 1, 1805.
10. Randolph, of course, turned the invitation down. See B.S. General Committee Minutes, February 19, 1810, Owen, Bible Society Origins, I, 471.
11. Papers occasioned by Attempts to Form Auxiliary Bible Societies in Various Parts of the Kingdom (1812), 25.
12. See F. K. Brown, Fathers of the Victorians (1961), 295 ff.
13. H. Marsh, A Reply to the Strictures of the Rev. Dr. Isaac Milner (1813), 141.
14. Owen, Bible Society Origins, III, 140 f. They were followed in 1816 by Samuel Goodenough, Bishop of Carlisle and Edward Bowyer, Bishop of Ely in 1817. For the remarks of the Bishop of Lincoln, see Bodl. MSS Eng. Misc. d 32, f. 17.
15. C. Wordsworth, An Remonstrance to the Lord Bishop of London (1806), 68 f.; Dealtry, Vindication, 108 f.
16. H. Marsh, A Letter to the Rt. Hon. N. Vansittart (1812), 25 f.; Cf., W. Otter, An Examination of Dr. Marsh's Answer to all Arguments in Favour of the British and Foreign Bible Society (1812), 17 f.; C. Simeon, The Excellency of the Liturgy .. to Which Is Prefixed an Answer to Dr. Marsh's Inquiry Respecting the Neglecting to Give the Prayer Book with the Bible (1812), 48 f.
17. This was the dilemma faced by Simeon. See Simeon, op. cit., 51 fn.
18. Cf., Dealtry, Vindication, 56; W. K. L. Clark, A History of the S.P.C.K. (1959), 104 f.
19. Cf., H. H. Norris, A Practical Exposition of the Tendency and Proceedings of the British and Foreign Bible Society (1814), 382 fn.
20. T. Sikes, An Address to Lord Teignmouth (1805), 21, 24. A similar criticism was levelled against Bishop Porteus. See T. Sikes, An Humble Remonstrance to the Lord Bishop of London (1806), 9 f.; Cf., Bodl. MS 133e723(1*), 14: "Minutes of a Conversation with Bishop Porteus by Thomas Sikes."
21. T. Sikes, Address to Teignmouth, 46 f.
22. J. H. Spry, An Enquiry into the Claims of the British and Foreign Bible Society (1810), 16.

23. T. Sikes, Humble Remonstrance to Porteus, 50.
24. Van Mildert, Letter to the S.P.C.K., 27.
25. Sikes, Address to Teignmouth, 11 f.
26. T. Sikes, A Second Letter to Lord Teignmouth (1810), 45.
27. An Address to the Committee of the Bible Society in Horsham and Its Neighborhood (1818), 28, 29.
28. H. H. Norris, A Respectful Letter to the Earl of Liverpool (1822), 41 fn. Cf., Norris, Practical Exposition, 483; W. Dealtry, A Review of Mr. Norris's Attack Upon the British and Foreign Bible Society (1815), 55.
29. T. Sikes, Address to Teignmouth, 24; W. Van Mildert, Letter to the S.P.C.K., 23 ff.
30. J. Owen, Letter to a Country Clergyman, 49 f.
31. H. H. Norris, Respectful Letter to the Earl of Liverpool, 116 fn.
32. T. Sikes, Humble Remonstrance to Porteus, 56 f.; Sikes, Second Letter to Teignmouth, 5 f., 11; Cf., H. Marsh, An Address to the Members of the Senate of the University of Cambridge Occasioned by the Proposal to Introduce in This Place an Auxiliary Bible Society (1811), 1.
33. N. Vansittart, Three Letters on the Subject of the British and Foreign Bible Society (1812), 53; Vansittart, Letter to the Rev. Dr. Marsh ... Occasioned by His Address to the Senate of [Cambridge] University (1811), 6.
34. T. Sikes, Address to Teignmouth, 32.
35. C. Daubeny, The Substance of a Discourse Delivered at the Abbey Church in Bath ... Giving a Churchman's Reasons for Declining a Connection with the Bible Society (1814), 6 f.
36. H. Marsh, An Inquiry into the Consequences of Neglecting to Give the Prayer Book with the Bible (1812), 58. "Take away the Prayer-book," Marsh said in 1817, "and though we remain Christians, we cease to be Churchmen." Cited in J. H. Overton, The English Church in the Nineteenth Century (1894), 280. Cf., W. Otter, Examination of Marsh's Answer, 34 f.
37. See J. W. Cunningham, A Sermon Preached Before the Prayer Book and Homily Society (1813).
38. H. Marsh, Letter to Vansittart, 44 f.
39. T. Gisborne, A Letter to the Right Reverend the Bishop of Gloucester on the Subject of the British and Foreign Bible Society (1815), 32.
40. B.S. Home Correspondence: H. W. Gardiner to C. F.

Steinkopf, April 25, 1822. Cf., B.S. Home Correspondence: J. Shewell to J. Hughes, November 26, 1822.

41. B.S. Paterson Letters, I, f 105: C. F. Steinkopf to J. Paterson, August 16, 1813. Cf., J. Leifchild, Memoir of the Late Rev. J. Hughes (1835), 252 f.

42. B.S. Home Correspondence: T. Gleadow to J. Tarn, March 30, 1815.

43. B.S. Home Correspondence: J. Coleman to J. Owen, July 30, 1818. Cf., B.S. Home Correspondence: R. Tolson to J. Tarn, June 19, 1816.

44. B.S. Home Correspondence: T. Jones Sr. to J. Tarn, June 13, 1818; Cf., B.S. Home Correspondence: J. Moody et al. to J. Tarn, April 14, 1818; T. Clubbe to H. Dobbs, March 29, 1817; J. Fletcher to R. Steven, March 31, 1821.

45. B.S. Home Correspondence: R. C. Wilson to J. Tarn, April 10, 1820.

46. Cf., B.S. Home Correspondence: J. Langley to J. Tarn, January 24, 1823; Cf., B.S. Home Correspondence: J. Mules to C. F. Steinkopf, December 8, 1819.

47. B.S. Miscellaneous Book, I, 27 f.: G. Sharp to Bible Society, August 8, 1804.

48. B.S. Minutes of General Committee, February 5, 1810.

49. Cf., B.S. Home Correspondence: L. Grant to J. Tarn, c. November 13, 1815; S. Alcorn to J. Tarn, December 26, 1815; N. McNeil and J. Russell to J. Tarn, September 11, 1816.

50. B.S. Home Correspondence: G. Burder to J. Owen, January 1818.

51. B.S. Minutes of General Committee, January 19, 1818.

52. B.S. Home Correspondence: C. Anderson to Bible Society, March 26, 1818.

53. B.S. Home Correspondence: E. Burn to J. Owen, April 23, 1818; B.S. Minutes of the Printing Subcommittee, May 1, 1818.

54. B.S. Home Correspondence: C. S. Dudley to Bible Society, May 14, 1817. Cf., C. S. Dudley, An Analysis of the System of the Bible Society (1821), 365, 370.

55. A Letter to the Church Members of the Auxiliary Society, Liverpool (1819), 18 f., 21.

56. Cited in B.S. Home Correspondence: R. Everett to J. Tarn, January 14, 1823.

57. Bod. MSS Montagu d. 12, II, f. 131: W. Conybeare to Mrs. Hodge, n.d.

58. B.S. Home Correspondence: R. B. Fisher to J. Hughes, March 18, 1817.

59. For example, Henry Brooke of Wells threatened to resign from the Society because he saw in Dudley's plan a plot to divide the parishes into subdivisions, to canvass the neighborhood so as to ascertain its state and to use all of this information in the overthrow of the establishment. B.S. Home Correspondence, H. Brooke to J. Owen, September 19, 1817.

60. B.S. Minutes of Printing and General Purposes Subcommittee, May 31, 1817. Cf., J. Scholefield, A Second Letter to the Right Hon. Earl of Liverpool (1822), 65 f.

61. B.S. Minutes of General Committee, November 17, 1817.

62. B.S. Home Correspondence: J. B. Stuart to J. Owen, January 30, 1822.

63. B.S. Home Correspondence: J. J. Gurney to Bible Society, May 31, 1817.

64. B.S. Home Correspondence: J. Langley to J. Tarn, March 17, 1821.

65. B.S. Teignmouth Letters, f. 72: R. Gray to Teignmouth, August 16, 1819.

66. B.S. Home Correspondence: G. White to J. Tarn, March 16, 1820.

67. A Letter to the Right Reverend the Bishop of Gloucester in Vindication of His Lordship's Refusal to Accept a Vice-Presidentship of an Auxiliary Bible Society at Gloucester (1813), 17 fn.

68. Bodl. MSS Montagu, d.9, f. 72: J. Owen to W. Bicheno, December 17, 1814.

69. B.S. Home Correspondence: E. Burn to J. Hughes, October 12, 1819.

70. B.S. Home Correspondence: W. C. Wilson to R. Cockle, August 11, 1822.

71. B.S. Home Correspondence: T. Tyndale to [A. Brandrum], November 18, 1825.

72. B.S. Home Correspondence: J. D. Wawm to J. Owen, January 9, 1822.

I.

The 1820's marked a watershed in the history of the Bible Society. By 1822, as we have seen, the controversy with High Churchmen had largely run its course, but it had sown many doubts in the minds of patrons. Attempts by the parent society in London to dictate Bible distributing policies in Scotland and to reassert control over the wayward activities of auxiliaries in England were largely unsuccessful. The Scots resented the hypocritical way the parent society made decisions on some very sensitive matters; English Anglicans were unhappy with the failure of the parent society to discipline irregularity. This unhappiness led to two further controversies that we must now examine in some detail.

The reaction in Scotland was complex. In part, the so-called Apocrypha Controversy was precipitated by the unreasonable and inconsistent way London managed its Scottish affairs. Later, however, it became apparent that the Presbyterian aversion to Apocryphal Bibles was rooted in an almost neurotic fear of Roman Catholicism. These factors, together with the discussion of Catholic Emancipation before Parliament, caused a secession of the Scottish auxiliaries from the parent society in 1825 although, for the most part, the Scottish Dissenters remained faithful to London. In England, on the other hand, dissident Anglicans within the Society, fearful of the sectarian dangers previously proclaimed by the Society's High Church critics, and inflamed by the repeal of the Test and Corporation Acts, saw need to force a "test" on the Society itself in the hope of weeding out not only the Unitarians, but other unorthodox "sectaries" whom they felt were dangerous to the establishment. The Society's refusal to accede to these demands forced a second secession in 1831.

Although the Bible Society survived these controversies, it was evident by 1830 that the pan-evangelical movement had been seriously weakened. And if the Bible Society,
with its simple constitution, found it difficult to weather denominational and theological warfare, the future of evangelical unity appeared bleak.

It was never the intention of the Bible Society in its
earlier years to circulate Apocryphal Bibles. This was certainly always true of the Bibles circulated in Britain, but
even on the Continent where Roman Catholics in particular
considered the Apocrypha an integral part of the Scriptures,
the Society explicitly disapproved of its circulation. Still,
many Continental societies circulated Apocryphal Bibles in
the Society's name though almost certainly without London's
knowledge or sanction.

By 1812, if not before, the Bible Society faced a
perplexing situation. Increasingly, many Continental agents
were complaining that Society Bibles did not sell because
they lacked the Apocrypha. Even C. F. Steinkopf, the Society's Foreign Secretary, sent to the Continent in 1812 to
impress upon the Continental societies the importance of
adhering strictly to London's rules, returned to England declaring that unless the parent society was rather more flex-
ible about issuing Apocryphal Bibles, it would lose a great
deal of its Continental patronage. On June 7, 1813, therefore, it was decided in committee "that the manner of printing the Holy Scripture by the Foreign societies, be left to
their discretion, provided they be printed without note or
comment."[1] This resolution was tactfully phrased, for even
though nothing was directly said about Apocryphal Bibles,
their circulation was to be permitted by implication. The
parent society did not wish this to be publicized and told its
provincial auxiliaries in Britain nothing of the decision.

By 1821, however, rumors were beginning to circulate that the parent society had illegally countenanced the
circulation of Apocryphal Bibles without the general approval
of its members. With the Society's regulation on Metrical
Psalms still fresh in their memories, these rumors must
have been particularly irritating to the Scots. In fact, it
was a Scotsman, Robert Haldane, who first exposed London's duplicity in the matter after discovering, quite by
chance, that the French Bible edited at Montauban and financed partly with his own money, had included the Apocrypha. Apparently, the directors had led him to believe

that the Montauban Bible would contain nothing but the "pure word of God."[2] The result of Haldane's investigations into the "secret" affairs of the Society was a strong letter of protest written on October 6, 1821, in which he warned London that if the practice of circulating Apocryphal Bibles was persevered in, "a very general secession of auxiliary societies & subscribers will take place."[3] Haldane's words were indeed prophetic!

Because Haldane was not a director of the Bible Society, the mantle of what would soon be called the "Anti-Apocrypha Party" fell on the shoulders of the Irish clergyman William Thorpe, former chaplain at the Lock Hospital in London who served the parent society with a notice that at their next meeting he would press for anti-Apocryphal legislation.[4] But when Thorpe presented his resolution on July 22, 1822, which, had it been adopted, would have outlawed the use of Society funds for the printing or circulation of Apocryphal Bibles on the Continent, he was opposed by an Anglican pressure group within the parent society (later to be known as the "Philo-Apocrypha Party") who hinted that the resolution would result in the unhappy resignation of many Anglican patrons in England, many of whom had always used the Apocrypha in Church services, and the possible loss of the Society's Continental patronage.[5] Consequently, Thorpe's resolution failed in committee.

Because of mounting pressures from provincial auxiliaries over the matter, the Scots' claim could not easily be overlooked. The parent society decided, therefore, that some sort of compromise was in order, and accepted a resolution drawn up by Lord Teignmouth on August 9, 1822, making it an invariable rule of the Society to finance only those books of the Bible which were generally received as canonical in Britain, but with the important proviso that the Continental societies would remain at liberty to apply their own funds to the printing and circulating of Apocryphal Bibles "in whatever way" they saw fit.[6] In other words, the Apocrypha would still be appended or interspersed with Society Bibles as long as the Continental societies financed the Apocrypha themselves. But this was an unhappy compromise. Not only did it still permit the circulation of Apocryphal Bibles (albeit, with Society funds used only for the canonical Scriptures), but London had underestimated the Scottish aversion to a "dangerous book" loaded with "Romish errors." The Scottish animosity towards the Apocrypha was, needless to say, stoked by the resentment lingering from the Metric Psalm affair.[7]

Two years of relative calm passed before the Scots could find an issue worthy of renewed agitation. They found this issue in Leander Van Ess, a Roman Catholic priest who served as an agent of the Society in Germany. Van Ess had complained that the non-Apocryphal Bibles he was receiving from the Bible Society were not selling because the Roman Catholic population in his area thought them to be Lutheran Testaments. He therefore requested permission to purchase 8,000 copies of the Bible in sheets to which, at his own expense, he would reintegrate the Apocrypha. Since Van Ess' request seemed to be legal under the resolution of August 1822, it was acceded to in committee without debate, and Van Ess was voted £500 for his project.[8] Unfortunately, the Scottish Anti-Apocryphist Edward Craig, minister of St. James Episcopal Chapel in Edinburgh who had attended the meeting, returned to Scotland with the news which ignited protests.[9] What kind of Bible had the Society been committed to? "Let us suppose," Thorpe wrote Teignmouth, "this Bible of Professor Leander Van Ess completed[10]

and let us suppose it laid on the table of our committee room. On taking it up, it is found to contain the Apocryphal books, as well as the Holy Scriptures; nay, to have the former intermixed with the latter, in such a manner as that the story of Bel and the Dragon appears as one of the chapters of Daniel's prophecy. A member of the Society, on observing this, remarks, "here is a violation of one of our fundamental laws." "Oh no," replies the Committee, turning to one side of a leaf which contains the word of God, "We paid for this," but turning to the other side, in which the Apocrypha appears, "some other person, we know not who, paid for that."

If the parent society continued to publish Apocryphal Bibles in any form, Thorpe predicted, the Society would face "consequences of the most disastrous description."[11] James F. Gordon, also of the Edinburgh Bible Society, hinted that unless Van Ess' grant was rescinded, "you will find the B&F Bible Society will lose all Scotland, both auxiliaries & also private subscribers."[12]

To head off impending disaster, a resolution was rushed through committee rescinding Van Ess' grant. Teignmouth hoped that this action would appease the Scots and that the August 1822 resolution would still authorize the com-

mittee at least to assist in the circulation of Bibles with the
Apocrypha appended. But he also feared that the Anti-Apocryphists would make a second attempt either to abolish the
resolution of August 1822 in its entirety or alter it in such
a way that the Society would be prohibited from circulating
Apocryphal Bibles in any form. If this was attempted, Teignmouth confided to Andrew Brandram (John Owen's successor
as the Anglican Secretary), there would be problems. In
the first place, a resolution condemning the Apocrypha whole-
sale would be more than Teignmouth and most of the Society's Anglican patrons could personally countenance, for
while the Church of England never regarded the Apocrypha
as canonical, it did permit the circulation of the Bible with
the Apocrypha appended to it. Indeed, lessons from the
Apocrypha were periodically read in Anglican worship. Secondly, if the Anti-Apocryphists succeeded in boycotting Continental societies that were willing to append privately financed Apocryphas at the end of Society Bibles, Teignmouth
feared that the great evangelical mission to Europe "would
be brought within very restricted limits."[13] Consequently,
on December 20, 1824, fearing that anti-Apocryphal legislation might be forthcoming from Scotland, Teignmouth proposed yet another compromise, this time mandating that Society grants would not aid in the printing of any Bible in
which the Apocrypha was mixed or interspersed, but allowing the Society to continue aiding auxiliaries which appended
the Apocrypha separately at the end of the Bible at their
own expense.[14] But no sooner was Teignmouth's compromise proposed than the Edinburgh Bible Society protested
that his resolution served to "administer a salvo to the con-
sciences of objectors at home; whilst abroad the evil remains exactly the same as ever."[15]

Meanwhile in England, a Philo-Apocrypha reaction,
supported by Anglicans headed by Andrew Brandram, began
to agitate for a return to what seemed in Scotland at least,
to be pro-Apocrypha rules. In fact, these Anglicans scarcely approved of the Apocrypha any more than the Scots.[16]
What they desired was a rule which encouraged the circulation of non-Apocryphal Bibles on the Continent, but which
also permitted the Society to circulate Apocryphal Bibles in
areas that would receive nothing else. Ironically, the Philo-
Apocryphists based their argument on the same foundation
the Scots had been using against the circulation of Apocryphal Bibles, namely that it would be a violation of the Society's fundamental principle, which united all Christians in
one common enterprise, to "cut off some of the largest &

most promising branches of the Society's labour--by giving up, in some quarters the only way in which any part of the word of God can be circulated."[17]   The result of this opposition was a resolution in committee on March 7, 1825, which rescinded all previous Apocrypha legislation.[18]

The Anti-Apocryphist reaction to this new development was predictably hostile, resulting in petitions and letters of protest.   A "Special Subcommittee" was soon formed in April to consider further compromise,[19] but nothing could be done to assuage the Scots who wanted nothing less than a complete break with the Continental societies that circulated Apocryphal Bibles in any form, with or without Society funds.[20] The result was a decision by the Edinburgh Bible Society in May of 1825 to take unilateral action and discontine remittances to the Bible Society as long as it continued to resist reform.[21]

The impact of the Edinburgh decision was catastrophic. Not only did several auxiliaries in Scotland follow suit by also cutting off funds, but so did some in England.[22]   The appointment of a second "Special Subcommittee" in October to cope with this new problem only intensified dissatisfaction, and when it was resolved on November 21, 1825, that all Bibles printed in England for circulation on the Continent would be issue-bound (i.e. not sent in sheets) thus making it impossible for the Apocrypha to be introduced,[23] the Scots protested that the foreign societies would now spend the whole of their own funds on the independent circulation of the Apocrypha.[24]   Soon the Presbytery of Glasgow, in whose hands rested the future of the important Glasgow Bible Society, was contemplating similar action against London.[25]

II.

By 1825, if indeed not before, Bible Society evangelicals were beginning to polarize over the Apocrypha issue. At first glance, there seemed to be two parties to the dispute.   The so-called Anti-Apocryphists appeared to represent all the Scottish evangelicals, most of the English evangelical Dissenters, and a rather large number of English churchmen.   The Philo-Apocryphists, on the other hand, seemed in the beginning at least, to be headed largely by a group of Clapham Sect evangelical Anglicans who dominated the parent society and, of course, representatives of the foreign churches like C. F. Steinkopf.   But in fact, the

lines of division were much more complex than this. In
the first place, most British evangelicals, to different degrees, opposed the Apocrypha. Scottish Presbyterians had
social and theological reasons for opposing its circulation
for not only was it condemned by the Westminster Confession, but it symbolized the continuing Scottish fear of Roman
Catholicism. English evangelical Anglicans also discouraged
the use of the Apocrypha though unlike their Northern brethren, they shared neither the same aversion to Apocryphal
Bibles nor quite the same intensity of anti-Popery emotion.
Consequently, they were willing to circulate Apocryphal Bibles in countries that would accept nothing else. Nonconformists in Scotland and England were also, for the most
part, Anti-Apocryphists, but though the Apocrypha had no
place in their Bibles, they, too, did not completely share
the Presbyterian anti-Roman Catholic neurosis.

        The polarization of Society evangelicals into Anti-and
Philo-Apocrypha groups was really determined by the degree
to which each group was willing to go in abolishing the Apocrypha from Society Bibles. Consequently, by 1825 there
were at least three parties to the controversy. The Anti-
Apocryphists, represented mostly by evangelicals of the
Scottish establishment and an extremist fringe composed of
the Haldanes, Edward Irving, and Andrew Thomson, wanted
the Apocrypha banned by the Society even if this action meant
sacrificing Continental patronage.[26] This feeling was so
strong that they were willing to leave the Society if their
demands were not met.[27] The Philo-Apocrypha Party, composed as it was of Anglicans, foreigners and others, was
not prepared to forfeit Continental support by banning the
Apocrypha. This party, as we have seen, was willing to
countenance Apocryphal Bibles when Continental societies
would receive nothing else. But by far, the vast majority
of British evangelicals fell into neither extreme camp, at
least in the beginning of 1825. If anything, they tended to
side with the Anti-Apocryphists. But when the Anti-Apocryphists became intransigent and separation seemed imminent,
the moderates tended more and more to back the parent society.

        Edinburgh's decision to withhold its funds portended a
schism, and this the parent society wanted to avoid if at all
possible. On January 2, 1826, an assurance was dispatched
to the Scots that the Apocrypha would never again be circulated with Society Bibles, but the parent society was not prepared to give in to Edinburgh's demand that support be with-

drawn from all Continental societies which still chose to
print and circulate the Apocrypha at their own expense. [28]
A deputation was subsequently sent to Scotland in March
1826 to negotiate, but success was limited. [29] That all
Apocryphal Bibles should be removed from the stock, and
the stereotype plates used for their printing should be destroyed were demands that London could readily accept.
But the delegation dug in its heels when it came to the demand for public repentance by the directors for breaches of
the fundamental principle: still more when the Scots insisted
on the severance of relations with Continental societies that
circulated the Apocrypha in any manner, and finally on the
removal of the Philo-Apocryphists from the Society's direction. These were demands that the deputation had no authority to meet. [30]

London was hardly prepared to demand the resignations of its three secretaries and Lord Teignmouth. In any
event, it was the opinion of the returning deputation that
nothing short of total acquiescence to Edinburgh's demands
would prevent schism. [31] So resigned to the fact that Edinburgh was probably a lost cause, the Society passed a series of resolutions between April and May 1826 which only
reiterated more definitely the resolution of November 1825. [32]
The result, as expected, was Edinburgh's final withdrawal
which was followed some months later by that of the Glasgow Bible Society. [33]

The Edinburgh and Glasgow separations left many
Scottish moderates in a very difficult position. The Eclectic Review, for instance, pointed out to Scottish Episcopalians that if they separated from the Bible Society on terms
that banned the Apocrypha from the Bible ("the Bible as it
exists, horribile dictu, on the reading desks of Episcopal
churches") they were impugning the traditions of their own
communion. [34] Neither Thorpe nor Craig and most of the
other Episcopalians in Scotland were willing to go this far. [35]
Most of the Scottish Baptists and Independents and even several members of the United Secession Church were also unwilling to follow their brethren in the Church of Scotland into separation. [36] Therefore in June of 1827, a group of
Scottish dissidents seceded from the Edinburgh Bible Society and eventually formed a new auxiliary still connected
with the parent society in London. [37]

The Edinburgh and Glasgow schisms and the adverse
publicity that followed had a disastrous effect in Scotland.

Of the forty-eight Scottish auxiliaries contributing to the
parent society in 1825, only eight continued to do so three
years later.[38] Nevertheless, the Society weathered advers-
ity and continued on its way as a major pan-evangelical institution though greatly weakened financially from its loss of
generous Scottish patrons. But before it could completely
recover, it had to face a second major test of its ability to
survive.

III.

          Just as the Apocrypha agitation began to calm down,
the Bible Society had to face a second disruption known as
the Socinian or Test Controversy in which some members
desired to institute a test of faith that would weed out Socinians and other "unorthodox" members. Accusations that
the Society harbored unorthodox elements were hardly new.
High Churchmen had pointed a critical finger not only at the
Society's small number of Unitarian patrons, but at otherwise orthodox Dissenters who were allegedly plotting to un-
dermine the establishment. By the beginning of the third
decade of the nineteenth century, a small group of evangelicals, mostly belonging to the Church of England, were beginning to believe that there was perhaps some truth to these
accusations especially when they witnessed the highly irregular activities of the women's associations and the "indiscretions" propagated by Dissenters at auxiliary meetings. Some
questioned the propriety of their continued patronage of the
Society. Others contemplated a purge of the dangerous
groups. Most evangelical churchmen, of course, did not
regard orthodox Dissent at large as dangerous. But the inability of the parent society to control irregularity in the
provinces gave many Anglicans second thoughts about co-
partnership with heterodox or radical elements in the alliance.

          A further development confirmed these fears. The
1820's witnessed, as we have seen in the history of the London Missionary Society, a revival of Nonconformist self-
identification which greatly modified the traditional political
relationship between Church and Dissent. In the first place,
evangelical Congregationalists and Baptists had, by 1812, ex-
perimented with their first denominational unions. With their
increasing numbers, Dissenters also discovered that they
possessed greater political leverage, and this realization
gave renewed vitality to the Repeal movement. The Dis-

senting Deputies and the recently formed Protestant Association began to entertain hopes for the immediate repeal of
the Tests.   Many evangelical churchmen now found themselves in a very difficult position.   Repeal, they believed,
was only the first step to disestablishment and while Repeal
itself might be supported by churchmen, disestablishment
would naturally have to be opposed.   At the same time,
evangelical Anglicans still felt far more spiritual affinity
with evangelical Dissenters than with their High Church colleagues.   The Bible Society itself, of course, had done much
to build bridges between Church and Dissent.   The problem,
then, was how to fend off political Dissent without weakening
the pan-evangelical cause.

A small number of Anglican evangelicals, like most
High Churchmen, felt that the only solution was to cease
from any kind of cooperation with Dissenters. [39]   Others
saw a simpler solution to the "sectarian" problem.   The
dangerous elements in the Bible Society would be located
and ejected, making cooperation with the more orthodox
Dissenters altogether safer and more straightforward.   Not
surprisingly, the alien group was to be found in the prominent party of the Repeal movement--the Unitarians.

The Unitarians were well cast for the role.   Though
never a major force in Britain's ecclesiastical life after the
eighteenth century, they had nevertheless enjoyed a minor
theological revival in the 1820's through the works of Thomas Belsham and Robert Aspland and in the recently formed
British and Foreign Unitarian Association which, since 1825,
bound them together for the first time into a denomination.
The idea of a united Unitarian movement immediately conjured up old fears of "rational Dissent" in its most dangerous form.   Therefore the small number of Unitarians who
patronized the Bible Society became the scapegoats of a
growing anti-Dissenting hostility among not a few evangelical
clergymen.   This hostility was inflamed, needless to say,
by the harsh High Church accusations of the previous decade.
After reading Henry Handley Norris on the subject, for example, Hugh Rogers, rector of Camborne in Cornwall, wanted to know in 1822, exactly how many Unitarians actually
belonged to the Society. [40]   But Rogers was only one among
many who were now asking the same question.   Robert Haldane increased the number of inquiries by reporting in 1825
that from one end of the Continent to the other "Christians
have very little weight in the several [Bible Society] committees, which, in general, are wholly under the direction

of Freethinkers ... Many Arians and Socinians ... are the
sole governors of several societies abroad."[41] In 1826,
another Anglican patron of the Society added that "Unitarian
teachers were systematically embraced and hugged by [the
Society's] Secretaries, at home."[42]

      In the beginning, agitation to exclude Unitarians from
the Society came from only one or two individuals like William Williams, curate of Dunsfold in Surrey who, in 1820,
warned of the "sin and evil consequences of entering into a
religious alliance with Socinians" in the Bible Society.[43] But
though Williams was thought to be insane, especially after
he broke into a meeting of the parent society and lectured
the directors on his obsession, his persistence had its effect.[44] Soon members were demanding the institution of
prayers at business meetings and anniversaries, possibly
designed to repel Unitarians.[45] Others were threatening to
leave the Society unless Williams' charges were disproven
publicly before an open meeting of the Society.[46] Concurrently, the extremists who had obstructed the Society during
the Apocrypha Controversy, collaborated in refounding a
newspaper entitled the Record, which was edited by Edward
Irving, Henry Drummond, Robert Haldane, Lord Mandeville,
and others.[47] Its members, one observer noted, were ob-
sessional, "under the influence of a monomania, which pre-
vents their reasoning coolly and impartially."[48]

      By the early spring of 1830, the "Pro-Test" Party of
the Bible Society, which consisted primarily of members of
the Church of England together with Haldane and his friends
on the Record, formally announced their intention to propose
at their earliest opportunity, that committee meetings be
opened by prayer.[49] But when the parent society, unwilling
to enforce a "modern Act of Uniformity" on its members
ignored this new attack, some of the militants decided to
take unilateral action.[50] Consequently, on September 9,
1830, the Derby Auxiliary announced that it would institute
prayers at business meetings, not necessarily as a test to
exclude Socinians, but because the Society as a whole was
"chargeable with the guilt of living without prayer."[51] The
Guernsey Auxiliary followed suit several days later with reasons less professedly devout, openly admitting that their aim
was to exclude Socinians.[52] Similar resolutions banning Socinians followed at Rugby, Hereford and Hastings.[53] But
when the Rugby Auxiliary asked the parent society "to de-
clare those, who deny the Divinity of our Lord and Saviour
Jesus Christ to be inadmissible to vote at any meeting ...

or to take part in the management of the society's affairs,"
it replied that it had no power to alter the Society's fundamental law which admitted into membership all Christians
who paid their dues. [54] On November 1 the parent society
passed an anti-Test resolution and implored its delinquent
auxiliaries to return to the simplicity of the Society's constitution.   But of those that had instituted the prayer test,
only the Hastings Auxiliary decided under protest to conform. [55] Meanwhile, many more auxiliaries, largely those
which relied on Anglican support, passed anti-Socinian laws.

By the spring of 1831, London was understandably
anxious because the approaching anniversary in May portended another confrontation which could not easily be evad-
ed.   So to defuse a potentially explosive issue, the Society
"unofficially" published a statement, signed by the majority
of the directors, which presented the case for opposing a
change in the Society's constitution. [56] It suggested that a
prayer test would create insurmountable difficulties if required of Society members.   Who would offer up the prayer
at Society meetings, clergymen or Dissenters?   If prayers
were allotted on a rotating basis, would this not lead to squab-
bling?   "One petitioner will be distrusted as not evangelical;
a second as not spiritual; a third as not educated; a fourth
as not discreet; and a fifth as not harmonious with his brethren. "[57] If prayer was only to be offered up by a clergyman,
as the Pro-Test Party later suggested, it was very doubtful
that the general body of orthodox Dissenters would acqui-
esce. [58]

There was also fear that tests established to exclude
Socinians might be extended to other "undesirable" groups
as well.   As J. D. Macbride, Principal of Magdalen Hall,
Oxford, told Joseph Hughes:[59]

> I am ready to concede that none depart further
> from orthodoxy than the modern Socinian, but if
> an erroneous creed is to exclude him, where is
> the line to be drawn, and who is to draw it?
> Probably no denomination has done more for our
> society in proportion to its members and its means
> than that which calls itself the Friends, and yet
> viewing them not as Christian philanthropists, but
> as theologians, who out of their own communion,
> will defend their rejection of both Sacraments.
> Many would hold no intercourse with a Roman
> Catholic even upon a Bible Platform.   Several re-

gard the Methodists as schismatics in separating
from a church, the doctrines of which they retain.
And there are not a few who would exclude all but
members of their own denomination.

Macbride's fears were real. James Haldane Stewart, an
Anglican, argued that the undue deference paid the Quakers
was "a very bad symptom in the modern profession of Christianity."[60] Robert Haldane repeatedly attacked the admission
of Arminians into the government of the Society. These he
considered were as much the bane of the Continental Bible
societies as the heterodox "neologians."[61] That an excuse
to winkle out Roman Catholics would delight many members
was well known. Furthermore, how were Socinians to be
identified? They existed not only in the churches professedly Unitarian but, more covertly, in other churches as well.
There were known to be individual Socinians in the Scots
Kirk and in the Church of England. Were they, too, to be
hunted out?[62]

The crisis again raised the familiar question whether
the Bible Society was primarily a business organization that
distributed Bibles or a religious organization that propagated
a particular brand of Christianity. If the Society was the
latter, as most Pro-Test people claimed, then it was only
natural to exclude unbelievers and heretics as other religious
institutions did. If it was the former, as the Anti-Test
Party claimed, then a test of orthodoxy was not only irrelevant, but a needless brake on the Society's activities.
The parent society argued that while the activities of the Society were religious to the extent that it distributed a religious book, it could not be considered a church institution
for several reasons. Its members did not come together in
church fellowship. It did not possess its own churches, ministers, liturgies, synods or convocations. And, of course,
it did not administer the sacraments.[63] Since prayer was
regarded as "the most solemn act in which a rational being
can be engaged," its place was in the temple and private
closet, not in "annual assemblages promiscuously drawn together to hear the business done and the money raised and
expended."[64] The Pro-Test Party, on the other hand, argued that from its inception, the Bible Society had considered
itself a religious organization for orthodox Christians only.
This was the inference drawn by men like George Washington Philips, the Oxford-educated South Carolinian and vicar
of Wendy, from the Society's ninth and thirteenth articles
which stated that the committee must be composed of laymen

professing the Christian religion and that the general voting
membership must be drawn from Christian ministers and
clergymen only.   Since the Unitarians were not yet legally
considered by British law a "Christian" denomination, they
were, in Philips' opinion at least, constitutionally excluded
from any kind of participation in the Society's activities save
the privilege of contributing money. 65   The Pro-Test party
professed only to make explicit what they held to be already
implied in the Society's laws.

On May 4, 1831, at Exeter Hall in London, the
dreaded confrontation between the Pro-and Anti-Test factions finally took place. 66   After Andrew Brandram read
an abstract from the Society's annual report which included
the Anti-Test resolution of November 1830, J. E. Gordon,
the Irish M. P. from Dundalk, proposed the following resolution before the report was officially entered into the minutes, viz. "that the British and Foreign Bible Society is
preeminently a religious and Christian institution" and therefore "no person rejecting the doctrine of a triune Jehova
can be considered a Member of a Christian institution. "
Seeing that Gordon's motion would not gain the support of
the Society, the Rev. Lundy Foot, rector of Long Bredy in
Dorset proposed a compromise resolution that would bar Socinians from the Society's governing body only.   But when
Luke Howard, a Quaker, threatened to resign if Foot's resolution was carried, it was quickly rejected.   Consequently,
the committee's annual report with the November 1830 Anti-
Test resolution was voted on and entered into the minutes,
and the Society's Anti-Test Party won the day by a majority,
some observers said, of six to one. 67

IV.

Party lines were much more clearly drawn in the
Tests Controversy than they ever had been in the Apocrypha
Controversy.   Essentially, there were two parties this time.
The Anti-Test party included many evangelical Anglicans and
with one or two exceptions, virtually all of the evangelical
Dissenters. 68   The Pro-Test Party, almost to a man, belonged either to the English or Scottish Established Church.
Nonconformist opposition to the Test was so strong, that it
seemed in the provinces not as a contest between Pro and
Anti-Test factions, but rather between churchman and Dissenter. 69   Needless to say, this had a very divisive effect
on provincial auxiliaries where only a few Anglicans actually favored tests and prayers.

The Pro-Test Party itself was composed of two factions. In the first place, there was the same extremist
fringe who had plagued the Society during the Apocrypha
controversy. In the beginning at least, these men felt the
same way that most Pro-Test evangelicals felt about Roman
Catholics and Socinians. They believed, as Edward Irving
did, that "the purity of the national faith was the safeguard
of its life, and the ark of national safety was in danger the
moment that unhallowed hands touched or approached it."[70]
Their mission, therefore, was to purge the Society of dangerous sectaries and heretics. But a far larger degree of
irrationality separated the radicals from the more orthodox
Pro-Test evangelicals. As early as July 1831, for example,
it was reported that Henry Drummond had written to a clergyman that because it was "the sign of the coming Son of
God" that the Bible Society was "breaking up," it was his
duty to destroy rather than to purify and reform it.[71] Whether or not this story was true, the pre-millennialist eccen-
tricities of the Irvingites alarmed many Pro-Test evangelicals almost as much as the heretical doctrines they were
all supposed to be combating.

The moderate Pro-Test evangelicals had a more rational or, at least, more political reason for their opposition to Socinians and Roman Catholics. The Test Controversy somewhat resembled the controversy with High Churchmen played over again except that the protagonists were now
evangelical clergymen. Like the High Churchmen who had
pointed to the defeat of Lord Sidmouth's Bill as a sign that
the Church was in danger, these men saw the repeal of the
Test Act and Catholic Emancipation as similarly prophetic
of the demise of the established church.[72] Where High
Churchmen feared that Bibles circulated by sectaries would
be used to propagate heretical beliefs, these evangelicals
now feared that Bibles circulated by proselytizing Socinians
would have the same effect.[73] The cry of "Church in Danger" was reechoed in many evangelical Anglican party jour-
nals at the beginning of the 1830's.[74] The crisis in Church-
State relations in the period 1828-29, the Reform Bill crisis,
and the fear of a Whig assault on aspects of the Church establishment all greatly exacerbated the crisis in the affairs
of the Bible Society.

Most evangelical Anglicans seem to have felt the conflict of two emotions during these critical years. On the
one hand, they were hesitant to condemn their Nonconformist brethren en bloc as enemies and subversives. On the
other, they could not help absorbing some of the panic fears

for the future of the National Church which were widespread
during these troubled times. It may be that the attack on
Socinians represented a means of reconciling these conflicting emotions by projecting onto a small, well-defined and
easily identified group of "radical" Nonconformists the gener-
alized but only half-formulated suspicions they sometimes
harbored against Nonconformity as a whole, but struggled
to suppress. The fact that almost all of the Pro-Test agitators were against Repeal and Emancipation while, generally speaking, their colleagues on the parent committee were
in favor of them, did much to precipitate test legislation in
the Bible Society.

The Pro-Test Party did not take its defeat at Exeter Hall gracefully. Indeed, J. E. Gordon later complained
that the meeting was packed with "infidels and blasphemers
who held up not only one, but in many instances both hands
against the amendment."[75] In retaliation, they aired their
accusations before a number of other evangelical organizations, further inflaming an already volatile situation.[76] They
had some measure of success. When, for example, the
Pro-Test Party pressed for similar legislation at the Naval
and Military Bible Society on May 10, 1831, they managed
to implement an anti-Socinian test.[77]

Heartened by this victory, the Pro-Test agitators re-
grouped for a last attempt to force the Bible Society to alter
its constitution. On July 16, 1831, they formed the so-
called Sackville Street Provisional Committee which, besides
Pro-Test regulars like George Washington Philips and T.
Pell Platt (the Society's Anglican librarian), included many
familiar names from the Apocrypha days including Henry
Drummond and the Haldane brothers. The Provisional Committee's avowed purpose was to rescind, by whatever means
possible, the Exeter Hall decision of the previous May.[78]
But in this they were totally unsuccessful for the parent society simply ignored them.

The strategy of the Provisional Committee was again
to evoke the dangers of Socinianism. Gordon, for example,
spread rumors that a host of Socinians belonged to the auxiliary committees.[79] Much more serious, however, was the
claim that Socinians made frequent speeches at the public
meetings of the Society in defense of their own creed, in-
sulting the feelings of the orthodox Christians present.[80]
But the parent society had evidence to discredit these exag-
gerations. Baptist Noel, minister of St. John's Chapel at

Bedford Row, for example, calculated that of the 37,500 committee members and collectors of the Society, only thirty-two were Unitarians.[81] Joseph John Gurney held that of the 10,000 office holders of the Society, three were Unitarians adding that during the twenty-seven years of its existence, not a single Unitarian had ever been a director of the parent committee.[82] To the allegations that Socinians foisted their evil doctrines upon innocent auxiliaries, Andrew Brandram replied that in all his travels as Secretary, he had never once witnessed such a case.[83] John King, incumbent of Christ Church, Hull could find only three well authenticated cases in which a Socinian had forced his sentiments upon a meeting of the Bible Society.[84] The Provisional Committee's propaganda, therefore, over-reached itself and as the parent society felt more secure of majority support, it brusquely rejected the Provisional Committee's demand for concession. Soon there were rumblings of an approaching schism.[85]

The final break came in December 1832 when the Pro-Test Party finally realized that it could no longer achieve compromise. Their new organization, called the Trinitarian Bible Society, numbered among its founders several M.P.'s including J. E. Gordon, Spencer Perceval, Jr., George Sinclair, and Alexander Pringle, together with most of the Provisional Committee. Its first resolution excluded not only Socinians, but also Roman Catholics. As Philips remarked in the inaugural address of December 7, 1832: "[The Trinitarian Bible Society] stands equally remote from the dark realms of Papal idolatry, and the blighted regions of Socinian infidelity."[86] Almost from the start, the new society ran into difficulties from its Irvingite faction which tried to force its beliefs on the whole organization leading not a few to suspect that they had rid themselves of one heresy only to gain another.[87] As a result, the Edinburgh Bible Society, which otherwise had every reason to affiliate with the Trinitarian Bible Society withdrew its support in 1832 as did several individuals like Baptist Noel, J. E. Gordon, and even the Haldanes.[88] Division within the Trinitarian Bible Society soon followed, and it achieved a measure of stability only when the Irvingites were forced to resign.

The ability of the Bible Society to withstand two consecutive controversies and to emerge victorious, though perhaps battleworn, is a remarkable testimonial to the institution's tenaciousness and will to survive. From a human perspective we must also admire the uncompromising way in which the Society's directors stood firm on the fundamental

principle thus preserving its interdenominational character
for future generations. The loss of prosperous Scottish auxiliaries in the aftermath of the Apocrypha Controversy hurt
the Society financially. Before it could recover, it had to
face the full force of an evangelical Anglican attack on its
affairs. Fortunately, the Test Controversy and the subsequent founding of the Trinitarian Bible Society attracted away
from the Bible Society very few of its clerical patrons. Had
the test issue appealed to as many Anglicans as the Apocrypha issue did to Scottish Churchmen, it is doubtful whether
the Society could have survived in the form we know it today. In the late 1830's the Society faced yet a third disruption known as the "Baptizo Controversy" due to a disagreement with the Serampore Baptists over how to translate the
word "immerse" in the Society's Bengalese Bible. This in-
cident led to the resignation of several prominent Baptists
and the founding of the Baptist Translation Society in 1840.
But like the Trinitarian Bible Society, it attracted away from
the Bible Society few of its former patrons.[89] The creation
of the Evangelical Alliance in the 1840's probably gave the
Society a new spiritual transfusion and a much needed rest
from the previous stormy decade. Today it happily survives
in the same interdenominational form in which it was founded
over one hundred and seventy-five years ago.

NOTES

1. B. S. Minutes of General Committee, June 7, 1813.
2. A. Haldane, The Lives of Robert Haldane ... and His
    Brother James Alexander Haldane (1855), 484 f. Ap-
    parently, these revelations were as startling to Lord
    Teignmouth as they had been to Haldane himself.
3. B. S. Home Correspondence: R. Haldane to J. Hughes,
    October 6, 1821.
4. B. S. Minutes of General Committee, July 15, 1822.
5. B. S. Minutes of General Committee, July 22, 1822;
    Cf., B. S. Home Correspondence: P. J. Heisch to
    Bible Society, August 9, 1822.
6. B. S. Minutes of General Committee, August 9, 19,
    1822. Cf., B. S. Home Correspondence: Teignmouth
    to C. F. Steinkopf, August 5, 1822.
7. Cf., T. Davidson, Second Statement of the Committee
    of the Edinburgh Bible Society (1826), 77, 132 f.
8. B. S. Minutes of General Committee, August 2, 1824.
9. Cf., B. S. Home Correspondence: T. P. Platt to A.
    Brandrum, August 27, 1824.

10. B.S. Home Correspondence: W. Thorpe to Teignmouth, August 14, 1824.
11. Loc. cit.
12. B.S. Home Correspondence: J. F. Gordon to J. Tarn, September 21, 1824.
13. B.S. Home Correspondence: Teignmouth to A. Brandram, September 4, 1824.
14. B.S. Minutes of General Committee, December 20, 1824.
15. B.S. Home Correspondence (Apocrypha Papers A.4): H. Gray, "Extracts from the Minutes of the Edinburgh Bible Society," January 17, 1825.
16. Thomas Biddulph, for example, had suffered ecclesiastical censure for refusing to read the Apocrypha in worship. Yet he was a Philo-Apocryphist. See B.S. Home Correspondence (A.P. A.12): T. Biddulph et al., to Committee, April 15, 1825.
17. B.S. Home Correspondence (A.P. A.6): J. Lamb, et al., to Bible Society, February 11, 1825. Signatures include William Farrish, Charles Simeon, Legh Richmond, George Milner, Baptist Noel, T. P. Platt, Henry Venn II, and William Cecil.
18. B.S. Minutes of General Committee, March 7, 1825.
19. Cf., B.S. Minutes of Special Subcommittee, April 9, 22, 1825, for the recommendation of the Special Subcommittee which read: "That it be recommended to the general committee not to print or circulate the Apocryphal books; and at the same time to use their best endeavours to aid the circulation of the Inspired Volume in all foreign countries, by grants of the Canonical Books, in whole or in part, without interfering with the future distribution of the same, whether with or without the Apocryphal Books."
20. B.S. Minutes of General Committee, April 4, 1825.
21. T. Davidson, et al., Statement by the Committee of the Edinburgh Bible Society, Relative to the Circulation of the Apocrypha by the British and Foreign Bible Society (1825).
22. In Scotland, besides the Edinburgh Bible Society, the Leith, Ayrshire and Haddington Auxiliaries refused to remit money. In England, the Newcastle and Surrey Auxiliaries did the same. The latter, significantly, was Drummond's auxiliary.
23. B.S. Minutes of General Committee, November 21, 1825. Cf., B.S. Minutes of Special Subcommittee, October 31, November 15, 1825.
24. Cf., B.S. Home Correspondence (A.P. B.13): J. Peddie to J. Hughes, December 12, 1825.

25. B.S. Home Correspondence (A.P. B. 31): P. McFarlan
    to Bible Society, January 31, 1826.
26. According to David Brown, Robert Haldane held a
    grudge against the Bible Society for two reasons--
    because of the Montauban Bible episode, and because
    his friend Ebenezer Henderson had been removed
    from his position as one of the Society's foreign
    agents. See D. Brown, Letters in Defence of the
    British and Foreign Bible Society (1826), 3 f.
27. Cf., B.S. Paterson Papers, II: R. Stevens to Pater-
    son, February 20, 1826.
28. B.S. Minutes of General Committee, January 2, 1826.
29. B. S. Minutes of General Committee, March 20, 1826.
30. B.S. Home Correspondence: W. Arnot to Bible Society,
    April 4, 1826. Cf., A. Haldane, op.cit., 498.
31. Cf., B.S. Home Correspondence: J. Hughes to A.
    Brandram, April 12, 1826.
32. B.S. Minutes of General Committee, April 21, 25,
    May 1, 1826.
33. Third Statement of the Committee of the Edinburgh
    Bible Society (1826), 53. Cf., Statement of the
    Committee of the Glasgow Bible Society (1826), 38.
34. Eclectic Review, 25 (1826), 372.
35. Cf., B.S. Home Correspondence: G. C. Gorham to
    A. Brandram, October 24, 1826. Cf., Eclectic Re-
    view, 25 (1826), 222.
36. Cf., B.S. Home Correspondence: R. Steven to J.
    Tarn, July 27, 1826.
37. Cf., B.S. Home Correspondence: H. Grey to J. Tarn,
    June 22, 1827. For a similar movement in Glasgow,
    see B.S. Home Correspondence: R. Wardlaw to J.
    Tarn, December 22, 1826; R. Wardlaw to A. Brand-
    ram, March 15, 1827. The dissidents in both the
    Edinburgh and Glasgow Societies included the Baptist
    Christopher Anderson and William Innes and the Con-
    gregationalists Greville Ewing, Ralph Wardlaw, and
    John Aikman. James Alexander Haldane decided to re-
    main a member of the Society, but this later turned out
    to be more of a curse than a blessing. See B.S. Home
    Correspondence: A. Haldane to A. Brandram, May
    10, 1826. Cf., H. Grey, View of the Character, Po-
    sition, and Prospects of the Edinburgh Bible Society
    (1827).
38. See 21st and 24th Annual Report of the British and For-
    eign Bible Society for a comparison of Scottish patron-
    age in 1825 and then in 1828.
39. Cf., R. Lloyd, Two Letters Addressed to a Young

Clergyman Illustrative of His Clerical Duties in These
Times of Innovation and Schism.   With an Appendix
Containing an Account of a Recent Attempt to Institute
an Auxiliary to the British and Foreign Bible Society
in Midhurst (1818), 43.   Cf., J. Bennett, The History
of Dissenters During the Last Thirty Years from 1808
to 1838 (1839), 222.

40.   B.S. Home Correspondence: H. Rogers to J. Tarn,
      August 21, 1822.

41.   R. Haldane, Review of the Conduct of the Directors of
      the British and Foreign Bible Society Relative to the
      Apocrypha and to Their Administration on the Con-
      tinent (1825), 119.

42.   W. Williams, The Pretensions of Socinians to the Priv-
      ilege of Partnership in the British and Foreign Bible
      Society Proved to Have Been Properly Precluded by
      the Fundamental Rules and Prospectus of that Institu-
      tion in a Series of Letters Addressed to C.F.A. Stein-
      kopf (1826), xxiii.

43.   W. Williams, The Truth Exhibited Between Extremes
      and the Progress of Error in the British and Foreign
      Bible Society (1820), i.

44.   B.S. Home Correspondence (Outward f.91): J. Tarn
      to W. Jackson, April 17, 1828; B.S. Home Corres-
      pondence: W. Jackson to J. Tarn, March 29, 1828.

45.   Cf., B.S. Teignmouth Letters, f.86: J. Hughes to
      Teignmouth, March 17, 1828; J. Hughes, The Subject
      of Prayer at Meetings of the British and Foreign Bi-
      ble Society Considered in a Letter to the Right Hon.
      Lord Teignmouth (1830); C.J. Shore, Memoir of the
      Life and Correspondence of John Lord Teignmouth
      (1843), II, 519.

46.   One such was John Dampier whose letter threatening
      resignation is missing from the Society's archives.
      Its contents, however, are recorded in the calendar
      of correspondence.   Brandram in his reply to Dampier
      wrote: "I can only say that it is a gross falsehood
      that Unitarian teachers are systematically embraced
      and hugged by its secretaries at home."   B.S. Home
      Correspondence (Outward f.142): A. Brandram to J.
      Dampier, May 7, 1829.

47.   For the refounding of the Record, see M. O. W. Oli-
      phant, The Life of Edward Irving (1862), II, 45 f.
      These men were also meeting at Drummond's home
      at Albury in Surrey in 1826 to discuss the pre-millen-
      ial ideas of Irving.   According to A. L. Drummond,
      nineteen Anglicans, two Dissenters and four Scottish

churchmen attended the early meetings. Many of
these men led the schism of 1831 in the Bible Society.
A. L. Drummond, Edward Irving and His Circle
(1938), 133. For an excellent study of the Irvingites,
see R. L. Lively, "The Catholic Apostolic Church
and the Church of Jesus Christ of Latter Day Saints:
A Comparative Study of Two Minority Millenarian
Groups in Nineteenth Century England" (Oxford D. Phil.
Thesis 1977).

48. Cited in J. Fletcher, The Constitution of the Bible Society Defended (1831), 20.

49. B. S. Minutes of General Committee, March 1, 1830.
Much of the agitation for prayers in the Bible Society
grew out of James Haldane Stewart's Prayer Move-
ment of the 1820's. See J. H. Stewart, Thoughts on
the Importance of Special Prayer for the General Out-
pouring of the Holy Spirit (1821). From 1825 on,
Stewart began to adopt the pre-millennial views of
Irving and attended the Albury conferences. See
D. D. Stewart, Memoir of the Life of the Rev. James
Haldane Stewart (2nd ed. 1857).

50. J. Hughes, op. cit., 9; Cf., Home Correspondence:
J. H. Stewart to [A. Brandram], June 19, 29, 1830.

51. B. S. Home Correspondence: T. Cox to Bible Society,
September 9, 1830.

52. B. S. Minutes of General Committee, September 20,
1830.

53. B. S. Home Correspondence: J. H. C. Moor to A.
Brandram, September 17, 1830; W. Brackenbury to
J. Tarn, September 17, 1830; W. Davis to Bible So-
ciety, October 28, 1830.

54. B. S. Home Correspondence: J. H. C. Moor to A.
Brandram, September 17, 1830; B. S. Minutes of
General Committee, September 20, 1830.

55. B. S. Minutes of General Committee, November 1, 1830;
B. S. Home Correspondence: W. Davis to Bible Society, November 15, 1830.

56. B. S. Home Correspondence (Outward f. 242): A. Brandram to E. H. Hoare, April 6, 1831.

57. J. Hughes, op. cit., 11.

58. Cf., J. Pratt, Jr., Memoir of the Rev. Josiah Pratt
(1849), 284f.

59. B. S. Communications from Auxiliaries, 295 f.: J. D.
Macbride to J. Hughes, April 19, 1831. Cf., Christian Guardian (1831), 346.

60. [J. H. Stewart], Letter to a Friend in Answer to the
Question "Ought Religious Societies to Commence

Their Meetings for Business with Prayer." By An-
tipas (1830), 5.

61. S. C. Wilks, The Bible Society Question (1832), 29.
Cf., Methodist Magazine (1831), 479.

62. J. Hughes, op. cit., 38; Cf., A Letter Addressed to
the Hon. Baptist W. Noel ... By Fiat Justitia (1831),
14 ff., 35 f.

63. J. Hughes, op. cit., 27 f.

64. B. S. Communications from Auxiliaries, 302 f.: Letter
from the Scarborough Auxiliary to the Bible Society,
April 30, 1831.

65. G. W. Philips, An Appeal to the Members of the British and Foreign Bible Society (1831), 2 f., 11. Cf.,
B. S. Home Correspondence: W. Wickes to Bible Society, August 12, 1831. Cf., J. Fletcher, The Constitution of the Bible Society Defended (1831), 58.

66. The following material is taken from the Monthly Extracts, May 31, 1831, no. 166. Cf., G. Browne,
The History of the British and Foreign Bible Society
(1859), I, 131.

67. See C. J. Shore, Memoir of the Life and Correspondence of John Lord Teignmouth (1843), II, 547. According to the same source, of the recipients of a
questionnaire sent to all of the Society's auxiliaries,
272 opposed a test while only 18 favored it. See
Ibid., 547 fn. Responses can be found in "Communications from Auxiliary and Branch Societies and Associations Relative to the Constitution of the British
and Foreign Bible Society" in the Society's archives.

68. Cf., G. Redford and J. A. James, eds., The Autobiography of the Rev. William Jay (1855), 317.

69. Cf., Extracts from Correspondence ... of the Provisional Committee, no. II, 2, filed with the Trinitarian Bible Society pamphlets in the Bible Society archives; B. S. Home Correspondence: G. Lewis to
J. Tarn, October 19, 1831. No doubt much of the
anti-establishment hostility created by the Tests Controversy was provoked by the decision of both the
Congregational and Baptist Unions unanimously to
condemn the test proposals. See B. S. Home Correspondence: J. Fletcher to A. Brandram, October
5, 1831.

70. Cited in Oliphant, op. cit., 383.

71. B. S. Home Correspondence: W. Brackenbury to J.
Tarn, July 23, 1831.

72. As J. Jowett of Sleaford pointed out to William Cockle
in reference to past times: "Tis the old story over

again--only now told by those whom we thought
friends." B.S. Home Correspondence: J. Jowett
to W. Cockle, May 25, 1831. Cf., Monthly Extracts, May 31, 1831, no. 166, 497.

73.   Cf., J. Scott, Trinitarian Bible Society. A Letter Addressed to the Editor of the Record Newspaper on
the Proceedings of the Above Institution (1832), 10 f.

74.   Cf., Christian Guardian (1831), 350.

75.   B.S. Home Correspondence: J. E. Gordon to A Brandram. May 18, 1831.

76.   See B.S. Home Correspondence (Outward f. 243): A.
Brandram to J. E. Gordon, May 13, 1831.

77.   Naval and Military Bible Society: The Speeches Delivered at the Anniversary Meeting (1831).

78.   B.S. Home Correspondence: G. W. Philips to Bible
Society, July 16, 1831; G. W. Philips to Bible Society, May 21, 1831. Members of the committee
included Henry Drummond, Thomas Erskine, James
Alexander Haldane, G. W. Philips and T. P. Platt.

79.   B. S. Home Correspondence (Outward f. 244): A.
Brandram to J. Brown, May 18, 1831.

80.   See J. King, The Comparative Claims of the British
and Foreign Bible Society and the Trinitarian Bible
Society Calmly Discussed (1832), 23.

81.   B. W. Noel, An Appeal on Behalf of the British and
Foreign Bible Society to Those Who Are Disposed to
Secede from It (1832), 13 f.

82.   J. J. Gurney, Terms of Union (1832), 23 f.; Cf., Monthly Extracts, no. 116, 490 fn.

83.   B.S. Home Correspondence (Outward f. 244): A.
Brandram to J. Brown, May 18, 1831.

84.   J. King, op.cit., 23.

85.   G. W. Philips, et al., Correspondence (1831), 5.

86.   Trinitarian Bible Society. Report of the Proceedings
(1832), 14 f.

87.   See Christian Observer (1832), 120.

88.   The First Annual Report of the Trinitarian Bible Society
(1832), 16.

89.   Literature on the so-called "Baptizo Controversy" is
extensive. See E. Steane, The Baptists and the Bible
Society (1840); E. B. Underhill, The Baptists and the
Bible Society (1868).

PART IV:

THE TRACT AND JEWS SOCIETIES

I.

Though the Bible Society was the largest and most ambitious of the great pan-evangelical organizations founded in the early years of the nineteenth century, and the first to really achieve pan-evangelicalism on a grand scale, it did not as a result stand above the other pan-evangelical societies in importance. In many ways, the Religious Tract Society, the third pan-evangelical organization that we shall examine, had as influential a role to play in the cause of evangelical union as the Bible Society to which it had given birth.

In the early years of the eighteenth-century Revival, tract distribution was among the more important activities engaged in by the evangelicals. The Book Society, founded in 1750, was an early tract distribution organization which attempted to unite the literary efforts of several Calvinistic denominations. Later, the free-lance contributions of Hannah More with her Cheap Repository Tracts written to counter the flood of Jacobinical chapbooks, and Mrs. Rebecca Wilkinson and her abridged works of Anglican and nonconformist divines, provided an additional source of religious books and tracts near century's end. [1]

By the last decade of the eighteenth century, several developments forced the evangelicals greatly to expand their concern for tract distribution and led to the foundation of a new and energetic tract society. Firstly, Hannah More had suddenly discontinued writing the Cheap Repository Tracts in 1798 because the task had proven too burdensome and expensive for one person working alone. [2] Many evangelicals admired the way that her tracts had counteracted the ungodly influence of the lewd chapbooks and half penny ballads hawked

148

to the lower classes, and a new organization was deemed
necessary to fill a role now left largely vacant. Secondly,
by the late 1790's, the Sunday School movement had done
much to create a literate British public that now craved for
reading material on a scale which could not easily be catered
to by a few individuals. It would probably be overstating the
case to claim that the Religious Tract Society grew directly
out of the Sunday School movement, but it cannot be denied
that by increasing the demand for religious literature, the
Sunday Schools had done much to advertise the need for an
evangelical publishing house.[3] Finally, the movement for
foreign missions increased the realization that Britain itself
was a mission field that still possessed a mass of "heathens"
crying out for the Gospel. The famine of the Word in Wales,
as we have seen, directed attention to the distribution of
Bibles, but England too had its "dark" counties and "unre-
generate" parishes, and by 1796, evangelicals were busy
establishing a network of village itinerancy societies and
county unions to spread the word of God in every city, village and hamlet. In part, the Religious Tract Society was
designed to be a subsidiary agency for these local institutions, producing tracts and pamphlets for circulation by itinerant ministers as they toured the country in search of converts. But it was also born out of the hope that while itinerants could reach only a limited number of people, the books
and tracts they circulated might by themselves convert an
even larger cross-section of the heathen population. The
Religious Tract Society, therefore, was intended to be far
more than a merely supportive organization. Through its
literature the Society became in its own right an important
agency of conversion, playing a primary role along with the
Bible Society in the great tide of domestic missions now
breaking over Great Britain.

One of those most interested in tract distribution was
George Burder, the Independent minister of the Fetter Lane
Chapel in London. Born in London to parents who had been
converted by George Whitefield, Burder became in 1778 pastor of the Independent chapel in Lancaster but spent most of
his time itinerating. Later, as the Independent minister in
Coventry where he founded the first Sunday School in the
city, and then in London at Fetter Lane, he was involved
in a number of pan-evangelical institutions including the London Missionary Society of which he was Secretary, the Evangelical Magazine which he edited after John Eyre's premature death in 1803, and the British and Foreign Bible Society.[4] But Burder's most important contribution to the

pan-evangelical movement was his involvement in the founding of the Religious Tract Society.

Burder's concern with tracts can be traced back to
1781 when he wrote a pamphlet entitled "The Good Old Way"
in which the fall and recovery of man was proved by Scripture and confirmed by quotations from the Articles and Liturgy of the Church of England. [5] Although an admirer of
Hannah More, Burder regretted that her tracts did not contain a more comprehensive statement of the evangelical principles of religion, but when he and Samuel Greatheed, the
founder of the Bedfordshire Union of Christians, set out in
1796 to write and publish a series of village tracts, the project quickly fell into bankruptcy in the hands of an incompe-
tent London book seller. This failure forced the realization
that only a general tract depository established on a much
larger and more comprehensive scale could cope with the
growing demand for inexpensive, popular, evangelical literature for the huge home market. [6]

As a distinguished member of the London Missionary
Society, Burder soon saw in the Society's May 1799 anniversary an excellent opportunity to promote his scheme for
a tract society. On May 8, before a congregation of London
Missionary Society directors in Rowland Hill's Surrey Chapel,
Burder announced his plan which, at a smaller meeting immediately afterwards, won the unanimous approbation of those
present. For the next two days, the directors met at St.
Paul's Coffee House to set Burder's plan into motion. [7]

These meetings were noteworthy not so much for the
discussions that took place as for the participants. It has
often been assumed that the Religious Tract Society, and not
the British and Foreign Bible Society, was the first institution in Britain to achieve pan-evangelicalism on a large scale
after the abortive attempt of the London Missionary Society
several years before. This belief rests on the assumption
that the Society's founders, and later its chief supporters,
represented the entire evangelical family, Particular Baptists, Wesleyans and Anglican churchmen included. In fact,
the Religious Tract Society was at first scarcely more rep-
resentative denominationally than the London Missionary Society. Among its founding members it claimed most of the
Calvinists who had founded the London Missionary Society
together with a group of influential Baptists. On the first
committee in 1799, for example, sat Joseph Hughes, whom
we have already met in the Bible Society and who later be-

came the Tract Society's first Secretary; William Newman,
the Baptist minister as the Old Ford meeting in Middlesex;
and John Ryland, Jr., Baptist minister at Broadmead Chapel
in Bristol.[8] But the Wesleyans and evangelical Anglicans
were not in evidence in the new society when it was founded.
Indeed, only several years after the Bible Society had been
established, did these groups support the Tract Society providing it with some of its more illustrious leaders.

II.

     There were two major reasons why the Wesleyans
and the evangelical Anglicans, missing from the Religious
Tract Society in 1799, finally consented to help it.   Both
hinged partly on precedents set by the Bible Society in 1804.
In the first place, when the Tract Society was established,
it almost immediately fell into debt.   The missionary societies, it seems, were far more able to capture the public's imagination than a less dramatic organization which
published tracts for domestic use, and as a result they
threatened the Society's existence by their competition for
funds.[9]   To counter impending bankruptcy, the Tract Society
adopted in 1810 an auxiliary system modeled on that of the
Bible Society, and through this system began to make a more
extensive appeal for funds among a much wider evangelical
constituency, Anglicans and Wesleyans included.[10]   Secondly,
the Bible Society, by setting the precedent for large scale
pan-evangelical cooperation in 1804, made possible the same
kind of cooperation in the Tract Society.   Before 1804, the
Wesleyans had probably withheld extensive support from the
Religious Tract Society not only because they had a tract
society of their own, but also because the R. T. S. was probably still too closely associated in their minds with the London Missionary Society and its Calvinistic directors.[11]   After
fraternization with the Calvinists in the Bible Society, the
Wesleyan were far more willing to support a similar enterprise at the Tract Society.[12]   The same was certainly true
of most evangelical Anglicans who at first were also reluctant to patronize the Tract Society.   The Church Missionary
Society had been founded one month before the R. T. S. had
been established partly to provide a foreign mission which
would command the respect of churchmen suspicious of the
London Missionary Society and its undenominational mission
churches.   In 1799, therefore, the Religious Tract Society
seemed as suspect as its parent body, the L. M. S., and too
closely associated with itinerant preaching societies which

were thrusting themselves into hundreds of Anglican parishes, provoking loud cries from angry incumbents who feared the home missionaries as crypto-Jacobins. [13]

Apart from Rowland Hill--scarcely to be cited as a respectable example--there were virtually no clergymen on the Tract Society's board until John Eyre became a director in 1802, and he was almost as irregular as Hill. [14] In fact, the clergymen who supported the Religious Tract Society, at least until 1808, were the same irregular Anglicans who had patronized the London Missionary Society since 1795. Anglican laymen, however, were less discriminating. Samuel Mills, an Evangelical leather merchant, was one of the Society's founders. [15] Zachary Macaulay became a director in 1800 and attended meetings with regularity. [16] It may have been these promising precedents, allied to the success of cooperation in the Bible Society and the concomitant expansion of the Tract Society's fundraising efforts through the newly established auxiliaries, that encouraged the R.T.S. to court "regular" clergymen and for these to respond. [17] By 1808 William Fancourt, Headmaster of St. Saviours Grammar School and Thomas Webster, Fellow of Queens College, Cambridge had both agreed to be Tract Society directors. They were followed the next year by William Gurney, Rector of St. Clement Dane in London and John Wilcox, Rector of Little Stonham in Suffolk and in 1810 by William Goode, Rector of the combined parishes of St. Andrew-by-the-Wardrobe and St. Ann's Blackfriars in London. [18]

In 1812, the Society took a major step and appointed Legh Richmond, rector of Turvey, as the first Anglican Secretary to serve alongside Joseph Hughes (the Society's only Secretary since 1799) and C. F. Steinkopf (who became Foreign Secretary in 1808). Richmond was an admirable choice, not least because he himself had been converted by the reading of a tract--Wilberforce's Practical View--and had already contributed a number of tracts for the Society's use. [19] The first of these, a poem entitled "The African Widow," was published by the Tract Society in 1810, but his greatest contribution was the classic Dairyman's Daughter which he allowed the Society to publish in 1811. [20] In that year, Richmond also preached at the Society's anniversary in London. [21] His credentials as a "regular" Anglican churchman were impeccable. Though perhaps somewhat prejudiced against the Baptists, he looked favorably upon the Wesleyans, and the Society needed Wesleyan patronage as badly as it needed Church patronage. When curate of

Brading and Yaverland on the Isle of Wight, Richmond had
many happy associations with the Wesleyans who lived in
his parish and who were employed in his household as ser-
vants. Indeed, the heroine of The Dairyman's Daughter was
Elizabeth Wallbridge, a member of the local Wesleyan chapel. 22

     The accession of Anglican directors by 1809 forced
the Tract Society to make two important constitutional modifications. In 1807, the committee of the Society consisted
of six ministers and twelve laymen, but since there were
no clerical members and only a few Anglican laymen, it
was unnecessary (indeed, it was impossible) to divide the
control equally between Church and Dissent as in the Bible
Society. 23 Once clergymen sat among the directors, however, provision of this kind had to be made, and in 1810 it
became a rule that at least one of the directors always had
to be an Anglican clergyman. 24 There was a second constitutional modification in 1816 when, to encourage more
Anglican support, it was decided to divide the control of
the Society equally between Church and Dissent. Ironically,
Legh Richmond opposed this decision as legalistic, fearing
that it might inhibit the choice of the best qualified committee members; but the resolution was passed in May 1816,
and the Religious Tract Society became constitutionally almost a carbon copy of the Bible Society. 25

     Unlike the London Missionary Society before it or the
Bible Society after, the Tract Society did not draft a "fundamental principle" on the basis of which the various denominations could cooperate. The Society's aim was simply taken
for granted. David Bogue came close to putting this aim into words when he remarked in a sermon at the Society's first
anniversary in London, 26

> It will be justly considered as a recommendation by
> not a few, that [the Religious Tract Society] is not
> the undertaking of a party; nor designed to con-
> demn or applaud any particular sect.... There is
> nothing in its tracts to recommend or to satirize
> episcopacy, presbytery, independency, methodism,
> paedobaptism or anti-paedobaptism. Nor is it the
> design to take part in the nice distinctions, or
> peculiar notions, or discriminating opinions of
> high-flying individuals, or puny sects. The object
> is to hold forth to view those grand doctrinal and
> practical truths which have in every age been mighty

through God, in converting, sanctifying, and com-
forting souls.

The same spirit was reflected in Tract One, also written by
Bogue and called by many the Tract Society's "Act of Parliament." Speaking of the kind of tract that the Society expected to produce, Bogue argued that there should be "nothing
in it of the shibboleth of a sect; nothing to recommend one
denomination, or to throw odium on another; nothing of the
acrimony of contending parties against those that differ from
them."[27] How this principle worked in practice we will soon
see.

Several years later, the Tract Society found it necessary to codify intentions which had originally been understood
but increasingly misinterpreted not only by the Society's own
members but also by its critics. In 1820, for instance, an
influential patron asked the Society to publish a tract on the
Cato Street Conspiracy and while it had always been tacitly
understood that political issues were to be avoided, the understanding was now made quite explicit for the patron was
told that "this society avoids publishing any article on political subjects."[28] However, it often remained difficult to decide whether a tract was political or religious, so the Society had to define its principles more precisely. During
the Catholic Emancipation debates in Parliament, for example,
the Society published an anti-Catholic broadsheet which brought
upon it severe criticism from some of its subscribers. Incidents of this nature compelled the Religious Tract Society
to make in 1825 the first comprehensive statement of its
fundamental aim, namely,[29]

that at the present period, this meeting considers
it most important fully to recognise the principles
upon which this Society has hitherto proceeded;
namely, "the evangelical principles of the Reformation in which Luther, Calvin, and Cranmer were
agreed," and trust, that without reference to points
of a secular or merely controversial nature, the
Committee will ever consider "the Luthers, the
Melanchthons, the Tindals, the Cranmers, the La-
timers, and the Bradfords of former days, as
their patterns in sound doctrine and active exertion."

Practical ground rules were slowly hammered out.
It was at first decided that the Society would not issue a

tract unless it was approved at a meeting of the General Committee by two thirds of the directors present,[30] though as the volume of submitted tracts increased, the process of selection was simplified by appointing an interdenominational subcommittee to screen tracts before they reached the general committee for final approval, and to weed out those which appeared unsuitable or offensive.[31] Thereafter, each tract was examined by every member of the General Committee. Comments and revisions were inscribed in the tract's margin if it offended denominational or theological sensibilities. Unless rejected outright, the revised proofs were then candidly discussed by the General Committee as a body. Since the names of the authors were always concealed to avoid prejudice, those committee members who submitted tracts of their own often had silently to suffer sometimes severe criticism at the hands of friends and colleagues.[32] This was often a difficult exercise in humility and self-restraint. Indeed, it was a miracle that so few friendships broke up at selection committee meetings.[33] If the views of the author contradicted "Scriptural truth taught by our reformers," the tract would be rejected. Only when this rigorous scrutiny had been accomplished and emendations generally agreed upon, could a tract win approval.[34] Heresy, denominational bias and stylistic infelicities were all purged away.

Even this tight filter failed sometimes to prevent embarrassments, most of them arising from incidents beyond the committee's control. In 1808, for example, the manager of the Tract Society's depository, under whose name Society tracts were published, circulated a tract at his own expense entitled "Popular objections to the Established Church" which created a minor scandal since subscribers, especially Anglican subscribers, believed that the tract was officially issued by the R.T.S. The manager was reprimanded for breaking a contract which allowed him only to publish Religious Tract Society material and the mistake did not occur again.[35] But other violations of the fundamental principle slipped past the committee. In 1815, the following letter was written by William McGavin, an Anti-Burgher minister in Glasgow with a complaint which merits quotation at some length:[36]

> There is another objection that has occurred to myself, and has been mentioned by others, i.e. there is rather too much of the Church of England in your tracts for our northern climate. An instance occurs,

--but as I have not the tract by me I cannot give
the precise words; they are descriptive of the character of a very worthy man of whom something like
this is said, "He would never endure the thought of
separating from the Established Church." Now
though we admit it to be the duty of every Christian
to keep by the church with which he is satisfied, yet
as the Church of England has no existence here except in a small chapel, and serious people don't like
the doctrine usually taught there, we don't think it
proper to put books into the hands of ignorant people by which they might be led to imagine that all
good was confined to the Church of England, or that
it would be a dreadful sin to separate from it.

The tract complained about in this letter was probably published or at least circulated in Scotland by mistake. The
reading and revising of tracts was a time-consuming business from the beginning and by 1815 it was becoming a her-
culean task. Though practically all manuscript correspondence of the Religious Tract Society was destroyed by a German air-raid in the Second World War, we may surmise that
McGavin was probably only one among many in the later
years who complained about "sectarian" tracts that had inadvertently slipped through the reviewing committee.

III.

In comparison to the London Missionary Society and
the Bible Society, the Religious Tract Society was a small
institution. But if the income and size of the R.T.S. was
tiny, it nevertheless reached hundreds of thousands of people with its tracts and pamphlets. By 1801 it had disposed
of 800,000 tracts; two million by 1805; and four million by
1807.[37] By the middle of the nineteenth century, the Society
was circulating works in 110 languages and a total of 4,363
titles appeared on its lists.[38] The literary reach of some
Tract Society authors must have exceeded that of any con-
temporary novelist or poet. George Burder's tracts achieved
a circulation of nearly a million in his own lifetime.[39] Legh
Richmond's reached over a million by 1850.[40] The religious
and moral influence of this immense flow of literature is difficult to estimate, but there can be little doubt that the Religious Tract Society became, as Maurice Quinlan has observed, one of the chief sources of literature for nineteenth
century readers.[41]

The scope of the tracts varied greatly. Many were
intended to awaken sinners. Others, like the enormously
successful Cottage Sermons of George Burder were designed
to instill the "Gospel scheme" into the minds of its readers.
The works of the Reformers--especially the English reformers like Owen and Baxter, the eighteenth-century evangelicals like Hervey and Cecil, and the Dissenting fathers like
Watts and Doddridge--were ransacked for suitable passages.
Here, as the Committee promised in 1799, were whole "vol-
umes ... condensed into a few pages."[42] As Burder's
Tract Number One promised, they aimed to disseminate
"pure truth ... uncontaminated with error, undisturbed with
human systems, clear as a crystal, like the river of life ...
pure, good natured Christianity [free of the] acrimony of
contending parties."[43] The First Series Tracts published
between 1799 and 1805 also concerned themselves with con-
troverting error as well as propagating truth. Apologetic
targets included Popery, infidelity and Socinianism. One of
these early publications, Bogue's Essay on the Inspiration
of the New Testament even achieved the fame of being read
and marked by the captive Napoleon on St. Helena.[44]

The market for Tract Society publications varied.
Occasionally it concerned itself with the well-to-do and the
highly educated as when 6,000 copies of Wilberforce's Practical View were distributed among the upper classes in London resulting in one of two spectacular conversions.[45] But
the chief targets were lower down the social scale. The
mass of the ignorant multitude were not seen as a very fruitful field for Tract Society propaganda, at least not until they
had already been awakened to a thirst for biblical truth.
More good could be done to them by godly conversation and
pastoral visiting than any literary production however simple
or arrestingly written.[46] The real quarry of the Tract Society were those already "awakened" to some extent and in
search of more religious instruction, or the growing multitude of the newly literate like Sunday School scholars whose
minds had been roused "to desire something beyond trash,"
or artisans of the type which would frequent mechanics in-
stitutes.[47] As the nineteenth century wore on, the larger
publications of the Tract Society such as bound books which
it eventually disseminated, were increasingly aimed at "the
numerous masses who will not rest satisfied without more
reading--who have a thirst for instruction, and who are often greedy for printed books."[48] The Tract Society, as lit-
eracy levels increased, set itself to capture the same classes
to which Cobbett's Political Register was aimed. Other like-

ly targets were those whom circumstance had placed in isolated or circumscribed environments like coastguards or pau-
pers in the union workhouses. [49]

R.T.S. tracts, like those of Hannah More before,
were intended to inculcate approved norms of morality as
well as religious doctrines. A large proportion of the Society's tracts were also concerned with social control and
the upholding of exemplary patterns of behavior for guidance
and imitation. Drunkenness, sexual licentiousness, theatre-
going, and idleness were constant targets of Tract Society
pamphlets and broadsheets. So was swearing. No single
Tract Society publication had by 1850 a circulation comparable to the Swearer's Prayer which had by this date sold a
million copies. [50] Starting in 1805, the Society brought out
its famous "Hawkers Tract Series." The series had a two-
fold purpose. First it produced and circulated inexpensive
tracts to counteract the cheap "profane and licentious trash"
that was being peddled on the streets and sold to the lower
classes by hawkers. Second, it provided the hawkers themselves with material to peddle, sell, and make a profit on.
The Hawkers Series had striking titles like "The Fortune
Teller's Conjuring Cap," "Tom Toper's Tale over a Jug of
Ale,", and "The Dairyman's Daughter." Though less edify-
ing than the more polite First Series Tracts, the Hawkers
Series nevertheless served the same purpose by spinning out
easily read morality tales on a number of topics that could
be cheaply bought and easily digested. The Dairyman's
Daughter, for example, indirectly attempted to justify the
prevailing social class structure by emphasizing future re-
wards in heaven over the deprivations of everyday life. Thus
Elizabeth Wallbridge, the tract's heroine, obsequiously wrote
to Legh Richmond, the tract's author: [51]

> Dear Sir, I thank you for your kindness and con-
> descension, in leaving those that are of high rank
> and birth in the world, to converse with me, who
> am but a servant here below. But when I con-
> sider what a high calling, what honour and dignity
> God has conferred upon me, to be called his child,
> to be born of his Spirit, made an heir of Glory,
> and a joint-heir with Christ; how humble and cir-
> cumspect should I be in all my ways, as a dutiful
> and loving child to an affectionate and loving Fa-
> ther! When I seriously consider these things, it
> fills me with love and gratitude to God, and I do
> not wish for any higher station, nor envy the rich.

The moral of the story after Elizabeth had died from a long
and painful disease, was predictable. "My poor reader,"
Richmond wrote, "the Dairyman's daughter was a poor girl,
and the child of a poor man. Herein thou resemblest her,
but dost thou resemble her, as she resembled Christ?"[52]
A similar message was later conveyed to factory workers.
In An Address to Young Persons Employed in Manufactories,
the working class was told: "To your employers you owe
much; they have devoted their time, talents, and fortunes
to business, and to that business you are indebted for your
maintenance."[53]

As the Tract Society grew in size and importance, so
did the scope and variety of the tracts which it produced.
In 1805, the Society began printing moral broadsheets which
could be posted on the walls of cottages and factories, perhaps over one of their "lewd" rivals. After 1809, it published books for children which not only provided Sunday
Schools with reading material but also with prizes for their
scholars. Many of these works were in the established
evangelical literary genre which held up holy lives and happy deaths for emulation. Children read tales like "An Account of a Woman saved from Self-Murder," and "The Happy Death of James Steven." By 1822, the Society had revived an earlier suggestion made by Robert Spear of Manchester to publish hand-bills that could either be pasted on
walls like the broadsheets, or circulated among crowds of
people especially at races, wakes and fairs.

It is very difficult to ascertain the impact of the
Tract Society on evangelical union primarily because of the
paucity of evidence. Like those of the Bible Society, its
minutes are bald and clinical, portraying business meetings
in which resolutions were recited and passed, and in which
business was transacted with a minimal amount of friction
and a great deal of efficiency. Hardly anything is said
about the influence of interdenominational cooperation in
tract selection and distribution on the evangelicals themselves. Printed sources are also unhelpful primarily because the biographies of Society directors concentrated more
on their activities in foreign missions and Bible distribution
than on their activities in the Tract Society. But the Society, especially in provincial areas, served as a very important agency of evangelical union. Legh Richmond lyrical-
ly compared the atmosphere of committee meetings to the
concord of the Apostles at Pentecost. "Although as individuals the Committee belonged to various denominations of
Christians," he wrote in the seventeenth report,[54]

and both thought and worshipped accordingly, yet
in the common principles of vital religion, in love
for the souls of their fellow man, in a disposition
to let every lesser consideration merge in the
grand effort to promote evangelical piety throughout the world, they constituted but one denomination. In the prosecution of their earnest wishes
to promote the temporal and spiritual welfare of
mankind, they have often met together "all with
one accord in one place"; they have "continued together in the apostles' doctrine and fellowship,"
and their communion with one another has been
sweet.

The great anniversaries of the Religious Tract Society, like
those of the other religious societies, were held in the spring
and were gala days for a host of subscribers and workers,
who met together for breakfast and devotions, sometimes in
huge numbers, much like the thousand folk who sat down to
the Tract Society anniversary breakfast in the London Tavern
in 1813.[55] These gatherings were important occasions for
inter-evangelical fellowship and friendship, as, in a spring-
like atmosphere (to quote one Tract Society author) the evangelical Christian was "accustomed to meet the thousands of
our British Israel, assembled to hear of the progress of
'pure undefiled religion,' and to renew to each other and to
God their mutual pledges of devotedness to the sacred cause
of their divine Redeemer."[56] As evangelicals corresponded,
conferred in committee, wrote, edited, and published for
the common cause, and met in huge and solemn anniversary
assemblies, their sense of unity in a single great endeavor
was continually renewed. It was in the work of the Religious Tract Society that many Baptists were first brought
into the pan-evangelical cause. The association in Tract
Society work brought increased fraternization between local
churches, as in Salisbury, where Baptist and Independent
supporters of the Society shared a common communion table.[57] In 1808, the Blackburn Baptists let Joseph Fletcher,
a prominent Independent patron of the Tract Society, and
his congregation worship in their meeting while the Independent church was being enlarged.[58] No doubt, many more
examples could be cited.

Yet while the Tract Society promoted union and fraternity among evangelicals, it was not entirely immune from
controversy and dissension, especially since many of the
tracts that it considered for publication were highly contro-

versial, even among evangelicals. We must therefore examine the Society from the perspective of its internal operations, bearing in mind the profound impact that it had on
the church outside of its committee room.

IV.

        Since we lack Tract Society correspondence for our
period, it is difficult to determine to what degree the Society suffered the same controversies that plagued the Bible Society. High Churchmen, of course, believed that Tract
Society publications were dangerous and potentially seditious,
but they reserved most of their animus for the Bible Society
which they believed to be a much more dangerous foe. Internal controversy was kept to a minimum because, unlike
the Bible Society which tried to accommodate all Christian
denominations and groups, the Tract Society considered itself an organization composed solely of orthodox Protestant
Dissenters and later, Churchmen. Its meetings were opened
and closed with prayer.[59] Many of its tracts were explicitly anti-Catholic and anti-Socinian.[60] Charity and the "catholic spirit" were never extended to the Roman Church nor
the Unitarians and other "unorthodox" Christian denominations.[61] Consequently, while the Bible Society was racked
by the Apocrypha and Test Controversies, the Tract Society
was able to step up its production of anti-Catholic and anti-
Socinian tracts with impunity.[62]

        Nevertheless, the Tract Society did face several mi-
nor internal conflicts which interest us for their effects on
the work of the R.T.S. and also as indices of fundamental
obstacles to the cause of evangelical union. The three problems discussed in this section did not arise accidentally.
Each raised a basic issue which divided members of the
"Gospel World." The first was the problem of the high and
hyper-Calvinists who shared the Reformed "doctrines of
grace" held by evangelicals, but pushed their predestinarian
tenets beyond the point considered tolerable by the devotees
of evangelical consensus. The second was, once again, the
irrepressible issue of Church versus Dissent which we have
already seen in other contexts. The third was the issue of
religious politics, especially Roman Catholic politics and the
stance to be taken by evangelicals on the thorny issue of
Catholic Emancipation.

        The first controversy we shall examine involved Robert

Hawker, Vicar of Charles near Plymouth. Born at Exeter,
the son of a surgeon, Hawker, after studying medicine himself, became an assistant surgeon in the Royal Marines. In
1778 he entered Magdalen Hall, Oxford, later becoming curate of St. Martin near Looe in Cornwall and then in 1784,
the Vicar of Charles after serving under John Bedford as
curate. In 1802, he founded the Great Western Society for
Dispersing Tracts, though he was still an enthusiastic patron
of the Religious Tract Society which he had helped to establish in 1799. [63] Hawker was something of an eccentric and
his high Calvinistic beliefs which bordered on speculative
Antinomianism, got him in trouble with Nonconformist and
Anglican evangelicals alike. There was much in the high
Calvinism of the Hawker variety to alarm the mission-minded evangelical. His insistence on predestined reprobation,
his belief that Christ died not for the sins of the world but
only for the elect, and his almost fatalistic view of Provi-
dence were not easily assimilated with the normal evangelical belief in universal offers of grace. More alarming was
the high Calvinistic tendency to stress the "finished work of
Christ" in justification at the expense of the continuing work
of sanctification. Simeon was shocked by Hawker's pronounce-
ment that the New Testament only spoke of personal holiness
because of the then infant state of the Church. Hawker believed that in later times such incitements to holiness were
unnecessary. He was always something of a bete noire in
evangelical circles. Edward Bickersteth, a secretary of the
Church Missionary Society and a director of the R.T.S.,
complained that Hawker's high Calvinism had often disrupted
C.M.S. meetings when Hawker attended them. [64] William
Jay the Independent and Adam Clarke the Wesleyan shared
Bickersteth's opinion of Hawker's extreme theological views. [65]
William Wilberforce would not allow his children to hear
Hawker when he preached at the Lock Hospital for fear that
he might influence them adversely. [66] It was only a matter
of time before Hawker's extreme beliefs would come into
direct conflict with the more moderate views of his col-
leagues in the Religious Tract Society.

        The potential for conflict was already evident as early
as June 1800 when Hawker submitted a tract to the R.T.S.
entitled "Solemn Questions." Since some of the tract's
phrases were provocative, it was recommended for revision and only after an unprecedented four meetings did the
committee finally decide to publish even the revised pro-
duct. [67] Another tract, a morality story, had to be rejected
outright. [68] For a Society that wanted Anglican patronage as

badly as the Tract Society did, Hawker's indiscretions (which
were never enumerated specifically) must have been fairly
serious.   Nevertheless, Hawker continued to preach collection sermons for the Society and could only write good things
about it as late as 1803. [69]   By 1808, however, Hawker had
not only declined to serve as a director of the London Missionary Society, but his interest in the Religious Tract Society had apparently diminished also. [70]   Why this had happened, however, was not yet made clear.

In 1824, Hawker founded the Gospel Tract Society,
the design and purpose of which seemed directly to oppose
the Religious Tract Society which he no longer supported.
Of his new organization, Hawker told a colleague in almost
predestinarian terms that "I feel a growing confidence that
the thing is of the Lord; and that the Lord hath from the
first ordained the formation of the Gospel Tract Society."[71]
The R.T.S., however, did not take this development lightly
especially since some evangelicals, confusing the new society
with the old, began to redirect their annual contributions.
At the Religious Tract Society's twenty-fifth anniversary,
for example, Spedding Curwin, an Independent minister from
Hull, allegedly made several abusive remarks about Hawker
and his new Society which brought on protests from Henry
Peto and Edward Palmer, the Gospel Tract Society's two
secretaries, and a demand from them for a public apology. [72]
The matter was only further exacerbated in 1825 when the
R.T.S. placed a notice in its annual report disowning any
association with Hawker's organization and the men who patronized it. [73]   This notice provoked Hawker not only publicly to agree that the two societies were "utterly unlike in
feature, in their origin, progress [and] pursuits," but to explain why the Gospel Tract Society had been founded in the
first place. [74]

Hawker was a Calvinist who believed, rather unfash-
ionably in evangelical circles, that the doctrines of predestination were so explicit in the Bible that they constituted an
unavoidable part of the Christian message, being essentials
and not circumstantials of the faith.   As a high Calvinist,
he soon found it impossible to support the calculated ambiguity over the Five Points which pan-evangelical associations
like the Religious Tract Society demanded.   Anticipating the
criticisms which have been leveled against many Christian
union movements (not least against the Ecumenical Movement
today), Hawker argued that the price of so-called union was
an emasculation of important theological issues, a dangerous

reluctance to preach the Gospel in all its fullness, and a
failure to face up to the issues which really divided professed Christians. This artificial concentration on the low-
est common multiple of beliefs, Hawker believed, only di-
luted the strong wine of Christian truth and led to vague and
cowardly compromises. As a result of these personal rev-
elations, Hawker not only questioned the benefit to be gained
by Churchmen uniting in an "unnatural" coalition with Dissenters, but also felt that the strict Calvinism of his forefathers would be severely accommodated by associating with
Arminian Methodists who also patronized the Religious Tract
Society. To Hawker, therefore, the difference between his
Society and the R. T. S. was incalculable:[75]

> The Religious Tract Society, considers all man-
> kind as alike salvable: The Gospel Tract Society,
> acknowledgeth none but the election of grace. The
> former, conceives that the common ground which
> the churchman, Dissenter, and foreigner jointly
> occupy, will bring about those evangelical princi-
> ples in which all are agreed; the latter, limits
> according to Scripture, "the remnant of Jacob in
> the midst of many people."

Though Hawker's protests paralleled in time and in
many ways the issues of similar protests against the Bible
Society during the Apocrypha and Test Controversies, its
effect on the Tract Society was apparently negligible. There
was no major division in the Tract Society over the issue,
nor does it appear that the Society lost a large number of
its patrons. What the controversy did indicate, however,
was that even in the Tract Society, reaction against evangelical union, which was becoming more and more evident
over questions of church polity, could also extend to doctrinal issues. Hawker's secession raised an important problem which faced, and continues to face movements for church
unity. How far can one press the theories of mutual toler-
ance and the cheerful acceptance of "unity in diversity?"
At what point do Christians have to speak out concerning
particular doctrines which they themselves hold devoutly,
but whose announcement may disrupt the carefully construct-
ed consensus of unity? Where does one draw the line between those beliefs which are the plene esse of Christian
faith and those which pertain merely to the esse?

The second major controversy which confronted the
Religious Tract Society during the mid-twenties was poten-

tially more serious because it pitted a denominational author-
ity--the Congregational Board--against Anglican opinion.   The
"Milnerian Controversy," so called since it involved the propriety of an R.T.S. edition of Joseph Milner's Church History, came into being when George Stokes of Cheltenham, a
wealthy Anglican patron of the Tract Society and its accountant, offered in 1825 to provide the stereotype plates of Milner's work free of charge if the Society agreed to republish
it.[76]   When the Congregational Board heard of this project,
however, it protested vigorously.[77]   The complaint was personally presented to the directors by a deputation from the
Board which, though allowing for Milner's piety, took exception to his thinly disguised defense of Anglicanism and
the implied rebuke to Nonconformity which ran through the
book's pages.[78]   Though primarily an historical account of
"real" or "vital" religion through the centuries, irrespective
of its particular denominational garb, Milner's History was
written partly during the Revolutionary period and contained
much to offend the sensitive Dissenter.   It defended episcopacy, infant baptism, and ecclesiastical establishments.   It
was hard on those who had separated from an unfallen Church,
like the Novations, and implied that English Nonconformity
originated in unjustified schism.   By contrast, it took a
surprisingly tolerant attitude towards aspects of medieval
religion stating that one should not be prejudiced against the
real Church simply "because she then wore Roman garb."
Thomas Haweis' rival Impartial and Succinct History of the
Church of Christ, published in 1800, was intended partly to
counteract Milner's apparent tendency to love some Romans
more than separatist Protestants.[79]   It was, therefore, not
surprising that the Congregational Board's deputation, should
urge the R.T.S. "to abandon a project, which cannot be ex-
ecuted by them, without violating the principles on which the
Society was first established; and by a strict adherence to
which its present prosperity can only be perpetuated."[80]

   In January 1826, a conciliatory Tract Society deputation, headed by Edward Bickersteth, met the offended Congregationalists and listened to their detailed complaints.[81]
Milner's History, the Board felt, was too favorable to Rome
and contained "details which would not be unworthy of the
credulity of a Roman Catholic historian" praising "canonised
saints of the Romish calendar" in extravagant eulogy.   Worse
were Milner's episcopalian asides on the heretics and sep-
aratists of church history, some of whom he clearly regarded as the ancestors of modern Dissent.   Finally, asked the
Board, how could the issue of such a polemical work be

squared "with the avowed principles of the Religious Tract
Society?" Had a similar biased history been written by a
Nonconformist and submitted to the Tract Society, the Anglicans would no doubt have protested bitterly. [82]   Twenty-five
years before, docile Independents would have left criticism
of Milner's History, as they indeed did, to irregular Anglicans like Thomas Haweis or Rowland Hill. [83]   Now, with a
denominational authority to back them up, they could speak
loudly and know that they would be listened to.

A compromise was quickly reached.   It was suggested
by the Congregational Board that the Society publish, solely
on its own responsibility and without Milner's name, bio-
graphical sketches rather than a church history.   The inclusion of Milner's name in the title, they felt, would only
recommend to readers the unexpurgated work which, as we
have said, advocated a particular form of church government and civil establishment.   The Tract Society deputation
agreed to omit Milner's name from the title if the book was
now entitled The History of the Church of Christ Previous
to the Reformation, Consisting Chiefly of Sketches of the
Lives, and Extracts from the Writings of Christians, During the Early and Middle Ages.   Both parties finally agreed
to this compromise. [84]

The Milnerian Controversy might have been more
serious had all the Dissenters been united in opposition to
the History, but this was not the case.   The Wesleyan Joseph Butterworth, the Baptist Joseph Ivimey and even the
Congregationalists John Campbell and John Clayton, favored
printing Milner's History in its entirety. [85]   Nevertheless,
the controversy demonstrated that by 1825 Nonconformist
associations and unions were already forces to be reckoned
with.

The final cleavage was precipitated by the problem
of anti-Catholic broadsheets, and echoed in some ways the
Test Controversy in the Bible Society which was raging at
this time.   The Tract Society generally avoided publishing
political tracts but, as we have seen, the distinction between
politics and religion was often hard to establish, and no-
where was this more evident than in the case of the great
debate over Catholic Emancipation which the R.T.S. could
not resist entering.

The Society's involvement in the politics of Catholicism reflected the bias of its leaders, particularly Richard

Waldo Sibthorp, the Anglican minister at Percy Chapel in
St. Pancras, London, who succeeded Legh Richmond as Secretary, as well as Baptists Noel and James Haldane Stewart,
who were also high enough in the councils of the Tract Society to be considered as possible secretaries in his place.[86]
All three were strong anti-Catholics as well as "regular"
Anglicans.[87] During the Test Controversy in the Bible Society, Stewart and Sibthorp had been among the seceders who
formed the Trinitarian Bible Society which expressly barred
Roman Catholics from membership.   The Bible Society and
the Religious Tract Society took a different view of the Catholic question.   The Bible Society, strongly influenced by its
complement of Parliamentary "Saints," generally favored
Catholic Emancipation and tried to repress anti-Catholic agitation within its ranks.   The Tract Society was far less liberal, tending instead to the anti-Socinian and anti-Catholic
side of the evangelical political spectrum, and hence found
it difficult to resist the lure of religious politics.

In 1827, when the Emancipation issue was shaking the
nation, the Tract Society issued an anti-Catholic broadsheet
entitled "Queen Mary's Days" which discussed at length and
in lurid detail the reign of "Bloody" Mary and featured on
its cover nine woodcuts displaying the tortures and burnings
of the Smithfield Martyrs.   Two years later, this tract was
attacked in Parliament by William Joseph Denison, a millionaire pro-Emancipationist M. P. from Surrey.   Denison, who
encountered the R. T. S. broadsheet at an anti-Emancipation-
ist rally in his constituency, was alarmed at the "inflamma-
tory handbills" which were scattered among the lower classes
in such a way as to incite them to violence.[88] The Tract
Society jumped to its defense, claiming that its broadsheet
never touched on secular or political questions, but merely
recorded "the faith, patience and sufferings of those who
were persecuted for their adherence to the truths of the
Gospel." They acted not as politicians but as Protestants,
the Society claimed, compelled for conscience sake "to con-
trovert the errors of the Church of Rome and to expose the
evil consequences arising from its doctrines."[89] Not all the
Society's supporters, however, were satisfied by this excuse.
John Burder of Stroud threatened that he and many of his
friends would resign if any more "pictures of Popish cruel-
ty" were disseminated at this time of political unrest.[90]
Even Joseph Hughes, on tour for the Society in Bristol, suggested that his society should disavow any intention of interfering with so controversial a topic, especially since it was
now being debated in Parliament, and so maintain its pro-

fessed neutrality.[91]   A number of auxiliaries concurred,
though some influential patrons like Lady Farnham urged
the Society on to greater "Protestant militancy."[92]

The danger of a disruption like that which shook the
Bible Society was forestalled by yet another compromise in
April 1829 which restated the Society's intention to propagate the agreed doctrines of the Reformation but adding the
important proviso that "in promoting this object it is particularly desirable to avoid any methods which are not fully
consonant to the spirit of the Gospel of peace and love or
which may excite or strengthen prejudices in the minds of
those whom we are anxious to convince."[93]   A special subcommittee was appointed to carry this through.[94]

In its internal relations, the Tract Society had obviously learned a great deal from the mistakes of the Bible
Society.   It tactfully avoided confrontation when matters
reached a boiling point.   Consequently it was better able to
maintain its stability as a pan-evangelical institution, emerging in this century as the Lutterworth Press.   The same,
however, could not be said of the London Society for Promoting Christianity Amongst the Jews which, of the four pan-
evangelical institutions examined in this book, was the least
successful in maintaining pan-evangelical accord.   It is to
the study of this society that we finally turn.

NOTES

1.   See W. Jones, The Jubilee Memorial of the Religious
     Tract Society (1850), 8.   Cf., E. P. Thompson, The
     Making of the English Working Class (1963), 141 f.
2.   M. J. Quinlan, Victorian Prelude (1941), 122.
3.   Cf., W. H. Watson, The First Fifty Years of the Sun-
     day School (1873), 40 f.; Jones, Memorial of the
     Tract Society, 12; Evangelical Magazine, 7 (1799),
     307.
4.   For the biography of Burder, see S. G. Green, George
     Burder (1888).
5.   Cf., Jones, Memorial of the Tract Society, 12.
6.   Ibid., 13.
7.   R. T. S. Minutes, May 9, 10, 1799; Evangelical Magazine,
     7 (1799), 253.   Ministers present at these early meet-
     ings were Richard Allen of Exeter, James Bennet of
     Romsey, David Bogue of Gosport, George Burder of
     Coventry, Joseph Hughes of Battersea, George Lam-

bert of Hull, Joseph Slatterie of Chatham, Robert
Sloper of Devizes, Thomas Towne of Royston, Matthew Wilks of London, and Rowland Hill, also of London.   With the exception of Hughes (a Baptist), Wilks
(Calvinistic Methodist) and Hill (Anglican), all of these
men were Independents.   With the exception of Hughes,
all were directors of the L. M. S.   See Jones, Memorial of the Tract Society, 15.

8.   See Evangelical Magazine, 7 (1799), 308.   Why the Particular Baptists decided to patronize a pan-evangelical
tract society in 1799 when three years before they
decided not to patronize a pan-evangelical foreign
missionary society is open to debate.   Several obvious reasons may be suggested: The Baptists had
a foreign missionary society of their own in 1799 but
no tract society.   Tract distribution also presented
fewer obstacles to Baptist-paedobaptist cooperation
than did undenominational missions where the subject
of Baptism was almost certain to arise.   But perhaps most important was the precedent set by cooperation in the Evangelical Magazine and in the
county unions and itinerancy societies where both
groups had joined hands in domestic missions.   The
tract society was intended largely as an extension
of these two activities.

9.   Cf., Evangelical Magazine, 9 (1801), 40 f.   Cf., R. T. S.
Minutes, January 13, 1801.

10.   Cf., R. T. S. Minutes, February 21, 1809.   Cf., Evangelical Magazine, 18 (1810), 253; Evangelical Magazine, 17 (1809), 171 f.   By 1815 there were 124 auxiliary Tract Societies throughout Britain.   Quinlan,
op. cit., 125.   It should be noted that branch societies
existed as early as 1801, but these did not, initially
at least, support the parent society financially as did
the Bible Society auxiliaries.   See R. T. S. Minutes,
September 29, 1801; Jones, Memorial of the Tract
Society, 179 ff.; G. H. C. Hewitt, Let the People
Read (1949), 29 f.

11.   The Wesleyan society was founded in 1782.   See A.
Stevens, The History of Methodism (1878), II, 2 fn;
Methodist Magazine (1847), 269 f.   Apparently it was
always in financial difficulty giving the Wesleyans
perhaps another reason to support the R. T. S.   Cf.,
R. T. S. Minutes, December 12, 1827.

12.   Cf., R. T. S. Minutes, April 15, 1806; November 17,
1807.   Christopher Sundius, a prominent Wesleyan,
became director of the R. T. S. in 1801.

13. Cf., Hewitt, op. cit., 21 fn.
14. Thomas Charles and Robert Hawker, two "irregular" Anglicans actively supported the Society shortly after it was founded, but neither men were directors of the parent society.
15. R. T. S. Minutes, August 26, 1799.
16. R. T. S. Minutes, December 23, 1800.
17. The Tract Society also won over some clerical good will by convincing prominent Evangelicals to produce tracts for publication. Thus, between 1799 and 1808, men of the stature of John Newton, Thomas Biddulph, Legh Richmond, Charles Simeon, and Richard Cecil, all agreed to have their works printed and circulated by the R. T. S. See R. T. S. Minutes, September 23, 30, November 5, 1799; July 8, 15, 1800; September 8, October 20, November 30, 1807; March 8, 1808.
18. Cf., R. T. S. Minutes, April 4, May 16, 1809.
19. For Richmond's biography, see T. S. Grimshaw, A Memoir of the Rev. Legh Richmond (3rd ed. 1828).
20. R. T. S. Minutes, March 6, 1810; February 19, April 2, 1811.
21. R. T. S. Minutes, May 14, 1811; Evangelical Magazine, 19 (1811), 199.
22. J. B. Dyson, Methodism in the Isle of Wight (1865), 209, 227, 237.
23. R. T. S. Minutes, May 5, 14, 1807.
24. R. T. S. Minutes, May 1, 1810.
25. Hewitt, op. cit., 42; Jones, Memorial of the Tract Society, 75.
26. D. Bogue, The Diffusion of the Truth (1800), 44.
27. Jones, op. cit., 18.
28. R. T. S. Minutes, March 8, 1820.
29. Jones, op. cit., 141.
30. R. T. S. Minutes, May 19, 1800. This regulation issued from the plan of union between the R. T. S. and the Evangelical Tract Society that year. See Evangelical Magazine, 8 (1800), 80.
31. R. T. S. Minutes, May 27, 1800. Members of the first committee included Joseph Tarn and Matthew Wilks (Calvinistic Methodists), Zachary Macaulay (Anglican), Joseph Hughes (Baptist) and Thomas Saddington (Independent?).
32. Hewitt, op. cit., 27 f.
33. Jones, op. cit., 117.
34. Rowland Hill, for example, who had written "Thomas Steady and John Wild" was criticized for a reference made to an Anglican clergyman which some thought

gave a sectarian appearance to his tract. Somewhat
offended by this criticism, Hill made the following
revision: "But then everybody says you have a very
good minister at the meeting. Our minister and he
are quite thick with each other." "There," said Hill
to the committee, "no one can find fault with it now."
Cited in Jones, op. cit., 27 f.

35. R. T. S. Minutes, November 15, 1808.
36. B. S. Home Correspondence: W. McGavin to Collins,
     June 27, 1815. This MS letter is probably one of
     the only extant pieces of R. T. S. home correspond-
     ence in existence. It was preserved from the in-
     cendiary raids of the last war by being kept by mis-
     take at the Bible Society. This error in itself shows
     how closely associated the two societies were.
37. See Evangelical Magazine, 9 (1801), 252; 13 (1805), 326;
     15 (1807), 284.
38. Jones, Memorial of the Tract Society, 150.
39. Ibid., 26.
40. Ibid., Appendix 5.
41. Quinlan, op. cit., 124. The adoption of the Auxiliary
     system as a fundraising device in 1809 also made
     the distribution of tracts more orderly and effective.
     After 1823, Loan Associations were organized where-
     by tracts could be lent to a family or a church and
     then passed on to other groups, thereby multiplying
     many times over the number reached by a single
     tract before it had worn out. With the aid of this
     innovation, the Society circulated the equivalent of
     10,012,760 tracts in 1824 alone.
42. Jones, op. cit., 17.
43. Ibid., 18.
44. Ibid., 40.
45. Ibid., 201.
46. Ibid., 122.
47. Ibid., 123.
48. Ibid., 122, 131.
49. Ibid., 186 ff.
50. R. T. S. Tract No. 76. This tract was probably written
     by the Quaker Luke Howard. See D. N. B.
51. L. Richmond, The Dairyman's Daughter (c. 1814), 40.
52. Ibid., 152.
53. R. T. S. Tract No. 419.
54. Cited in Jones, Memorial of the Tract Society, 69.
55. G. Pritchard, Memoir of the Rev. Wm. Newman (1837),
     266.
56. Jones, op. cit., 70.

57. T. Eisdell, A Circular Letter from the Associated
    Ministers of the Gospel in Hampshire Convened at
    Salisbury (1800).
58. W. A. Abram, A Century of Independency in Blackburn
    (1878), 22 f.
59. The R. T. S. always held quarterly prayer meetings,
    but in 1824 it was mandatory that Society meetings
    be opened with prayer. R. T. S. Minutes, July 13,
    20, 1824.
60. Jones, op. cit. , 118.
61. Hewitt, op. cit. , 42. A Unitarian "Christian Tract So-
    ciety" existed early on. See Bodl. Montagu MSS,
    d. 13, III, f. 93; W. Frend to N. Gould, June 7, 1821.
62. Cf. , R. T. S. Minutes, May 13, 1831. There were,
    nevertheless, several warm debates at the Tract So-
    ciety over Catholic Emancipation. See W. Urwick,
    The Life and Letters of William Urwick (1870), 71 f.
63. For Hawker's biography, see R. Hawker, The Works
    of the Rev. R. Hawker (1826-30).
64. T. R. Birks, Memoir of the Rev. Edward Bickersteth
    (3rd ed. 1852), I, 320.
65. C. Jay, Recollections of William Jay (1859), 339; J.
    Everett, Adam Clarke Portrayed (1844), II, 147 f.
66. R. I. and S. Wilberforce, The Life of William Wilber-
    force (1838), III, 473. For Hawker's hypercalvinism,
    see J. Stoughton, Religion in England from 1800 to
    1850, I (1884), 303 fn.
67. R. T. S. Minutes, June 17, 1800; July 1, 8, 22, 1800;
    Cf. , Evangelical Magazine, 7 (1799), 75 f.
68. R. T. S. Minutes, August 3, 1802.
69. R. T. S. Minutes, May 10, 1803; R. Hawker, Works,
    VII, 667.
70. L. M. S. Minutes, May 30, 1808; Cf. , L. M. S. Home
    Correspondence (2. 7. A): H. Mends to G. Burder
    August 20, 1812. In 1826, Hawker disassociated
    himself from the Bible Society. B. S. Home Cor-
    respondence: H. Gandy to Bible Society, January
    11, 1826.
71. Bodl. Eng. Misc. MSS, b. 93, f. 25: R. Hawker to H.
    Peto, July 4, 1825.
72. R. T. S. Minutes, September 7, 14, 28, 1824.
73. R. T. S. Minutes, July 18, 1825.
74. Hawker, Works, VII, 614.
75. Ibid. , 621 f. ; Cf. , R. Hawker, The Glory of God in
    Gathering His People to Himself, the First and Final
    Design of the Gospel Ministry (n. d.), 11. This was
    the first tract of the Gospel Tract Society.

76.   R.T.S. Minutes, August 9, 1825.
77.   R.T.S. Minutes, November 21, 1825.
78.   R.T.S. Minutes, November 22, 1825.
79.   For an account of Milner's History, see J. D. Walsh,
      "Joseph Milner's Evangelical Church History," Jour-
      nal of Ecclesiastical History (1959), X, 174 ff.
80.   R.T.S. Minutes, November 22, 1825. Cf., R.T.S.
      Minutes, December 6, 20, 27, 1825.
81.   R.T.S. Minutes, January 10, 17, 1826.
82.   R.T.S. Minutes, January 24, 1826.
83.   Cf., T. Haweis, Impartial and Succinct History of the
      Church of Christ (1800).
84.   R.T.S. Minutes, January 24, 1826; Cf., Congregational
      Magazine, 9 (1826), 110.
85.   R.T.S. Minutes, January 10, 17, 1826.
86.   R.T.S. Minutes, May 24, 1827; June 5, 8, 1827; July
      31, 1827.
87.   Ironically, Sibthorp, at first anti-Catholic, migrated to
      the Roman church many years later.
88.   R.T.S. Minutes, March 17, 1829; Cf., Hansard,
      XX (n.s.), 907.
89.   R.T.S. Minutes, March 11, 1829. These sentiments
      were conveyed to Parliament on behalf of the Society
      by two anti-Emancipation M.P.s, C.N. Palmer and
      Sir R. H. Inglis.
90.   R.T.S. Minutes, March 17, 1829.
91.   Loc. cit.
92.   R.T.S. Minutes, March 17, 24, 1829.
93.   R.T.S. Minutes, April 10, 1829.
94.   R.T.S. Minutes, April 20, 21, 1829.

I.

Side by side with the growing evangelical involvement in domestic missions which produced the Religious Tract Society in 1799, was an increasing interest in Britain's Jewish population. At first, this interest was minimal. Tiny communities of European Jews, resident in England before the Reformation, had been assimilated into the dominant Anglo-Saxon culture so thoroughly by the eighteenth century, that in many cases they went practically unnoticed by early Christian evangelists. But by the second half of the eighteenth century, the situation had changed dramatically. Repressive anti-Semitism in Central Europe and later the rumblings of revolution elsewhere on the Continent, induced a fairly large number of European Jews to cross the Channel into England in search of a haven free of religious persecution. Within a matter of years, the Jewish community in England had grown dramatically.

Unlike the older and more established Jewish community, these Jewish immigrants were poor and often unemployed. Moreover, they confined themselves largely to the ghettos of London and other large cities and refused to assimilate Anglo-Saxon cultural values or even learn English. But to the evangelicals, imbued now by mission fever, the Jews presented a novel challenge. Anglicans and Dissenters alike became fascinated, almost obsessed with the notion that far from being infidels, these people were really "half Christians" sharing the same Old Testament faith. When evangelical prophets of the millennium began to make predictions, based on their interpretation of the apocalyptic books of the Bible, that the Jews, like the heathen, would also be brought within the Christian fold, the Jewish place in evangelical missionary thought took on urgent proportions almost overnight.

Initially there was great disagreement between these prophets of the millennium over whether the Jew or the infidel should be given mission priority. Most evangelicals concurred that when the heathen was converted to Christianity, the Jews would follow as a matter of course. Consequently, they favored a mission to the former rather than the latter.[1] However, a small but growing group of evangelical millennialists disagreed with the majority, and argued instead that before the infidel was converted, a remnant of the Jewish nation would first be brought into the Christian fold. An attempt was even made by this party in 1796, to establish an independent evangelical missionary society dedicated solely to evangelizing among the Jews, but those who favored a mission to the foreign infidel finally won the day.[2] Only when Joseph Samuel Christian Frederick Frey came to England in 1801, under the auspices of the London Missionary Society, did the appeal for an evangelical mission to the Jews really begin to gain momentum.

The history of the London Missionary Society's Jewish mission between 1800 and the foundation of the London Society for Promoting Christianity Amongst the Jews is largely the history of one man, Joseph Frey, and his frustrated attempts to make the Jewish mission as integral a part of the evangelical movement as foreign and domestic missions. But, as Frey quickly found out, most evangelicals were not yet prepared to make a full-time commitment of money or man-power to an enterprise which at best only interested them somewhat speculatively. Millennial prophecy was discussed as much as ever, but the actual implementation of a Jewish mission was not yet regarded as an overriding concern.

Joseph Samuel C. F. Frey (pronounced "free") was born in 1771 at Mainstockheim near Kitzingen in Franconia.[3] Though he intended to be a Rabbi like his father and brothers, he was subsequently converted to Christianity by a Lutheran merchant and was baptized in 1798 in New Brandenburg. As was the tradition on such occasions, Frey adopted two Christian names to replace the old ones. Henceforth he was called Christian Frederick Frey. Briefly under the influence of the Moravians, Frey was soon called to be a missionary and entered the newly established Protestant academy in Berlin founded by Baron Von Schirnding and Father Janicke, and supported in England by the Church and London Missionary Societies.

In 1801, Frey emigrated to London where he con-

vinced several London Missionary Society directors that his
services were needed in Britain as a missionary to the Jews. [4]
Consequently, in 1805, with the approval of David Bogue under whom he had received further theological training, and
other L.M.S. directors, he was set apart for his unique
mission, and began a weekly series of Saturday night lectures for potential Jewish converts at John Ball's Calvinistic Methodist Chapel in Jewry Lane, Algate. [5]

   Unfortunately, Frey's early mission was plagued by
two interrelated problems which the directors of the London
Missionary Society seemed unwilling to confront. In the
first place, Frey felt that the directors had not made ade-
quate provision for the financial support of recently converted immigrant Jews who, because of the prejudices of the
older Jewish community and unsympathetic Christians, could
not find proper employment. If jobs were found, these converts would often apostatize and either rejoin the synagogue
or become social miscreants attached to no religious body. [6]
A second problem involved the London Missionary Society's
"Free School," established in 1807 to provide religious training for Jewish children. [7] The Free School, Frey complained,
had little control over the religious development of its students since they would return at the end of each day to the
"anti-Christian" influences of the Jewish community. To
solve the employment problem and at the same time dis-
courage apostasy, Frey wanted the Society to establish a
house of industry where poor Jewish immigrants could be
employed until they found permanent work elsewhere, pref-
erably with a Christian merchant or industrialist. In the
area of education, Frey proposed that the London Missionary Society found a boarding school where Jewish children
would be taken away from their parents and isolated from
the "negative" influences of family and synagogue while being educated in the Christian faith. [8] But the Committee for
Jewish Affairs, also known as the "Jewish Committee" and
established in 1805 to superintend Frey's mission, resisted
both schemes. Not only were its members unwilling to spend
money on projects which seemed to detract from more urgent
concerns in the foreign mission field, but they also were
probably offended by the seemingly sacrilegious and hypocritical practice of apostasy which only reinforced their
stereotype of the "guileful" Jew. [9]

   The rejections, between 1805 and 1809, of most of
Frey's innovative and highly controversial projects only provoked him to press for reform more militantly, creating in

the process acute tensions between himself and most of the London Missionary Society's more conservative and cautious directors. When his proposal to form a semi-autonomous Jewish mission with the power to raise its own money and establish its own policy was rejected by the L.M.S. in the spring of 1808,[10] Frey, together with several other dissidents, formed the "London Society for Visiting the Sick and Distressed and Instructing the Ignorant especially such as were of the Jewish Nation."[11]

Frey's new society was more an organization on paper than an active mission. Its early directors merely sought to reconcile Frey's differences with the London Missionary Society in the hope that schism would only be temporary. But they were not willing to compromise on three issues, namely Frey's demand for the establishment of a house of industry for poor Jewish laborers, a boarding school for Jewish children, and finally, a measure of organizational autonomy to raise money and formulate policy independently of the parent society.

Negotiations between Frey and the London Missionary Society, however, were fraught with hostility. David Bogue told Frey that his act of separation was an ungrateful way of treating a society that had paid for his education. Bogue also let it be known that Frey's idea of setting up a boarding school and a house of industry was repulsive to most evangelicals because it was tantamount to "bribing people to be Christians."[12] The London Society, in retaliation, pointed out that Frey's mission to the Jews had been impeded not only by the London Missionary Society's indisposition to initiate reform, but also because its "affairs [were] under the direction of a society either professedly or by reputation Dissenters." Frey and his colleagues were insinuating that "regular" Evangelical Anglicans, who had originally chosen not to patronize the London Missionary Society because of its Nonconformist affiliations, might be willing to support the London Society if it were officially and permanently separated from the parent institution.[13]

When negotiations finally reached an impasse, and it was seen by both sides that a rapprochement would be impossible, Frey formally resigned his position in the London Missionary Society, and the London Society for Promoting Christianity Amongst the Jews was officially incorporated in 1809.[14] Several more months of bitter controversy followed, producing a protracted pamphlet warfare be-

tween the belligerents and a breakneck competition for converts.   Only when the older but less thriving L. M. S. mission to the Jews was forced to terminate operations in 1810
did the London Society finally emerge as the recognized
evangelical mission to the Jewish people.[15]

II.

Because the Jewish Mission had been under the management of the London Missionary Society prior to 1809,
many evangelicals refused to patronize its activities.   Indeed, it was partially for this reason that Frey and his colleagues wanted their mission to be institutionally separate
from the L. M. S.   "Regular" Anglican churchmen would not
patronize the Jewish mission for the same reason they refused to support the London Missionary Society and, initially at least, the Religious Tract Society.   Baptists and Wesleyans, on the other hand, had probably stayed away for theological reasons, not wanting to patronize an organization dominated by paedobaptists or Calvinists.   But once separation
was completed in 1809, all of these groups supported the
new mission with varying degrees of enthusiasm.   In the
Particular Baptist camp, for example, a number of men
took part in the activities of the Society after 1809.   They
included Andrew Fuller, minister of the Baptist meeting at
Kettering; John Ryland, Jr., minister of Broadmead Chapel
in Bristol; Robert Hall, minister at Harvey Lane Baptist
church in Leicester; and James Hinton, the prominent Baptist minister at Oxford.   Though the Wesleyans never joined
the Society in large numbers, their chapels, nevertheless,
were opened to London Society fundraisers.   Even several
Independents and Presbyterians who had originally patronized the L. M. S.'s Jewish mission, rallied to the support
of the London Society when it was firmly established as a
separate entity.   They included men like John Pye Smith,
theological tutor at Homerton College; Thomas Raffles, Independent minister at George Yard Chapel Hammersmith;
and Alexander Fletcher, Scottish born Presbyterian minister
at Miles Lane Chapel, London Bridge.[16]

The most important recruits after the separation
were the Anglicans.   As early as 1806, the Christian Observer had called upon evangelical Anglicans to repair the
"evil effects" of past indifference, and show a more active
interest in the Jews.   "Why should the Church of England,"
the magazine asked, "be the last to engage in this "work of

faith and labour of love?'"[17] But for reasons of church
order, the Anglicans would not patronize the London Missionary Society's Jewish mission.   After 1809, however,
prominent churchmen like Thomas Scott, Chaplain of the
Lock Hospital in London and rector of Aston Sandford;
Charles Simeon, incumbent of Holy Trinity, Cambridge and
by now, virtual leader of the evangelical party within the
Church of England; Legh Richmond, rector of Turvey and
future Secretary of the Religious Tract Society; and William
Marsh, rector of Basildon and a leading millennialist, served
the Society in one capacity or another.   Anglican laymen of
the stature of William Wilberforce, the famous abolitionist
M. P. for Yorkshire, and Lewis Way, the millionaire philanthropist, joined their clerical brethren.

Though the Society initially found it difficult to re-
cruit prelatic patronage,[18] the English nobility joined in
respectable numbers.   By 1810, Society Vice Presidents
included the Earl of Crawford and Lindsay and Lord Calthorpe.   The second President of the Society, after Frey
had voluntarily resigned the position in March 1809, was
Lord Barham, the first Lord of the Admiralty.   The Duke
of Kent, father of Queen Victoria, became the Society's
first Royal patron four years later.

Even though several of the Society's auxiliaries took
on a sectarian appearance,[19] the parent society in London
was divided equally between Church and Dissent.   Joseph
Fox, a London Nonconformist layman, was the Society's
first Secretary, but he was joined in 1810 by Thomas Fry,
sometime Fellow of Lincoln College, Oxford and rector of
Emberton in Buckinghamshire, as the Anglican Secretary.
On Fox's retirement in 1812, William Bengo Collyer, Congregationalist minister at Hanover Chapel in Peckham and
friend of the Royal family, assumed the secretarial position
for the Dissenters.   As far as we can tell, the thirty-six
directors of the London Society after 1812, including twelve
ministers and clergymen and twenty-four laymen, were also
divided equally between Church and Dissent.

As with the Religious Tract Society, a fundamental
principle around which the various denominations could unite
was developed in stages by the London Society.   The germ
of such a principle was already evident in the Society's first
half-yearly report, in which the founders "thought it proper
and suitable, to the glory of God, to establish a Society for
the SOLE purpose of exciting the attention of the Jews to the

words of eternal salvation." In this statement, the founders
said that it was their "earnest desire, that the word denomination, may be lost in that of Christianity, in support of
an institution of such great importance."20 This declaration
of policy was reiterated several months later at the founding
of the Olney Auxiliary, when Thomas Fry pledged to his
Anglican colleagues that the London Society "would confine
themselves to the promotion of Christianity among the Jews,
unconnected with any other object & that they would not give
unnecessary offence to the Established Church."21 Though
the London Society never codified its fundamental principle
in one document as the London Missionary Society had, at
least one critic of the Society, in summarizing the Society's
first and third reports, stated such a principle in the following way:22

> As it was the simple object of the Bible Society
> to circulate the Bible without note or comment,
> and thus enlist under their banners all who re-
> ceive the Bible as the Word of God; so was it
> the object of the London Society ... to limit them-
> selves to the simple object that Jesus is the Mes-
> siah, the Saviour of the world, leaving them, when
> thus instructed, to search the Scriptures and judge
> for themselves respecting all inferior points on
> which Christians themselves were not agreed; such
> being "the Catholic spirit" indulged amongst them-
> selves, "that they should equally rejoice in the
> conversion of a Jew, whether within or without
> the pale of their own regular establishment."

This principle was interpreted in different ways by
different denominations. For example, G. B. Mitchell,
vicar of St. Mary, Leicester and a member of the Society
was already concerned about the charge of irregularity which
might be leveled against the Society when he told an assembly in 1813 that if the London Society interfered "in the
slightest degree, with the sentiments of religion which the
Jew might adopt when he embraced Christianity, I, for one,
would cease to be a member of it; but being fully convinced
from observation, that it takes no part in endeavouring to
persuade the Jews to join one or the other Society of Chris-
tians--that it leaves the matter entirely to themselves, I
can cordially as a churchman unite with this society."23
A Quaker from Huntingdon, equally concerned about the role
that the Society of Friends would play in the Society, told a
similar assembly one year later that "if the Episcopalian,

by his outward and visible sign, can cause the poor Jew to
see the need he has to be clothed in the inward and spiritual grace--if the Baptist, by his water, can cause the Jew to
see the need he has of being washed in the laver of Regen-
eration--if we, by our internal light, can bring them to the
knowledge, that the Lord's ear is ever open to the cry of
the poor and the destitute, to revive the spirit of the hum-
ble--if by any means, and by any instrument, they are
brought to the heaven of rest, we do rejoice, and we will
rejoice."[24]

The Society's fundamental principle, however, contained the seeds of its own destruction, rather as the fundamental principle of the London Missionary Society proved
unworkable, especially for the Anglicans. The London Missionary Society and the London Society for Promoting
Christianity Amongst the Jews were interdenominational missionary organizations (unlike the Bible and Tract Societies
which were basically publishing houses) and as such, their
objectives were similar. The London Missionary Society,
as we have seen, hoped to establish undenominational mission stations to which the various evangelical denominations
in Britain would send missionaries and financial support, but
as an experiment in cooperation, this plan proved to be unworkable for "regular" Anglicans, Wesleyans and Baptists.
In theory, the London Society was based on the same undenominational missionary principle. The Jews who were gathered in and converted would decide for themselves the denomination to which they would affiliate. But in reality, the
London Society faced the same problems that the London
Missionary Society had faced ten years before. For example, when the London Society purchased the French Church
in Spitalfields, London in 1809 (which they renamed the
"Jews Chapel"), the directors found it difficult to agree on
which denominational polity, if any, it should be established.
Nor could the directors cope with related theological and denominational questions that would eventually disrupt the Society's delicate interdenominational balance. By what theological formula would Jewish converts be nurtured in Christian doctrine once the Jews Chapel was opened? By whom
and in what mode would the Jews be baptized? Indeed, how
would converted Jews decide which denomination to affiliate
with once they had completed their Christian training? These
and other unanswered questions, as we shall see, portended
serious denominational conflict and eventual schism.

III.

Since most of the London Society's early energies
were sapped by the controversy with the London Missionary
Society, its programs were slow to start, but when it was
properly launched, its activities were carried on in three
major areas. From the beginning, weekly lectures were
provided for interested Jews and recent converts in the newly established Jews Chapel. The chapel, however, almost
immediately created a dilemma for the Society's Anglican
clergymen since Bishop Randolph of London, a notorious
High Church opponent of the evangelicals, refused to license
it, [25] causing some Anglicans to wonder "how the chapel
would be conducted upon the [undenominational] principles
held out to the public since ministers of the Established
Church could not consistently officiate with the Protestant
Dissenters in the same place of worship. "[26] The problem
was only resolved when the Society decided to establish two
lectures: one given by the Dissenters in the unconsecrated
Jews Chapel, and the other given by Anglican clergymen in
various Evangelical strongholds around London until Ely
Episcopal Chapel was open to them on a more or less permanent basis. [27]

The second area of activity involved the controversial
problems of Jewish education and employment. Shortly after
the Jews Chapel was opened by the Society, a "Free School"
with the capacity to enroll between three and four hundred
Jewish and Christian children was established on the popular
Lancastrian Plan. But this attempt at christianization through
integration appears not to have been very successful. [28] The
Society also opened its controversial "boarding school" where
Jewish children were housed and educated in isolation from
community and synagogue, and then bound apprentices to a
Christian businessman or industrialist when their education
was completed. [29] Concomitant with the boarding school was
another controversial project that had been debated at the
London Missionary Society in former days. This was the
establishment of a house of industry for poor Jewish laborers. For a time, converts were employed by the Society
to manufacture candlewicks and baskets, but the project was
unprofitable and had to be terminated. The same fate faced
numerous other enterprises including an asylum "for the re-
ception and employment of Jewesses," and a printing office.

The final area of activity involved Society publications.
Tracts and pamphlets together with Bibles and Testaments

had always been published and circulated by the Society.
Translated into Hebrew, these were directed primarily to
the older Jewish community which the Society thought could
be converted by rational argument. A house journal called
the Instructor was soon established, but like so many other
of the Society's enterprises, it too proved a financial failure
although it was replaced in 1813 by the Jewish Repository.

With the opening of Palestine Place on July 16, 1814,
all of these activities were centralized in one large complex
of buildings. Palestine Place at Bethnal Green consisted of
a Chapel for Christian Jews, an "Operative Jewish Convert's
Institution," a chaplain's residence, and a school.[30] As we
shall see, the management and financial support of Palestine
Place proved to be the undoing of Anglican-Nonconformist
cooperation in the London Society and indirectly led to schism
in 1815. As might have been anticipated, the conflict was
over the chapel which, when it was finally licensed by Bishop Randolph, could only be used by the Anglican clergy.

In retrospect, the successes of the early London Society, both as a missionary enterprise and as an experiment
in interdenominational cooperation were mixed. As a mission, the Society was a paradoxical mixture of all that was
good and bad in the early pan-evangelical missionary impulse. Some of the Society's conversionist techniques, for
instance, upset even some of its most mission-minded patrons. One of the Society's critics left the following account
of the methods used by Frey and his associates to bribe
Jewish children away from their parents:[31]

> The mode of introducing themselves among these
> fruit and silk merchants was, first by purchasing
> some article to the value of a few pence and leav-
> ing a dollar or seven shilling piece for it, to the
> delight and astonishment of the youth, who returned
> thanks to the God of Israel for such a fortunate
> event; the same benevolent deed was acted again
> and again, when, at length, the snare-laid youth
> humbly solicits to know to whom he is indebted
> for such mighty goodness. The answer is--My
> dear child, this is nothing at all; I mean to make
> your fortune, if you take the friendly advice I shall
> give you,--accompanying the last words with a
> guinea or two. Before the youth has time to re-
> cover himself from his surprise, he is informed
> that such a lovely fine lad would look handsome in

> a new suit of clothes, and that if he would come
> next Sunday and hear Mr. Frey preach, he shall
> have as fine a suit of clothes as can be made.

To many evangelicals, these methods seemed uncomfortably
reminiscent of the days of persecution, when Roman Catholics had allegedly removed Jewish children from their parents to educate them as Christians.   Though the London
Society had no power of physical coercion, yet, as another
critic pointed out: "They know the power of money, and
therefore ... they TEMPT the Jews, by the offer of gratis
maintenance and education, to do violence to their con-
sciences by delivering up their children to them, to be fed
the food forbidden by the Jewish nation, and educated as
Christians."[32]

On the other hand, the London Society performed a
very important function for poor Jewish immigrants as an
early welfare agency.   Its house of industry, for example,
provided employment for Jewish laborers who might otherwise have starved along with their families.   Increasingly,
many of the more reform-minded evangelicals, concerned
with the social and political disabilities under which Jews
were forced to live, shifted their energies away from former conversionist activities to more humane and urgent concerns.   Some of these evangelicals became the vanguard of
a movement in the 1830's to remove, through Parliamentary
legislation, Jewish civil disabilities, a movement, incidental-
ly, that indirectly culminated in the vision of a Jewish state
in Palestine.[33]

As an interdenominational institution, however, the
London Society was a failure.   If the evangelicals had learned
only one thing from their experiences in other pan-evangelical associations, it was simply that interdenominational cooperation succeeded or failed depending on the objects pursued by them in common.   If the object did not require communal worship and the sharing of the sacraments, but rather
concentrated on simpler things like the distribution of tracts
and Bibles, then cooperation usually proved fruitful as it
did in the Bible and Tract Societies.   On the other hand, if
cooperation involved projects that threatened denominational
autonomy, or violated some sacred theological premise held
by one denomination but not by the others, then cooperation
usually did not succeed.   As we shall see, the London So-
with its controversial undenominational chapels in London,
was placed in this second category along with the London

Missionary Society and its highly suspect undenominational
mission churches abroad.

IV.

        Almost from its inception, the London Society was
tormented by three interdependent and recurring crises which
greatly hampered the effectiveness of its operations and
eventually polarized the Dissenters and Anglicans into separate and antagonistic camps.   These three crises--a disappointing harvest of Jewish converts, denominational conflicts, and financial problems--have already been alluded
to.   They merit re-examination now as the primary issues
around which the Society finally became divided.

        Unhappily for the evangelicals, the London Society
was never able fully to realize the hopes of early millennialists who had predicted that large numbers of Jews would
be converted to Christianity with relatively little effort.   Although a precise record of the Society's adult conversions
is not extant, the indications are that a relatively small number of Jews adopted the Christian faith.[34]   Many of these,
as we have suggested, returned to the synagogue once jobs
were secured and financial aid was no longer needed.   The
evangelicals had seriously underestimated the opposition
their mission would receive from the local synagogue.   Moreover, they never quite grasped the fact that the Jews, though
often divided from each other physically and geographically,
were nevertheless united spiritually by a similar cultural
identity and strong religious faith that was almost imper-
vious to conversion.   Instead, the supporters of the Society
began to blame themselves for the Mission's failure.   Many
questioned whether a coalition of Dissenters and Anglicans,
themselves long divided, could ever present a united front
to the Jews: undoubtedly the excuse of denominational division became the rationalization for the Society's failure
to realize millennial prophesies.   Not a few of the Society's
Anglican patrons were coming to the conclusion that a mission directed and patronized solely by members of the Church
of England, would be much more successful than one jointly
patronized by Anglicans and Dissenters.

        Underlying the Mission's failure to win large numbers
of Jewish converts was a second and perhaps more serious
crisis.   Pan-evangelicalism in the London Society was based
on the hope that if Anglicans and Dissenters could cooperate

in a common mission to the Jews, they could also resolve
ecclesiastical differences that had divided them for centuries.
But in practice this proved an illusion.   Evangelical Churchmen were still inclined to set their allegiances to the Church
of England above their commitment to Protestant unity and
as a result, Society resolutions often favored the Church
cause.   Whether the directors were discussing how to administer the sacraments in the Jews Chapel, [35] or the rite
by which the Chapel services would be held, [36] the Anglicans
always insisted that only by conforming to the usages of the
Church of England, would clergymen be able to minister
alongside their Dissenting brethren.   Although the Dissenters
usually acquiesced they no doubt came to distrust their Anglican colleagues whom they feared were trying to force upon them the principles of conformity. [37]   If the evangelicals
had underestimated the communal and religious solidarity of
the Jews, they had even more seriously underestimated the
weakness of their own.

    One incident will serve to illustrate not only how
divisive, but also how absurd these differences could sometimes become.   In 1805, Frey was ordained by the London
Missionary Society in a very peculiar way.   Unsure of the
validity of an ordination performed by an undenominational
society and not a proper church, the Missionary Society's
cautious directors limited Frey's ministry to the Jews only
and even then would not permit him to administer the sacraments. [38]   Never happy with this arrangement, Frey naturally, once the London Society was established in 1809,
pressed for an ordination that would give him full sacra-
mental powers. [39]   Unfortunately, the London Society, with
half its directors "order-minded" Anglicans, fared little better than the Missionary Society in the resolution of this
problem.   For instance, in 1811 some of the directors
thought that a Lutheran ordination might be a compromise
acceptable to Anglican and Dissenter alike, but apparently
neither group favored the idea.   Even three years later,
when the Jews Chapel was used exclusively by the Dissenters,
Frey could not convince the Anglicans to let Dr. Collyer ordain him as a Congregational minister. [40]   It was not until
1827 that Frey was finally able to secure a Baptist ordination, but by then he had left the Society and was a Hebrew
instructor at the University of Michigan in America. [41]   Yet
while he was a member of the London Society in good standing, the whole issue of ordination only proved once again
how embarrassingly divisive denominational concerns could
be in a professedly undenominational organization.

If failures in the mission field and disagreements over issues of polity and church order had not completely divided the Society by the second decade of the nineteenth century, a third crisis involving its financial stability, was finally to render the union of Dissenters and Anglicans economically unfeasible if not totally impractical. Times were hard all over England in 1811, and economic depression had taken its toll of several voluntary associations. To aggravate matters for the London Society, a history of unwise institutional planning involving the expensive duplication of worship in two separate chapels together with the financial collapse of so many of its projects was beginning to have an adverse effect on the mission's economic stability. When financial assistance was sought from wealthy Anglicans hitherto unconnected with the Society, the response was disappointing. Influential Anglican churchmen were apparently still questioning the feasibility of supporting a mission plagued not only by internal dissension, but now also by a severe lack of funds.

Several evangelicals hoped that the internal and financial woes of the Society could be ameliorated while still maintaining the semblance of interdenominational unity. Consequently, in 1811 the Society planned the construction of a large complex of buildings at Bethnal Green known as "Palestine Place" in the hope that its diversified concerns, including possibly its chapels, could be centrally located on one large site allowing the Society to close down its operations elsewhere. [42] Unfortunately, as we have seen, an all too familiar problem subsequently arose. The new chapel was licensed by the Bishop of London in such a way that only ordained Anglican clergymen could officiate there. [43] The Dissenters nobly pledged to continue their support of the complex--most probably with the understanding that the Jews Chapel would still be maintained for them--but unhappily the unexpected high cost of construction in a period of inflation forced them to default on their pledge, and the Society was thrust to the point of total bankruptcy. [44]

Some of the more skeptical Anglican directors, who by now were certain that the Mission would, in any case, be better off without the Dissenters, pointed out to their more moderate episcopalian colleagues that if the Dissenters withdrew from the Society completely, wealthy Anglican Churchmen, who previously had scruples about the "unnatural coalition" of Church and Dissent, might rally to the Society's salvation. [45] Several more plans to salvage the remains of

pan-evangelical cooperation were proposed and rejected[46]
before Lewis Way, the wealthy Anglican philanthropist, offered to assume most of the Society's debt if the Dissenters
agreed to retire from the committee post haste.[47] With no
option open to them, the Dissenters met in caucus and finally accepted the offer.[48]

Immediately after the Dissenters had withdrawn, the
Society's constitution was revised so that Jewish children
under its patronage would be "instructed in the principles
and according to the formularies of the United Church of
England and Ireland." The revision also stated that public
worship in the Society's chapels would be "conducted in
strict conformity to the liturgy and formularies of the Church
of England as by law established."[49] As an afterthought,
Dr. Collyer and the other Dissenters on the old committee
were offered honorary life memberships, but apparently this
they would not accept.[50] After 1815, the evangelical mission to the Jews was carried on under the auspices of the
Church of England and remains so today as the Church's
Ministry Among the Jews.

NOTES

1. Interestingly, however, several L.M.S. directors fa-
     vored sending a mission to the South Sea Islands
     because they believed that one of the ten tribes of
     Israel had been scattered there. L.M.S. Minutes,
     December 15, 1800.
2. Evangelical Magazine 4 (1796), 403; M. Margoliouth, The
     History of the Jews in Great Britain (1851), II, 147
     ff.
3. For the biography of Frey, see Evangelical Magazine,
     14 (1806), 3 f.; Dictionary of American Biography.
4. L.M.S. Minutes, September 21, 1801; December 1, 1801.
5. L.M.S. Minutes, April 9, 1804; June 10, 1805.
6. L.M.S. Minutes, July 22, 1805; August 19, 26, 1805;
     September 13, 1805.
7. This school had been opposed by Rabbi Solomon Hirschel
     of the Great London Synagogue and as a result, the
     school proved to be a failure. See Evangelical Maga-
     zine, 14 (1806), 572. For opposition from Hirshel,
     see L.M.S. Minutes, January 8, 12, 1807.
8. See L.M.S. Jewish Committee MSS: L. Langton to W.
     Alers-Hankey, April 15, 1807; "Memorandum on the
     Jewish School to the Jewish Committee," October 19,

1807. Cf., C. F. Frey, Narrative of the Reverend
Joseph Samuel C. F. Frey (1809), 122 f.

9. L. M. S. Minutes, July 22, 1805; August 19, 26, 1805;
September 13, 1805; October 19, 26, 1807; February
29, 1808. Cf., Frey, Narrative, 141.

10. L. M. S. Minutes, November 9, 23, 1807; April 27,
1808.

11. See An Address from the Committee of the London Society (1808).

12. Cited in Frey, Narrative, 172.

13. L. S. Minutes, October 20, 1808. Cf., Frey, Narrative,
190 ff.

14. L. S. Minutes, February 15, 1809. Cf., City of Re-
fuge: An Address from the Committee of the London
Society to Christians of every Denomination (1809).
The Society later changed its name to the "London
Society for Promoting Christianity Amongst the Jews."

15. See L. M. S. Minutes, February 26, 1810.

16. There were, however, several evangelicals who opposed the Jewish mission for reasons quite independent of the dispute with the L. M. S. One such was
William Jay of Bath. See C. Jay, Recollections of
William Jay (1859), 143.

17. Christian Observer (1806), 254.

18. See L. S. Minutes, April 1, June 9, December 8, 1809;
January 12, 16, 1810. Cf., T. Halstead, Our Missions: History of the Principal Missionary Transactions of the London Society (1866), Appendix B.

19. See L. S. Minutes, November 17, 1809; January 12,
1810; April 24, 1810. Cf., W. T. Gidney, The History of the London Society (1908), 45.

20. Report of the Committee of the First Half-Yearly Meeting of the London Society (1809), 9.

21. L. S. Minutes, January 2, 12, 1810.

22. H. H. Norris, The Origin, Progress and Existing Circumstances of the London Society (1825), 26. Norris
is quoting in part from The Third Report of the Committee of the London Society (1811), 13.

23. Norris, Origin, 25 fn.

24. Ibid., 25 f.

25. L. S. Minutes, January 26, 1810; February 9, 1810.
Cf., Norris, Origin, 29 f.

26. Norris, Origin, 29 f.

27. L. S. Minutes, October 23, 1810; Norris, Origin, 29 f.

28. L. S. Minutes, June 2, 1809; Norris, Origin, 38.

29. Norris, Origin, 38; Frey, Narrative, 270 f.

30. Gidney, op. cit., 41 f.

31. Cited in M. Sailman, The Mystery Unfolded or an Ex-
    position on the Extraordinary Means Employed to Ob-
    tain Converts by the Agents of the London Society
    (1817), 45 f.

32. T. Witherby, The Wisdom of the Calvinistic Methodists
    Displayed (1810), 17.

33. In 1826, a group of evangelicals founded the "Philo-
    Judean Society." Nominally interdenominational, this
    organization concentrated almost solely on providing
    temporal assistance to distressed Jews. It also
    sponsored legislation in Parliament favoring Jewish
    emancipation. See U. Henriques, Religious Toler-
    ation in England (1961), 177 f.

34. This is suggested by Norris. See Norris, Origin,
    passim. An examination of the Society's baptismal
    register for the years under study leads one to the
    same conclusion. See L.S. "Register of Baptisms"
    1810-1814.

35. L.S. Minutes, November 28, 1809; April 30, 1810.
    Cf., A. L. Williams, Mission to the Jews: An
    Historical Retrospective (1897), 49 f.

36. L.S. Minutes, June 2, 1809; January 16, 26, 1810;
    January 22, 1811.

37. Cf., L.S. Minutes, October 30, 1810; August 20, 1811;
    November 12, 1811. Cf., Margoliouth, op.cit., II
    221.

38. See Frey, Narrative, 165

39. L.S. Minutes, November 28, 1809.

40. L.S. Minutes, January 22, 1811; February 5, 16, 19,
    1811; November 29, 1814.

41. For Frey's rather checkered career after 1815 and his
    subsequent removal to America, see Sailman, op.cit,
    45 f.; J. Rumyanek, "Early Conversionist Activities
    in London: A Missing Chapter in Anglo-Jewish His-
    tory," The Jewish Guardian, May 29, 1931, 8 f. Cf.,
    E. Jay, The Religion of the Heart (1979), 95 fn. In
    1820, Frey founded the "American Society for Ameli-
    orating the Conditions of the Jews." See L. Ratner,
    "Conversion of the Jews and Pre-Civil War Reform,"
    American Quarterly, XIII (1961), 43 ff.

42. L.S. Minutes, June 11, 1810; February 27, 1811. Cf.,
    Norris, Origin, 62, 70 fn.

43. Cf., L.S. Minutes, April 26, 1814. Cf., Gidney,
    op.cit., 46.

44. Cf., L.S. Minutes, May 31, 1814; September 27, 1814;
    October 25, 1814.

45. Cf., The Seventh Report of the Committee of the London

Society (1815), 35; Cf., L.S. Minutes, February 6, 1815.

46. L.S. Minutes, December 23, 27, 1814; January 31, 1815.

47. See Norris, Origin, 104 ff.; L.S. Minutes, February 17, 1815.

48. L.S. Minutes, February 17, 21, 24, 1815.

49. L.S. Minutes, February 28, 1815.

50. Loc. cit.; L.S. Minutes, April 25, 1815.

PART V:

CONCLUSION

The Pan-evangelical impulse was not dying by 1830.
Though the London Society had emerged as an Anglican organization by 1815, and the London Missionary Society, for
all practical purposes, as a Congregational one three years
later, the Religious Tract and British and Foreign Bible Societies continued to expand as interdenominational operations.
In 1825, the total annual receipts of the Tract Society were
a little over £10,000. By 1830, they had doubled to almost
£25,000 and by 1840 had doubled again to £59,000.[1] The
Bible Society also grew. Though hurt financially by the
Apocrypha and Tests controversies, it nevertheless managed to circulate over 280,000 Bibles in 1825, 434,000 in
1830, and 776,000 in 1840.[2] Both societies continued to
function as a major unitive force in British ecclesiastical
life. As auxiliaries expanded they drew into the pan-evangelical movement even larger numbers of people linking them
and the religious bodies they represented into a network of
formal and informal liaisons that by 1840 could be found
operating in virtually every city and town and in many vil-
lages and hamlets in Britain. The central committees of
the various Tract and Bible Society auxiliaries, like the
parent committees in London with their elected and appointed officials representing almost every denomination, were
also linked to each other by a sophisticated system of interlocking directorates making each separate auxiliary part
of one grand movement for church unity. Patronage of one
society usually implied patronage of the other.

There were, of course, many other societies and
they played an equally important role in the continuing surge
of pan-evangelicalism. The range and variety of these institutions was extraordinary. As Sir James Stephen so apt-
ly put it in 1848: "Ours is the age of societies. For every
redress of every oppression that is done under the sun,

there is a public meeting. For the cure of every sorrow
by which our land or race can be visited, there are patrons,
vice presidents and secretaries. For the diffusion of every
blessing of which mankind can partake in common, there is
a committee."[3] The proliferation of fundraisers became so
oppressive, that a pamphlet was written instructing would-
be targets of the fundraiser's trade how to evade their hard
(and not so easily resisted) salesmanship. [4]

      Smaller interdenominational organizations like the
Sunday Schools continued to grow apace and many new ones
appeared. Some, like the British Society for Promoting the
Religious Principles of the Reformation and the Young Men's
Christian Association resembled the Tract and Bible Societies
in their avoidance of controversial theological issues, choos-
ing instead as their agreed points of cooperation concerns
that would not offend denominational sensibilities. Others,
like the Association for Promoting Rational Humanity towards the Animal Creation and the British and Foreign
Temperance Society cooperated in issues that were entirely
secular in nature. For the most part, interdenominational
societies for religious purposes in which evangelicals worshipped side by side ceased to appear after the London Society and the London Missionary Society fell into denominational hands. This in itself was significant, for though the
spirit of evangelical union continued into the nineteenth century, it lacked the kind of idealism so characteristic of
men like Samuel Greatheed and John Eyre and the early pan-
evangelical organizations they had been instrumental in founding. Indeed, by 1808, only ten years after Greatheed published his General Union Recommended, the great manifesto
of the pan-evangelical "idealists," he was compelled to warn
the interdenominational Devon Union against the rising tide
of sectarianism. "Beware," he wrote,[5]

> lest selfish and interested motives pollute, in the
> smallest degree, the measures that you use for
> the benefit of others. Are you displeased, when
> your brethren differ from you in opinion concern-
> ing the steps by which your common object is to
> be pursued? Is it only in proportion as converts
> are added to your religious party, or as the num-
> bers of your own congregation increase, that you
> are gratified? Examine yourselves, my brethren.

Seven years later, Greatheed's own Bedfordshire Union of
Christians was rocked by a schism of several prominent
Baptist patrons. [6]

By 1830 most evangelicals agreed that the early fervor of their "idealistic" forefathers had been somewhat di-
luted. Looking back in 1834 on the halcyon days of the London Missionary Society when "the very union of Christians
... excited the attention of the religious public," Richard
Cope, a former L. M. S. director, lamented that the fading
of the old fraternal spirit had led to a deterioration in evangelical spirituality as a whole. "Since that period," he
wrote, "the zeal of Christians has generally declined; or-
dinary and extraordinary Prayer Meetings have no longer
an attractive influence; our places of worship are but thinly
attended [and] the number of communicants at the Lord's
Table is comparatively few."[7] That same year, the Evangelical Magazine declared its intention to adhere to "the
true principles of catholic and comprehensive piety" in which
the Magazine had originated but added that "in that adherence
it will be impossible ... to overlook the spirit of the age."[8]
That the "realists" of pan-evangelical union had triumphed
there could be no doubt. Even James Bennett, friend and
co-author of the classic history of Nonconformity with David
Bogue, the man who declared in 1795 that bigotry was dead,
wrote in 1839: "The perfection of union is ... not to be
hoped for, but by the perfection of holiness in heaven ...
There never was ... and never will be, on earth, and, perhaps, we may add, heaven too, any other union among Christians, but that of affection."[9]

How can one account for the decline not only of pan-
evangelical "idealism," but of the urge towards associated
cooperation between evangelicals, so powerful a few decades
before? One answer lies in the troubled political state of
the nation by 1830, not least in the politics of churchman-
ship. In a few years, the old ecclesiastical constitution of
England had changed drastically and seemed on the brink of
yet more drastic remodeling. In 1828, Dissenters were
freed from one of the symbols of their second-class citizen-
ship, the disabilities imposed upon them by the Test Acts.
Many Anglican evangelicals approved of the repeal of the
Tests, but not all. To some "Ultras" this seemed a step
toward disestablishment and the laicization of government.
Far more divisive was the issue of Roman Catholic Emancipation which reached its climax in 1829. Evangelicals,
anti-Romans to a man, fell apart over the Catholic question.
There was sharp division among Anglican evangelicals as
Wilberforce's Parliamentary "Saints" (for the most part)
supported Catholic relief on the grounds of charitableness
and political necessity, and the "Ultras" like Sir Robert

Inglis (and a large number of evangelical clergymen) opposed it. 10   Nor were the evangelical Dissenters of one
mind.   Middleclass Nonconformists tended to take a liberal
line, seeing an analogy between the Catholic and Dissenting
campaigns for greater religious equality.   On the other hand,
their lower-class colleagues, including most Methodists, opposed Emancipation vehemently in an outburst of no-Popery
hysteria. 11   We have already seen the repercussions of this
tension in the affairs of the Bible and Tract Societies, but
it continued to bedevil relations between Nonconformists.

The issue of Parliamentary reform also had its re-
percussion on evangelical relations.   Wilberforce's "Saints"
supported the extension of the franchise to wider sections of
the middle class, believing that in these lay the heart of the
great "religious public" which had loyally abetted so many
moral reform campaigns.   Their inclusion in the political
nation would only strengthen the cause of godliness and morality in English government.   Evangelical Tories, especially
among the Anglican clergy, tended to fear the new leverage
given to the enemies of the Anglican establishment, understandably since the Reform Bill crisis had given new ve-
hemence to critics of the state church.   In the 1830's, it
seemed as though the establishment might fall beneath the
attack of a motley army of would-be reformers including
Utilitarians demanding a more practical and educational use
of church endowments, Chartists calling for "more pigs and
fewer parsons," Irish Catholics unwilling to pay tithes to a
Protestant establishment, and, above all, Nonconformist ra-
dicals--most of them good evangelicals. 12   The alarming
increase of Nonconformist militancy disturbed many Anglican
exponents of evangelical union.   Though many Wesleyans
still saw themselves as half way between Church and Dissent and kept aloof from the campaigns for disestablishment,
many Quakers, Baptists, and Congregationalists waxed belli-
cose against the enormities of a state church.   Few were
more fiery than Thomas Binney, John Clayton's successor
at King's Weigh House Chapel, who declared in 1833, 13

> it is with me, I confess, a matter of deep, ser-
> ious, religious, conviction, that the Established
> Church is a great national evil; that it is an ob-
> stacle to the progress of truth and godliness in
> the land; that it destroys more souls than it saves;
> and that, therefore, its end is most devoutly to
> be wished by every lover of God and man.

Comments like these provoked the evangelical clergyman

Josiah Pratt, once a fervent supporter of interdenominational
cooperation, to warn his colleagues one year later:[14]

> The Dissenters are suffering as a religious body,
> irrecoverable injury, from having submitted them-
> selves to the guidance of a few ambitious men
> among them. It is no longer Dissent for con-
> science sake, with the thankfulness for the quiet
> enjoyment of the privilege of worshipping and
> preaching according to their own judgment; but
> it is a claim to be placed on equal footing with
> the Church, and to have the Church separated
> from the State.

William Urwick, the Irish evangelical, lamented the havoc
created by these divisions to the cause of evangelical fraternization. "The consequence has been, in one respect,
distressing," he wrote a friend in 1833. "It has, in many
instances, caused a rupture between ministers of the Establishment and those of Dissenting communities, who had
previously been in habits of cordial Christian friendship."[15]

    In the long run, theology was a more powerful sol-
vent than politics of the early "idealist" attitude toward evangelical union. Behind the pan-evangelical spirit lay, as we
have often seen, the assumption that the essential doctrines
of the Gospel were few, held by all the regenerate, and dis-
tinguishable from truths more peripheral which pertained
(perhaps) to the fullness but not the kernel of Christian
faith. The movement was based on the idea of consensus:
that issues divisive to unity could be suppressed or rele-
gated to the outer margins. But could they? It seemed to
some that enforced moderation and compromise was sometimes purchased at too high a price. Even the "idealists"
felt this from time to time. In 1808, for example, at a
time when the London Missionary Society and the Bedfordshire Union of Christians were passing through a period of
tension, David Bogue spoke of the "reprehensibility" of those
evangelicals who fell out over trifles, yet added significantly
that there was an opposite extreme of doctrinal vagueness
and flabbiness which was equally culpable. "When men
yield, for the sake of peace, to impositions against which
conscience revolts, and which conscience condemns as sinful," he wrote, "they merit at least an equal degree of
blame."[16] In the same year, the Anglican-sponsored Christian Observer wrote feelingly: "What we dislike above all
things, is an association of abundant profession with scanty

performance; a junction of exact notions on general doctrine, with an indifferent judgment as to particular points of duty and of conduct."[17] There seemed a danger that the glib, shallow, platitudinous, popular evangelicalism--the cheapened, trivialized Gospel of which they were beginning to complain--might be a legacy of too much interdenominationalism and the reduction of the Gospel to its minimal bones. Great and comprehensive religious systems like that of historic Calvinism seemed to have been shrunken and disfigured by the demands of organizational amity. This, as we have seen, is why Robert Hawker left the Religious Tract Society. His action was "condoned" long afterwards from a very different quarter when R. W. Dale wrote of the Moderate Calvinists:[18]

> They thought that while preserving the strong foundations of the Calvinistic theology and its method, they could modify some of the Calvinistic doctrines, which in their rigid form had become incredible to them. But they were attempting an impossible task, and doing injustice to the constructive genius of their great master. They had not learnt that theologians who begin with Calvin must end with Calvin. "Moderate Calvinism" was Calvinism in decay.

The critique of pan-evangelicalism was here very similar to that leveled at American revivalists in the age of Moody and Sankey.[19]

Another threat to the cause of evangelical unity lay, as we have seen continually, in the growing power of denominationalism.[20] The Congregationalists had established a denominational union in 1806, but it quickly collapsed when influential Independents refused to support it. Critics still believed that if there was to be a union, it should be one that comprehended all Protestant evangelicals. The London Missionary Society, of course, helped to serve this function. By the 1830's, however, feelings had changed. As the older ministers died or retired, their younger successors, in reaction to a brand of pan-evangelicalism that seemed to negate denominational tradition and heritage, repudiated the lofty "catholic" ideals of their fathers, and supported the denominational movement with enthusiasm. The formation of denominational magazines to supplement or replace the interdenominational Evangelical Magazine set off a chain reaction which fed the movement to establish the Baptist and

Congregational Unions between 1831 and 1832.[21] As the denominations expanded, they acquired their bureaucracies, official and unofficial, and competed energetically for membership according to the canons of free trade to which their
members generally subscribed. Indeed, the anti-church
movement rested its case partly on the way an established
Church of England denied the law of "free competition." Historic interest, tinged by romanticism, revived in the Puritan past of the Dissenting denominations and the peculiarities of each denomination seemed increasingly something to
prize and accentuate. Throughout the course of the movement for evangelical unity, there had, as we have seen,
been reactions against the submerging of heritage and tradition in the interests of consensus and unity. The Scots
Presbyterians and the English Anglicans were restive in the
Apocrypha and Tests Controversy at the Bible Society; the
Congregationalists uneasy in the Tract Society altercation
over Milner's Church History. A correspondent of the Baptist Magazine expressed this pride in denominational identity
well when he wrote in 1832: "I would yield to no man in af-
fectionate regards for the interests of other religious communities, but I love my own denomination with strong attachment, and would not sacrifice my designation as a Baptist at any shrine."[22] By this time the alarming reductio
ad absurdum of the principle of Christian union seemed to
have been reached by Broad Churchmen like Thomas Arnold,
whose project for unity would, as J. H. Overton disapprov-
ingly wrote, "have made the church so wide as to admit
within its pale Dissenters of all kinds--Roman Catholics,
Quakers and Unitarians excepted--without any compromise
of principle on either side."[23]

        The period after 1830, then, saw growth for many
charitable and some religious organizations in which evangelicals of all kinds cooperated fraternally. But much of
the bloom of the initial impulse seemed to have faded. Nothing, perhaps, mirrored this more than the Evangelical Alliance of 1845. The spirit of men like Greatheed, Bogue
and Haweis had been positive, optimistic, mission-minded;
that of the Alliance was defensive and anxious, even in some
ways negative. It rested on hostility to the growth of Roman
Catholicism and the Tractarian Movement whose Rome-ward
tendencies, mirrored in the secession of Newman in 1845,
was alarming. The Alliance was designed, as one of its
circulars stated, "to associate and concentrate the strength
of an enlightened Protestantism against the encroachments
of Popery and Puseyism."[24] Though the Alliance made, in

many respects, an important contribution to church unity,
its base was far narrower and more exclusive than its predecessors.   Andrew Reed, an early patron of the Alliance,
complained that though it "declared itself a Christian alliance [it] adopted a Protestant platform."[25] Catholics, of
course, were to be excluded, but so were Quakers and Unitarians.   Wesleyans and Baptists, though included, were
skeptical about patronizing the Alliance for many of the same
reasons which had led them to withhold support from the
London Missionary Society fifty years before.[26] So began
a new movement in pan-evangelical unity, but one that resembled little the pan-evangelical impulse of the late eighteenth and early nineteenth centuries.[27]

It will be apparent that the history of evangelical
union movements before 1830 has implications for the ecumenical movement today.   The controversies that this book
has described at length may appear to be barren, but they
often raise important problems which could be profitably
studied by the architects of ecumenicism, if the same pit-
falls are to be avoided.   The first problem involves the recurring issue of church polity and government.   Will it ever
be possible to find common ground upon which Christian denominations can join organically as one unified and undenominational Christian church?   Can we close our eyes to the
fact that not only are there basic differences between denominations, but that in Britain at least, Free Churches
and National Establishments are based on different principles?
The London Missionary Society and the London Society for
Promoting Christianity Amongst the Jews unsuccessfully tried
to overlook these differences either by regarding them as un-
important, or by pushing them into the background, hoping
that in the general enthusiasm to convert the heathen and
the Jews to Christianity, denominational peculiarities would
pale into insignificance and Christians would be of one mind
in their common mission.   For English Independents and
Presbyterians and Calvinistic Methodists, of course, this is
exactly what happened.   Anglicans, however, refused to patronize the L.M.S. because it ranked the national church as
only one denomination among many and threatened to involve
them in the founding and management of highly irregular undenominational mission churches which, by no stretch of the
imagination, could be regarded as episcopally sanctioned.
The London Society faced the same problem.   Its Anglican
patrons demurred from supporting, and worshiping in, an
episcopally unconsecrated chapel.   Only by cooperating in
enterprises that avoided denominational issues--like the dis-

tribution of tracts and Bibles--could all denominations successfully cooperate with each other.   But even then, the
Tract and Bible Societies functioned under the continual fear
that their simple alliance might break up over issues of
polity and church government as indeed almost happened during the Milnerian Controversy at the Tract Society.

The second problem involves the issue of theology.
To what degree can the ecumenical movement base itself on
a theology of consensus; that is, a theology that is so qualified that it offends no sensibilities?   The reason why the
London Missionary Society functioned so successfully as a
pan-evangelical organization was because most of its patrons
were Calvinists and paedobaptists, and the views of L. M. S.
missionaries and directors did not have to be muffled.   The
situation at the Bible and Tract Societies was very different.
Here, opinions likely to cause discord were suppressed.
Nevertheless, some began to question whether cooperation
was worth the sacrifice of principles held to be sacred and
important.   Many committed Christians, as we have seen,
were lost to the pan-evangelical movement because in it
they saw the dangers of an emerging theological liberalism
that required little belief or commitment.

Finally, there was (and still is) the crucial problem
of what church union implied.   Was the association of evangelicals in their great societies to be an end in itself leading to cooperation and fraternization but no more?   Or was
this activity merely a prelude to organic union at some future date in which evangelicals were to come together in one
great church, as Greatheed and other "idealists" envisaged?
Was the union brought about in evangelical-inspired societies
intended to bring in merely those who shared the evangelical
consensus, or to bring in those far beyond it?   In adopting
the latter tactic, the Bible Society enjoyed a remarkable degree of success but also faced a large degree of internal
strife as a result of its inclusion of Quakers, Unitarians
and Roman Catholics.   Many saw this as intolerable.   "Ecclesiastical anarchy," Socinianism, and Romanism were
three undesirable systems to most evangelicals.   Who could
predict what kind of harmful influence they might have on
Protestant orthodoxy?   Of course, many evangelicals, especially the type of Anglican associated with the Clapham
Sect, would have argued that the inclusion of non-evangelicals
in the alliance might predispose them in favor of evangelical
principles.   Here "union" might be seen as a concealed
agency of proselytism, an organ of evangelical "imperialism."

This aspect of some movements toward church unity has aroused criticism from modern opponents of ecumenicalism. Ian Henderson, for example, in his Power Without Glory, has viewed the ecumenical movement in Britain as a cloak for an Anglican take-over of other denominations.[28] The same fears found expression in our period, when alarmed High Church Anglicans warned their evangelical colleagues of the cloth that they were being lured away from the national, episcopal Church towards a brand of interdenominationalism which abandoned the apostolic order and was Dissent in disguise. Concurrently, some Dissenters, viewing the large degree of control exerted by Anglicans in the affairs of the societies, saw them as Trojan horses of the establishment. For all its carefully planned and well-publicized equality, the pan-evangelical societies (with the exception, perhaps, of the London Missionary Society) were in reality always dominated by the Anglicans who on a number of occasions--and the London Society is the best example--imposed their system on docile Dissenters who blindly submitted.

The ecumenical movement has not solved--perhaps many never solve--the problem of choice between the idea of organic unity and its alternatives of diversity-in-unity, or mere fraternization. Many would incline to Zinzendorf's conception, and cheerfully accept the benefits of pluralism within a framework of Christian amity. All, no doubt, would support the maxim sometimes attributed to Baxter and often quoted by the exponents of pan-evangelicalism:

<blockquote>
In things essential, unity;

In things non-essential, liberty;

In all things, charity.
</blockquote>

NOTES

1. W. Jones, The Jubilee Memorial of the Religious Tract Society (1850), Appendix One.
2. G. Browne, The History of the British and Foreign Bible Society (1859), II, 544.
3. J. Stephen, Essays in Ecclesiastical Biography (1907), II. 248.
4. The Art of Evading Charitable Subscription by Nabel Junion (1815).
5. S. Greatheed, The Regard Which We Owe to the Concerns of Others (1808), 34 f.

6. Cf., H. G. Tibbut, Cotton End Old Meeting (1963), 18.
7. R. Cope, The Autobiography and the Remains of the
    Rev. Richard Cope (1857), 93.
8. Evangelical Magazine, 22n. s. (1834), iv.
9. J. Bennett, The History of Dissenters During the Last
    Thirty Years from 1808 to 1838 (1839), 379.
10. See I. Bradley, "The Politics of Godliness: Evangel-
    icals in Parliament 1784-1829" (Oxford University
    D. Phil. Thesis, 1974), 178-9.
11. See J. H. Hexter, "The Protestant Revival and the
    Catholic Question in England 1778-1829," Journal of
    Modern History, VIII (1936), 305 f. G. I. T. Ma-
    chin, The Catholic Question in English Politics (1964),
    55; D. N. Hempton, "Methodism and Anti-Catholic Poli-
    tics 1800-1846" (St. Andrew's University PhD., 1977).
12. See J. D. Walsh, "Religion: Church and State in
    Europe and the Americas," in C. W. Crawley, ed.,
    The New Cambridge Modern History (1965), IX, 178.
13. Cited in E. Kaye, The History of King's Weigh House
    Church (1968), 67.
14. J. Pratt, Memoir of the Rev. Josiah Pratt (1849), 292.
15. W. Urwick, The Life and Letters of William Urwick
    (1870), 144.
16. D. Bogue and J. Bennett, History of the Dissenters
    (1808), I, 289 f.
17. Christian Observer, 7 (1808), 737.
18. R. W. Dale, History of English Congregationalism
    (1907), 588.
19. See J. W. White, "The Influence of North American
    Evangelism in Great Britain on the Origin and Devel-
    opment of the Ecumenical Movement" (Oxford Uni-
    versity D. Phil. Thesis, 1963), Chapters 2 and 8.
20. For parallel developments in America, see L. A.
    Loetscher, "The Problem of Christian Unity in Early
    Nineteenth Century America," Church History,
    XXXII (1963), 13 f.
21. See A. Peel, These Hundred Years (1931), 12 f.
22. Baptist Magazine, 24 (1832), 100 f.
23. J. H. Overton, The English Church in the Nineteenth
    Century (1894), 121.
24. Cited in G. J. Slosser, Christian Unity (1929), 175.
25. A. Reed, Memoirs of the Life and Philanthropic La-
    bours of Andrew Reed (2nd ed. 1863), 228.
26. See W. R. Ward, Religion and Society in England
    (1972), 219.
27. Cf., A. D. Gilbert, Religion and Society in Industrial
    England (1976), 169.
28. I. Henderson, Power Without Glory (1967), passim.

EDWARD BICKERSTETH (1786-1850). After being employed in a number of occupations, Bickersteth settled down in 1806 to the work of a solicitor's clerk. He was also active at this time in the administration of the Widow's Friend and Spitalfield Benevolent Societies. In 1812, he entered into partnership with his brother-in-law as a solicitor in Norwich, but gave the legal profession up after three years to receive deacon's orders in the Church of England and to serve in Sierra Leone as an agent of the C.M.S. After his return to England, Bickersteth was engaged by the C.M.S. as one of its secretaries and traveled throughout Britain in its service. When he was in London, which was very rare, he was assistant minister at Wheler Episcopal Chapel. In 1830, Bickersteth resigned the C.M.S. secretaryship and accepted the living at Watton Herts though he continued to travel as a C.M.S. agent. He provided the same service for the Tract and Jews Societies. A strong millenarian who had attended the Albury Conferences with Edward Irving, Bickersteth supported the Pro-Test Party during the Tests Controversy at the Bible Society, but he did not leave it in 1832. Instead, he patronized both the older society and the Trinitarian Bible Society. Prominent in the Evangelical Alliance of 1845, Bickersteth was a militant anti-Tractarian. He was a director of the R.T.S. from 1816 to 1825.

THOMAS TREGENNA BIDDULPH (1763-1838). Born at Claines in Worcestershire, Biddulph spent his early life in Padstow Cornwall where his father was vicar of the local parish church. He was educated at the Truro Grammar School and at Queens College Oxford from which he gradu-

---

*The biographies of well-known evangelicals, whose life histories are readily available, have not been included in this section. Unless otherwise indicated, material has been drawn from the Dictionary of National Biography. All of these evangelicals patronized the Bible Society.

ated in 1784.   Ordained deacon one year later for the Curacy
of Padstow, Biddulph became in 1793 the Incumbent at Benge-
worth near Evesham and from 1799 until his death, Rector
of St. James's Bristol where he became famous as an Evangelical preacher.   In 1798 he established the Zion's Trumpet,
which later evolved into the Christian Guardian.   Biddulph
was a strong advocate of both the Bible and the Jews Societies.

DAVID BOGUE (1750-1825).   Bogue was born at Hal-
lydown Berwickshire and educated at the University of Edinburgh.   After a number of ministerial positions, he became
the Independent minister at Gosport where, in 1780, he
opened an academy for Independent ministers.   Active in
many pan-evangelical enterprises, Bogue was a founding
father of the L. M. S. and a director from 1795 to 1825.
His academy was later used by the L. M. S. as a seminary
for its missionaries.

ANDREW BRANDRAM (d. 1850).   Brandram was educated at Oriel College Oxford from which he graduated in
1813 to become Curate of Beckenham in Kent.   Following
John Owen's death in 1822, he was the Anglican Secretary
of the Bible Society.   See W. Canton, A History of the
British and Foreign Bible Society (1904), I, 333.

GEORGE BURDER (1752-1832).   Born in London to
parents who had been converted by George Whitefield, Burder was early interested in art and subsequently took drawing lessons from Isaac Taylor, the famous line engraver.
After studying at the Royal Academy, however, he was converted by the sermons of Romaine and Whitefield and with
the encouragement of Fletcher of Madeley became an evangelical preacher.   In 1778, Burder was ordained pastor of
the Independent chapel in Lancaster, but spent most of his
time itinerating.   He later removed to West Orchard Chapel
in Coventry where, in 1785, he established the first Sunday
School in the area.   Burder was also instrumental in founding in 1793, the Warwickshire Association of Ministers for
the Spread of the Gospel at Home and Abroad.   After moving to London as minister of Fetter Lane Independent Church,
he became involved in a number of pan-evangelical activities.
He was a founding father of the L. M. S. serving as one of its
secretaries from 1803 to 1827.   He was also editor of the
Evangelical Magazine in 1803 in succession to John Eyre, and
the founder of the R. T. S. which he also served as a director
from 1803 to 1806.

JOSEPH BUTTERWORTH (1770-1826). The son of a
Baptist minister in Coventry, Butterworth at an early age
went to London where he founded a large and lucrative book-
selling business on Fleet Street. His home was a central
meeting place for the leading evangelical philanthropists of
the day and it was here that some of the early Bible Society meetings took place. Butterworth was M. P. for Coventry from 1812 to 1818 and then for Dover from 1820 to 1826.
A convert to Methodism, he was General Treasurer of the
Wesleyan Methodist Missionary Society from 1819 until his
death. Butterworth was also prominent along with Adam
Clarke, his brother-in-law, in Bible and Tract Societies
activities.

JOHN CAMPBELL (1766-1840). A schoolmate of Sir
Walter Scott in Edinburgh where he was born, Campbell was
a founder of the Edinburgh Tract Society in 1793 and also
an early advocate of Sunday Schools in Scotland. It is said
that he and James Haldane once established sixty Sunday
Schools in one week. At first an itinerant preacher, Campbell was later ordained to become in 1802 the Independent
minister at Kingsland Chapel in London. Two times (1812-
1814 and 1819-1821) he served the L. M. S. as an agent in
South Africa, traveling over four thousand miles in its service. He was a director of the L. M. S. from 1796 and of
the Tract Society from 1804.

ADAM CLARKE (1762?-1832). Born in Northern Ireland, Clarke was educated at Wesley's Kingswood School
near Bristol. In 1778 he became a Methodist passing through
the stages of local to regular preacher without much formal
education. He was appointed to his first circuit in Wiltshire
in 1782. A great admirer of Wesley, Clarke was also on
very friendly terms with a number of prominent Anglicans.
He was a popular preacher and three times (1806, 1814,
1822) filled the presidential chair at Conference. Clarke
was also a noted scholar of Oriental languages and could
read Hebrew, Syriac, Persian, Sanskrit, and several other
Eastern tongues with great facility. He was so valuable to
the Bible Society as a translator, that his denomination took
the unprecedented action of allowing him to stay permanently
in London. Clarke's most important literary achievement
was his commentary on the Bible in which he maintained,
among other things, that Eve was tempted by a baboon rather
than a snake and that Judas Iscariot was saved. Though he
maintained the divinity of Christ, he denied the eternal son-
ship.

WILLIAM BENGO COLLYER (1782-1854). Educated
at Homerton College in 1798, Collyer became minister of a
small Independent church in Peckham in 1800 which was subsequently rebuilt and reopened as Hanover Chapel in honor
of the monarch. A close friend of the royal family, he was
the Nonconformist Secretary of the London Society and a director of the L. M. S. from 1802 to 1829. In later years
he also occupied the pulpit at Salters' Hall.

WILLIAM DEALTRY (1775-1847). Dealtry was educated at Trinity College Cambridge where he became a Fellow in 1798. He served as a professor of mathematics at
the East India College in Haileybury between 1805 and 1813
later succeeding John Venn as the Rector of Clapham which
he served from 1813 to 1843. Dealtry was Chancellor of
the Diocese of Winchester from 1830 to 1835 and the Arch-
deacon of Surrey from 1845 until his death. He was an
advocate of the Bible Society and defended it from High
Church attacks in several important pamphlets.

GREVILLE EWING (1767-1841). Born in Edinburgh
and educated at the university there, Ewing was licensed in
1793 as assistant minister in one of Lady Glenorchy's chapels. He took an active part in the founding of the Edinburgh
Missionary Society becoming its first Secretary in 1796.
Ewing also served as editor of the Missionary Magazine.
In 1798, he resigned his position in the Scottish establishment to become minister of the first Independent church in
Glasgow, a position that he held until 1836. Ewing was tutor of the Glasgow Theological Academy from its foundation
in 1809 until 1836 and in 1812 helped to form the Congregational Union of Scotland.

JOHN EYRE (1754-1803). Eyre was born at Bodmin
in Cornwall and educated at the Bodmin Grammar School.
He was apprenticed a clothier in Tavistock when fifteen but
soon afterwards became an itinerant preacher in the town.
After receiving further education at Trevecca College, he
itinerated for Lady Huntingdon. In 1778 Eyre entered Emmanuel College Cambridge and was shortly afterwards ordained a priest by Bishop Thurlow. In 1799 he was Curate
of Weston, then in 1781 Curate to Cecil at Lewes before
moving to St. Giles Reading where he served under W. B.
Cadogan. From 1785 until his death, Eyre was minister at
Ram's Chapel in Homerton where he was involved in a number of pan-evangelical activities including the Village Itinerancy Society which he founded in 1796, the L. M. S. of

which he was a director and Secretary from 1795 to 1802,
and the Tract Society which he served as a director from
1799 until shortly before his death. He was also a founder
of the Evangelical Magazine and its editor from 1793 until
1802.

THOMAS FRY (1775-1860). Born in Somerset, Fry
was educated at Oriel College Oxford from which he graduated in 1796. He later became a Fellow of Lincoln College
Oxford before being elected in 1803 Chaplain of the Lock
Hospital in London in succession to Thomas Scott. Here
he met Legh Richmond, his life long friend. In 1804 he
was instituted on his own presentation Rector of Emberton
near Olney, but with the aid of a curate, continued his London chaplaincy. Fry was the Anglican Secretary of the London Society from 1810 until 1814. See J. Foster (ed.),
Alumni Oxonienses (1887).

WILLIAM GOODE (1762-1816). Goode was born in
Buckingham and received his education at the Newport Pagnell Academy and from Magdalen Hall Oxford from which he
graduated in 1784. He was Curate of Abbots Langley and
then Kings Langley in Herts before moving to London in
1786 as the Curate to William Romaine at St. Andrew's.
When Romaine died in 1795, Goode became the rector. He
was Secretary of the Society for the Relief of Poor Pious
Clergymen of the Establishment Residing in the Country in
1795 and a director of the R. T. S. from 1810 to 1814.

SAMUEL GREATHEED (d. 1823). Born in London,
Greatheed spent the early years of his life as a military
engineer in Canada before studying for the ministry at the
Newport Pagnell Academy in 1784. After a brief ministry
in Woburn, he returned to Newport Pagnell to become minister of the local Independent church and to teach at the
Academy. Greatheed was the founder of the Bedfordshire
Union of Christians in 1797 and the first Editor of the Eclectic Review in 1805. He was a director of the L. M. S.
from 1795 until 1821. See J. Morison, The Fathers and
Founders of the London Missionary Society (1839), II, 287.

JOSEPH JOHN GURNEY (1788-1847). Gurney was
born at Earlham Hall near Norwich, the son of John Gurney
the well known Quaker banker. He studied in Oxford under
the tuition of a private tutor though he never became a member of the University because he was a Dissenter. In 1818
he was called to be a minister among the Friends and com-

menced his evangelical activities. Gurney was involved
in prison reform with his sister Elizabeth Fry and in the
anti-slavery movement with Granville Sharp and William Wilberforce. On a tour of the United States many years later,
he was invited to speak before the House of Representatives
after which he was greeted by President Van Buren. A director of the Tract Society from 1829, Gurney was perhaps
best known in evangelical circles for his patronage of the
Bible Society.

ROBERT HALDANE (1764-1842). Born in London of
wealthy parents, Haldane began his education at the University of Edinburgh, but failing to complete his course of study,
went to sea as a midshipman in the navy. After his tour of
duty was over, he came under the influence of David Bogue
who convinced him to return to the university to finish his
theological studies, but after two sessions at Edinburgh followed by a "grand tour" of the Continent, he settled down
to the life of a country gentleman on his ancestral estate at
Airthrey. With the outbreak of Revolution in France, Haldane, along with Bogue and several other evangelicals, made
some unfortunate political statements which discredited him
in the eyes of Evangelical churchmen and ruined his bid in
1796 to establish a mission in India under the auspices of
the East India Company. In 1799, Haldane left the Church
of Scotland to become an Independent and to organize with
his brother James, chapels on the Whitefieldite model
throughout Scotland. To provide pastors for his chapels,
he founded a seminary which he maintained at his own expense. In 1808, Haldane became a Baptist precipitating a
bitter controversy between himself and his former colleague
Greville Ewing several years later. In 1816, he moved to
Geneva where he launched an evangelical campaign on the
Continent largely aimed against the Socinians. The next
year he moved to Montauban where, under Bible Society
auspices, he published at his own expense, an edition of
the Bible in French. Haldane returned to Scotland and his
new estate at Auchingray Lanarkshire in 1819 and played a
key role in both the Apocrypha and Tests Controversies at
the Bible Society. He was a director of the L.M.S. from
1796 to 1804.

ROBERT HALL (1764-1831). Hall was born at Arnes-
by the youngest of fourteen children. A precocious youth, it
was said that before he was nine, he had written several
hymns and that at eleven he preached at a religious meeting in the house of Beeby Wallis of Kettering. In 1776, Hall

studied at Northampton under the tuition of John Collett Ryland entering two years later the Baptist Academy in Bristol
then under the supervision of Caleb Evans. He was subsequently set apart for the ministry in 1780 but continued his
education at Kings College Aberdeen from which he graduated in 1784. One year later he was back in Bristol as
Evan's assistant at Broadmead Chapel but resigned in 1790
to succeed Robert Robinson in Cambridge. Because of bad
health (reported to be touches of insanity that was treated
with opium), Hall removed to Harvey Lane Baptist meeting
in Leicester in 1807 where ten years later he preached his
famous sermon on the death of Princess Charlotte. In 1826
he moved once again to Bristol to succeed John Ryland at
Broadmead where he died five years later of heart disease.
Hall, perhaps one of the most catholic-minded Baptists, patronized the London Society, Bible Society and R.T.S.

WILLIAM ALERS-HANKEY (d. 1859). Educated at
the University of Edinburgh from which he graduated in 1789,
Alers-Hankey moved to London to establish a banking house
on Fenchurch Street. A member of the Stepney Independent
Church of which he was a deacon in 1801, he was also actively engaged in several pan-evangelical enterprises. He
was a director of the L.M.S. from 1801 to 1828 serving as
its Secretary after 1816. He was chairman of the Committee for Jewish Affairs but later patronized the London Society after its separation in 1809 forced the L.M.S. to dis-
continue its mission to the Jews. A director of the Tract
Society from 1801 to 1813, Alers-Hankey also attended the
founding meeting of the Bible Society. See J. Kennedy, A
Sermon Preached on Occasion of the Death of William Alers-
Hankey (1859).

JOSEPH HARDCASTLE (1752-1819). A merchant by
profession, Hardcastle was a member of the Independent
chapel at Bury Street in London though he often communi-
cated in the Church of England. He was a friend of Clarkson and the Anti-Slavery Society often met at "Hatcham" his
country home. Hardcastle was a close friend of many Clapham Sect Evangelicals, a position which earned him an appointment in the Sierra Leone Company as one of the only
non-Anglican directors. The Missionary, Tract and Bible
Societies, of which he was a director, all met for a time
at his business premises in London. Hardcastle was Treasurer of the L.M.S. and the Village Itinerancy Society. See
J. Morison, Fathers and Founders, I, 295 ff.

THOMAS HAWEIS (1734-1820). Haweis was born in

Redruth Cornwall and educated at the Truro Grammar School.
His university career was spent first at Christ Church Oxford and then Magdalen Hall from which he graduated in 1755.
In 1757 he was appointed Chaplain to the Earl of Peterbor-
ough and Curate of St. Mary Magdalen Oxford but was removed from the latter because of his Methodist sympathies,
He was subsequently Martin Madan's assistant at the Lock
Chapel in London and then from 1764 until his death, Rector
of Aldwinckle in Northamptonshire. Haweis was also Chaplain to the Countess of Huntingdon and a Trustee of her connexion from 1791. He was a founding father of the L.M.S.
and a director from 1795 to 1819.

ROBERT HAWKER (1753-1827). Born in Exeter, the
son of a surgeon, Hawker became an assistant surgeon in
the Royal Marines after studying medicine. In 1778 he entered Magdalen Hall Oxford becoming the same year the Curate of St. Martin near Looe in Cornwall and then in 1784,
Vicar of Charles near Plymouth after a period there as
curate to John Bedford. In 1802, Hawker founded the Great
Western Society for Dispersing Tracts among the Poor but
he was also a patron of the Tract Society from its founding
until about 1808. Hawker was also a director of the L.M.S.
from 1802 to 1808.

ROWLAND HILL (1744-1833). Educated at Eton and
St. John's College Cambridge from which he graduated with
honors in 1769, Hill was refused ordination by six bishops
in succession before he was finally ordained in 1773 to dea-
cons's orders as Curate of Kingston in Somerset. But he
never became a priest. An itinerant preacher much of his
life, Surrey Chapel was erected for him in 1783 where he
remained until his death. Hill was a proponent of Sunday
Schools, thirteen of which were connected with his chapel.
He was a director of the L.M.S. from 1795 and of the
R.T.S. from 1799 to 1804.

JOSEPH HUGHES (1769-1835). Hughes was educated
at Aberdeen University where he founded the first Sunday
School in the district. For a time a tutor at the Baptist
College in Bristol, he subsequently moved to London as the
Baptist pastor in Battersea where he was close friends with
many Clapham Sect Evangelicals. Hughes was Secretary
of both the Tract and Bible Societies. See J. Leifchild,
Memoir of the Late Rev. J. Hughes (1835).

WILLIAM JAY (1769-1853). A pupil of Cornelius

Winter of Marlborough, Jay, at the tender age of nineteen, preached a series of discourses for Rowland Hill at Surrey Chapel in 1788 which brought him some fame. For a time he was a minister at Christian Malford near Chippenham and at Hotwells where he officiated in Lady Maxwell's Hope Chapel, but moved in 1791 to Bath where he was ordained the Independent minister of Argyle Chapel. Jay remained in Bath for the rest of his life though for a time he supplied Surrey Chapel six weeks during the year. He was a director of the L. M. S. from 1812.

JOHN LOVE (1757-1825). Educated at the University of Glasgow, Love served as a minister in Paisley, Rutherglen, and Greenock before accepting a call to the Artillery Street Presbyterian chapel in London. He was subsequently one of the first secretaries of the L. M. S. before moving back to Scotland to serve as minister of the Clyde Street chapel in Anderston in 1800. Love was later Secretary of the Glasgow Missionary Society.

CHARLES MIDDLETON, LORD BARHAM (1726-1813). Middleton was born in Leith Scotland. A sailor by profession, he won many honors while the captain of several warships. In 1778 he was appointed comptroller of the Navy, an office he held until 1790. He was created a Baronet in 1781, and after being elected an M. P. for Rochester, was promoted to the rank of Rear Admiral in 1787, Vice Admiral in 1793 and Admiral in 1795. From 1794 to 1795, Middleton was one of the Lords Commissioners of the Admiralty under the Earl of Chatham. After the resignation in 1805 of Lord Melville, a near relative, he was appointed First Lord of the Admiralty and raised to a peerage. Lord Barham was second President of the London Society from 1810 to 1811.

SAMUEL MILLS. Mills was a leather merchant who resided at Russell Square in London. He subsequently sold his business to Robert Steven. Mills was the only Anglican founder of the R. T. S. which he served as director from 1799 to 1809. He was also a founding father of the Bible Society and drafted its first plan in 1803 when it was being discussed at the Tract Society. In 1810, he was elected a director of the L. M. S. See J. Morison, Fathers and Founders, II, 577.

WILLIAM NEWMAN (1773-1837). Newman was born in Enfield Middlesex. A student of John Collett Ryland, he subsequently became pastor of the Baptist church at Old Ford

in 1794 and later, the first theological tutor at the Stepney
College. A founding father of the R.T.S., Newman served
as a director from 1799 to 1812. See G. Pritchard, Memoir of the Rev. Wm. Newman (1837).

JOHN OWEN (1766-1822). A graduate of Corpus
Christi College Cambridge in 1788, Owen was appointed
Curate of Fulham in Middlesex by Bishop Porteus in 1795
after a tour on the Continent which, significantly, brought
him into contact with religious conditions in revolutionary
France. He later served as Rector of Pagleshan in Es-
sex in 1808 afterwards becoming minister of the Park Street
Chapel in Chelsea when Bishop Randolph deprived him of
his living for being Secretary of the Bible Society.

LEGH RICHMOND (1772-1827). Richmond was born
in Liverpool and educated at Trinity College Cambridge
from which he graduated in 1794. After a short residence
in Cambridge, he was ordained Curate of Brading and Yaverland on the Isle of Wight where, shortly afterwards, he
was converted to evangelical principles by reading Wilberforce's Practical View. It was also here that Richmond
collected material for his famous Dairyman's Daughter which
was subsequently published by the R.T.S. In 1805, Richmond was appointed a chaplain of the Lock Hospital in London where he became close friends with Thomas Fry, future Secretary of the London Society. He then moved to
Bedfordshire as Rector of Turvey in succession to Erasmus
Middleton and stayed there until his death. Richmond was
the first Anglican Secretary of the R.T.S.

JOHN SHORE, LORD TEIGNMOUTH (1751-1834). Educated at Harrow, Shore went to India in 1768 as a writer
in the East India Company. After holding several important
offices, he gained the confidence of Lord Hastings and subsequently became in 1793 the Governor General. In 1798
he moved back to England where he was created Baron
Teignmouth. Teignmouth was a member of the Board of
Control and Privy Council, but he devoted most of his time
to the Bible Society which he served as President. A recognized scholar of Persian and the Indian dialects, Teignmouth made several important contributions to Bible Society
translations.

WILLIAM SHRUBSOLE (1759-1829). Apprenticed to
a shipwright in Sheerness, Shrubsole came to London in
1785 as a clerk in the Bank of England. He subsequently

became Secretary of the Committee of the Treasury.   An
occasional communicant at Blackfriar's parish church, Shrubsole became a member of Whitefield's Tabernacle in 1791
where he was close friends with Matthew Wilks, the minister.   He was a director of the L. M. S. from 1798 to 1829
serving as one of its secretaries, and a director of the
Tract Society from 1800 to 1819.

    RICHARD WALDO SIBTHORP (1792-1879).   Born at
Canwick Hall near Lincoln, the son of Colonel Humphrey
Waldo Sibthorp, M. P. for Lincoln, Richard was educated
at the Westminster School and Magdalen College Oxford.
Attracted from youth to the Roman faith, he spent a university term in Wolverhampton with Bishop Milner with the
intention of entering its communion, but he was forcibly
prevented from doing this by his family who sent him back
to Oxford.   After graduating in 1813, Sibthorp was appointed
Curate of Waddington and Harmston in Lincolnshire and
three years later, Curate to John Scott at St. Mary's Hull.
In 1818 he was elected Fellow of his college and one year
later received the living at Tattersall in Lincolnshire.   In
1825 Sibthorp was appointed minister of Percy Chapel in
London which he served simultaneously with an evening lec-
tureship at St. John's Chapel Bedford Row then under the
ministration of Baptist Noel.   In 1829 he gave up his connection with the London chapels to reside on his Fellowship
at Magdalen College Oxford.   From then until 1841 he was
also the incumbent at St. James' Church Ryde on the Isle
of Wight.   Between 1841 and his death, Sibthorp entered the
Roman Church twice: the first time in 1841 as a priest at
the Cathedral Church of St. Chad in Birmingham and the second
time in 1865 at the Cathedral of St. Barnabas in Nottingham.
However he was buried in Lincoln Cathedral according to
the rites of the Church of England.   Sibthorp was an agent
for the Bible Society following the Apocrypha Controversy
and inspected the Continental societies.   He was also Secretary of the Tract Society in succession to Legh Richmond.

    C. F. STEINKOPF (1773-1859).   Born at Ludwigs-
burg in Germany, Steinkopf was educated at the Evangelical
Theological Seminary at Tübingen which he entered in 1790.
In 1795, he was appointed Secretary of the Christian Society
in Basel, which was a central clearing house for a number
of evangelical enterprises.   In 1801, Steinkopf came to London as Pastor of the German Lutheran congregation assem-
bling in the Savoy.   He was engaged in many evangelical activities and at one time served simultaneously as the Foreign

Secretary of the Missionary, Tract and Bible Societies.
See W. Canton, Bible Society Hist. I, 43.

ROBERT STEVEN (1754-1827). Steven was born in
Glasgow where he attended the university for a time before
joining his father's business as a tanner. In 1775 he moved
to London where he established his own leather business after buying the factory owned by Samuel Mills, his future
colleague in a number of pan-evangelical activities. Steven
was brought to evangelical principles under the ministry of
James Knight, the Independent pastor at Collier's Rent. He
then became a member of George Clayton's Independent chapel at Walworth. Steven was an intimate friend of a number
of Evangelicals including Richard Cecil, John Newton and
Thomas Scott and knew most of the prominent evangelical
Nonconformists of the day. A founder of the Hibernian Society, he was also involved in the L. M. S. of which he was
a director from 1795 to 1825, and the R. T. S. which he
served in a similar capacity from 1804 to 1818. Steven
was also a frequent agent of the Bible Society especially
during the Apocrypha Controversy. See J. Morison, Founders and Fathers, II, 575.

CHRISTOPHER SUNDIUS (d. 1835). Sundius was born
at Allerum in Sweden, the son of the rector of the local
parish church. After a period of study at the University
of Lund, he entered the naval college at Carlskrona as a
naval cadet. During the War of American Independence,
Sundius fought on the British side but resigned from the
Swedish navy in 1780 when ordered to transfer his services
to France in that country's war against Britain. He subsequently became a British citizen and served as the Government Translator to the Board of the Admiralty, a position
he held until 1829 while engaged in a number of private com-
mercial ventures. Sundius was converted by Wesley around
1780 and became a Wesleyan shortly afterwards. He later
married Jane Vazeille, Wesley's step-granddaughter and
played a very influential role in the Methodist Conference.
A director of the L. M. S. from 1797 to 1802 and of the
R. T. S. from 1801 to 1806, Sundius was also present at the
founding meetings of the Bible Society in 1804 and later received an appointment as Honorary Governor for Life. See
Wesleyan Methodist Magazine, March 1904, 215 f.

JOSEPH TARN (1766-1837). A convert of Cecil, Tarn
was a lay trustee of the Spa Fields Chapel and numbered
himself a Calvinistic Methodist. He was a founder in 1800

of the Society for Distributing Evangelical Tracts Gratis which merged that year with the R.T.S. Tarn was the Accountant of the Bible Society and its Assistant Secretary from 1804 until his death. He was also a director of the Tract Society from 1800 to 1820 and of the L.M.S. from 1802. When he moved to Islington, Tarn joined the undenominational Union Chapel where he served as a deacon. See E.M. May 1837, 212 f.

JOHN TOWNSEND (1757-1826). Townsend was educated at Christ's Hospital in London and Trevecca College. In 1781 he was ordained pastor of the Independent Church at Kingston in Surrey before moving to Bermondsey where, with the assistance of H. C. Mason, the local rector, he founded the London Asylum for the Deaf and Dumb in 1792. Townsend was a director of the L.M.S. from 1796 to 1825 and of the R.T.S. from 1800 to 1819.

ALEXANDER WAUGH (1754-1827). Waugh was born at East Gordon in Berwickshire and educated at the Universities of Edinburgh and Aberdeen. Minister of the parish church at Melrose in 1780, he received a call to the Wells Street Congregational Chapel in London two years later. Waugh was a director of the L.M.S. from 1795 to 1827 and of the R.T.S. in 1799.

MATTHEW WILKS (1746-1828). Born in Gibraltar, the son of an army officer, Wilks was converted to evangelical principles by the Rev. W. Percy, the Rector of Bromwich. After receiving his theological training at Trevecca College, he accepted a call to Whitefield's Tabernacle in London. He was a founder of many evangelical enterprises including the Evangelical Magazine, the catholic principle of which was adopted at his suggestion. Wilks was a director of the L.M.S. from 1795 to 1828 and of the R.T.S. from 1799 to 1807.

BASIL WOODD (1760-1831). Woodd was born at Richmond in Surrey and educated at Trinity College Oxford from which he graduated in 1783. He was Lecturer at St. Peter's Cornhill in 1784 and Morning Preacher at Bentinck Chapel one year later. Bentinck was a proprietory chapel and Woodd purchased its lease in 1793. In 1808 he was instituted Rector of Drayton Beauchamp in Buckinghamshire. A patron of the Bible Society, he was Secretary of the London Society in succession to Thomas Fry.

Aikman, John 142
Albury Conferences 143f., 205
Alers-Hankey, William 73, 211
Allen, Richard 168
American Society for Ameliorating the Condition of the Jews 190
Amyraut, Moyse 16
Anderson, Christopher 142
Anglicans see Church of England
Antiburghers 54, 155
Antinomianism 6, 162
Apocrypha see Bibles
Apocrypha Controversy see British and Foreign Bible Society
Arminian Methodists see Methodists
Arnold, Thomas 200
Aspland, Robert 132
Association for Promoting Rationality Toward the Animal Creation 195
Assurance 8, 14
Atkinson, Miles 7
Atonement, Limited 17
Augustine 15

Baker's Coffee House 43
Bala (Wales) 80ff.
Ball, John 13, 176
Banwell, George 66
Baptism 18f., 63, 78
Baptist Academy (Bristol) 211f.
Baptist Magazine 62, 200
Baptist Missionary Society 40f., 46, 48f., 61-64

Baptist Translation Society 140
Baptist Union 73, 111, 131, 145, 199
Baptist, General 90, 96
Baptists, Particular 9, 14, 18f., 23, 32, 48f., 57, 61-64, 74, 81, 130, 150f., 166, 169, 178, 181, 195, 197, 201
  Chapels: Broadmead (Bristol) 151, 178, 211; Harvey Lane (Leicester) 178, 211; Old Ford (Middlesex) 151, 213; Park Street (Nottingham) 48
Baptizo Controversy see British and Foreign Bible Society
Barham, Lord see Charles Middleton
Bathurst, Bishop 25
Battersea (London) 86, 94
Baxter, Richard 157, 203
Bedford, John 162, 212
Bedfordshire Union of Christians 32, 150, 195, 198, 209
Beidenback, Henry 48
Belsham, Thomas 132
Bennett, James 58, 168, 196
Berridge, John 12f.
Berry, Joseph 65, 76
Best, Geoffrey 16
Bethnal Green (London) 183
Bibles
  Apocrypha 114, 124ff.
  Bengalese 140
  Chinese 113
  General 82

Marginal Reference 112
Metrical Psalms 112f.,
    124f.
Montauban 124f., 142, 210
Welsh 80ff., 99f.
Bible Society see British and
    Foreign Bible Society
Bickersteth, Edward 162, 165,
    205
Biddulph, Thomas 70, 77, 89,
    141, 170, 205f.
Binney, Thomas 197
Blackburn 160
Blacow, Richard 71
Bogue, David 27, 29, 42ff.,
    49, 57, 66, 72, 153f.,
    168, 176f., 196, 198,
    200, 206, 210
Book of Common Prayer 105ff.,
    108f., 120
Book Society see Society for
    Promoting Religious Knowl-
    edge
Bowyer, Edward 119
Bradford, William 154
Brandram, Andrew 127f., 136,
    139, 143, 206
Bristol Baptist College 86
British and Foreign Bible Soci-
    ety 24, 54, 80-146, 149,
    151f., 153, 156, 161,
    168, 171, 194f., 197,
    200, 202f., 205ff.
    Activities (domestic and inter-
        denominational) 91ff.
    Apocrypha Controversy 111,
        124-131, 140, 161, 164,
        194, 200, 210, 215, 216
    Baptizo Controversy 140
    Church Order, Controversy
        over 116ff.
    Denominational Patronage
        84f., 87f., 89ff.
    Founding 80ff.
    Fundamental Principle 84,
        87, 101, 111f., 127, 130,
        134, 139
    High Church accusations
        against 102ff.
    Internal divisions 111f.
    Ladies Bible Associations,
        Controversy over 92,
        114f.

Metric Psalm Controversy
    112ff., 125
Sackville Street Provisional
    Committee 138f.
SPCK, Controversy with
    99ff., 105f.
Test Controversy 89, 107,
    112, 131-140, 161, 164,
    166f., 194, 200, 211
Welsh Bible Controversy
    99ff.
British and Foreign Bible So-
    ciety Auxiliaries
    Ayrshire 141
    Birmingham 114
    Barnstable 110
    Bristol 112
    Chatham 117
    Colchester 103f.
    Derby 118, 133
    Edinburgh see Edinburgh
        Bible Society
    Glasgow see Glasgow Bible
        Society
    Gurnsey 133
    Hackney 104
    Haddington 141
    Harleston 108
    Hastings 133f.
    Henley Ladies 115
    Hereford 133
    Hertford Ladies 114
    Hibernian see Hibernian
        Bible Society
    Leith 141
    Newcastle 141
    Norwich 94, 96
    Reading 91
    Rugby 133f.
    Shrewsbury 116
    Southwark 107, 115
    Stafford 96
    Sunderland 117
    Surrey 141
    Tavistock 92
    Tunstall 117f.
    Wallingford 115
    Walsal 110
    Workington 117
    Yeovill 110
British and Foreign Temper-
    ance Society 195
British and Foreign Unitarian

Association 132
British Society for Promoting
the Religious Principles of
the Reformation 195
Broadbelt, George C. 60
Brooke, Henry 122
Brooksbank, Joseph 13, 57
Brothers, Richard 29
Brown, David 142
Brown, Ford K. 58, 92, 96
Bunting, Jabez 68, 76
Bunyan, John 19
Burder, George 25, 41, 73, 113,
149f., 156f., 168, 206
Burder, John 167
Burgess, Thomas 89, 100
Burke, Edmund 102
Burn, Edward 117
Butterworth, Joseph 68, 77,
166, 207

Cadogan, W. B. 42, 208
Calthorpe, Lord 179
Calvin, John 16, 154
Calvinism
High (Hyper) 17, 44, 161ff.
Moderate 16ff., 50, 199
Calvinistic Controversy 2, 6,
9, 14, 16, 35, 49f.
Calvinistic Methodists see
Methodists
Cambridge University see University
of Cambridge
Cambridge University Press
100f., 105
Cameron, John 16
Campbell, John 166, 207
Capetown South Africa 53
Carey, William 41f., 49, 55, 61f.
Cato Street Conspiracy 154
Cecil, Richard 12, 42, 89,
157, 170, 208, 216
Cecil, William 141
Charity School Movement 25
Charles I 17
Charles, Thomas 26, 80ff.,
99ff., 170
Charlotte, Princess 211
Chartism 197
Cherokee Indians 40
Christian Guardian 206
Christian Observer 32

Christian Society of Basil 215
Christian Tract Society 172
Church of England (Evangelical)
3f., 6ff., 9, 12, 14ff.,
32f., 50ff., 59, 68-71,
82, 102, 115, 117, 129,
131ff., 137f., 151ff.,
153, 178f., 185f., 187,
201, 203
Chapels:
All Saints (Aldwinckle) 12,
42, 51, 57
Bentinck Chapel (London)
217
Christ Church (Hull) 139
Ely Episcopal Chapel (London)
182
Holy Trinity (Cambridge)
85, 179
Park Street Episcopal Chapel
(Chelsea) 214
Percy Chapel (London) 167,
215
St. Ann's Blackfriars and
St. Andrews (London)
13, 70, 152, 209, 215
St. Brides (London) 70
St. Clement Dane (London)
152
St. Giles (Reading) 208
St. James (Bristol) 206
St. Johns Chapel (London)
105, 138f., 215
St. Leonards (London) 70
St. Marks (Liverpool) 71
St. Martin's (Cornwall)
162, 212
St. Mary Magdalen (Oxford)
51f., 212
St. Mary Woolnoth (London)
86
St. Mary's (Birmingham)
117
St. Mary's (Leicester) 27,
180
St. Mary's (Hull) 215
St. Mary's (Liverpool) 71
St. Mary's (Wallingford) 60
St. Michael's (Macclesfield)
12
St. Peters (Cornhill) 217
St. Saviours (London) 51,
70

Wheler Episcopal Chapel
(London) 205
Church Order 3, 6f., 12,
52f., 70, 102, 105,
108f., 116f., 179, 186,
201
Itinerating 7f.
Church of England (High
Church) 83, 99ff. 105ff.,
110f., 115, 131f., 161,
181f., 197f., 203
Church of Scotland 11
Church Missionary Society 48,
51f., 60, 68-71, 74, 87,
95, 151, 175, 205
Auxiliaries: Bristol 77;
Cork 71
Church's Ministry Among the
Jews 188; see also Lon-
don Society for Promoting
Christianity Amongst the
Jews
Clapham (London) 86, 94
Clapham Sect 86, 128, 202,
211f.
Clarke, Adam 85, 89, 162,
207
Clarke, Edward D. 90, 104
Clayton, George 216
Clayton, John 166, 197
Cobbett, William 157
Cockle, William 145f.
Coke, Thomas 25, 29f., 49,
59, 64ff., 76
Coleman, John Nobel 110
Collins, W. E. 20
Collison, George 66, 76
Collyer, William Bengo 179,
186, 188, 208
Colombo, Ceylon 65
Colquhoun, Patrick 36
Communion 18f., 31, 62
Congregational Council for
World Missions 74; see
also London Missionary
Society
Congregational Union (England)
73, 111, 131, 145, 200
Congregational Union (Scot-
land) 208
Congregationalists 11, 13,
61, 72-74, 130, 164ff.,
186, 197, 199f., 201

Chapels:
Argyle Chapel (Bath) 64,
213
Barbican (London) 56
Bermondsey (London) 47
Bury Street (London) 211
Cannon Street (Manchester)
57
Carr's Lane (Birmingham)
57
Collier's Rent (Southwark)
56, 216
Fetter Lane (London) 149,
206
George Yard (Hammersmith)
178
Gosport (Hampshire) 42
Haberdasher's Hall (London)
54, 57
Hanover Chapel (Peckham)
179, 208
Holywell Mount (London) 56
King's Weigh House (London)
197
Kingsland Chapel (London)
207
Kingston (Surrey) 217
Old White Chapel (Leeds)
68
Ram's Chapel (Homerton)
208
Stepney (London) 211
Walworth Chapel (Dorset)
216
Well's Street (London) 42,
217
West Orchard (Coventry)
206
Conversion, Instantaneous 8
Conybeare, William 115
Cook, James 40
Cooper, Edward 96
Cooper, William 54, 96
Cope, Richard 196
Corresponding Society 107
Countess of Huntingdon's Con-
nexion see Lady Hunting-
don's Connexion
Coventry 25, 149, 206
Cowie, George 57
Craig, Edward 126, 130
Cran, George 62
Cranmer, Thomas 154

Crawford and Lindsay, Earl of
    179
Crosse, John 28
Cunningham, John W. 104ff.
Curwen, Spedding 117, 163

Dale, R. W. 199
Dampier, John 143
Daubeny, Charles 102, 108f.
Davenant, John 16
Dealtry, William 89f., 103f.,
    108, 208
Denison, William J. 167
Denominationalism 199f.
Des Granges, August 62
Devon Union 195
Disestablishment 8, 118, 132,
    196
Dissenter's Library (London) 42
Dissenting Deputies 118, 131f.
Dobbin, Orlando 48
Doddridge, Philip 23, 157
Dore, James 26
Dort, Synod of 16
Douglas, Archibald 13
Drummond, A. L. 143
Drummond, Henry 137f., 141,
    143, 146
Dudley, Charles 107, 114f.,
    122

Earlham 94
East India College (Haileybury)
    103, 208
East India Company 87, 210,
    214
Eccles, William 68
Eclectic Review 130, 209
Eclectic Society 33, 52
Ecumenical Movement 163f.,
    201-203
Edinburgh Bible Society 113f.,
    127ff., 139, 142
Edinburgh Missionary Society
    208
Edinburgh Tract Society 207
Edward, David 80f.
Edwards, Jonathan 5, 23,
    40
Eimeo (Society Islands) 53
Election, Particular 17

Elland Society 8
Emancipation, Catholic see
    Roman Catholic Emancipa-
    tion
English Calvinistic Methodists
    see Methodists
Episcopalians, Scottish 130
Erskine, John 23
Erskine, Thomas 146
Evangelical Alliance 140,
    200f., 205
Evangelical Magazine 14, 56,
    62, 67, 149, 169, 196,
    199, 206, 209, 217
Evangelical Theological Sem-
    inary (Tübingen) 215
Evangelical Tract Society see
    Society for Distributing
    Evangelical Tracts Gratis
Evangelicals see Church of
    England, Evangelical
Evans, Caleb 211
Ewing, Greville 142, 208, 210
Exeter Hall (London) 136, 138
Experience, Christian 14f., 31
Eyre, John (of Homerton) 12,
    14, 42ff., 50, 59, 149,
    152, 195, 208f.
Eyre, John (the missionary)
    54
Eyre, Thomas 14

Fancourt, William 152
Farnham, Lady 168
Farrish, William 141
Fetter Lane (London) 5
Fisher, John 89
Fisher, R. B. 115
Fletcher, Alexander 178
Fletcher, Irene 58
Fletcher, John 41, 206
Fletcher, Joseph 160
Foot, Lundy 136
Fox, Joseph 179
Fox, William 25
France 29f.
French Revolution 27f., 40,
    52, 70
Frey, Joseph Samuel 175ff.,
    184, 186, 190
Fry, Elizabeth 210
Fry, Thomas 179f., 209, 214

Fuller, Andrew 17, 29f., 33,
    49, 62f., 64, 74f., 178

Gambier, Lord 109
Gaskin, George 100
German Bible Society 90, 112
Gisborne, Thomas 89, 109
Glasgow, Presbytery of 128
Glasgow Bible Society 128,
    130, 142
Glasgow Missionary Society
    213
Glasgow Theological Academy
    208
Glenorchy, Lady 208
Goodall, Norman 55
Goode, John 13f.
Goode, William 13f., 152,
    209
Goodenough, Samuel 119
Gordon, J. E. 136, 138f.
Gordon, James F. 126
Gospel Tract Society 163ff.,
    172
Gosport Academy 42, 66,
    206
Gossner, Johann 90
Grace, Prevenient 17
Grant, Charles 89
Gray, Robert 117
Great Namaqualand (Africa)
    53, 64
Great Western Society for Dis-
    tributing Tracts 162,
    212
Greatheed, Samuel 30f., 43f.,
    48ff., 58, 65, 150, 195,
    200, 202, 209f.
Greenland 40
Gregory, Olinthus 114
Griffin, John 73
Grimshaw, William 7, 12
Gurney, John 209
Gurney, Joseph John 92, 94,
    96, 116, 139, 209f.
Gurney, William 152

Hackney College 76
Haldane, James Alexander
    138f., 142, 146, 210
Haldane, Robert 13, 27,

    124f., 132ff., 135, 138f.,
    140, 142, 210
Halevy, Elie 94
Hall, Robert 18, 30, 62, 178,
    210f.
Hamilton, George 54
Hardcastle, Joseph 211
Hare, August 94
Harris, Howell 11
Hastings, Lord 214
Haweis, Thomas 12f., 24,
    42f., 47, 51f., 54, 57,
    62, 75, 165f., 200, 211f.
Hawker, Robert 12, 26, 124f.,
    162ff., 170, 199, 212
Henderson, Ebenezer 142
Henderson, Ian 203
Hervey, James 157
Hibernian Bible Society 105,
    216
Highfield, George 66
Hill, Rowland 6, 12f., 26,
    43, 50f., 52, 83, 150,
    152, 166, 169f., 212f.
Hinton, James 13, 178
Hirschel, Solomon 188
Home Missionary Society 74
Homerton College 208
Horne, Melville 41f., 46f.,
    51, 57
Howard, Luke 136, 171
Hughes, David 90
Hughes, Joseph 74, 86f., 94,
    117, 134, 150, 152, 167f.,
    170, 212
Hunt, John 66
Hunt, Legh 67
Huntingdon, Selina Countess of
    6, 10, 24, 212; see also
    Lady Huntingdon's Con-
    nexion
Hypercalvinism see Calvinism

Illuminati 28, 107
Independents see Congrega-
    tionalists
Inglis, R. H. 173, 197
Innes, William 142
Instructor 183
Ireland 92, 97, 105
Irving, Edward 129, 133, 137,
    143, 205

Isle of Wight 153f., 214
Israel 184
Ivimey, Joseph 166

Jacobinism 27f., 40, 107,
    109, 115, 152
Jamaica (West Indies) 65
James, John Angell 73
Jane, Joseph 52
Janicke, Father 175
Jay, William 13, 50, 63, 97,
    162, 189, 212f.
Jefferson, John 54
Jerram, Charles 92
Jewish Emancipation 190
Jewish Repository 183
Jews Society see London So-
    ciety for Promoting Chris-
    tianity Amongst the Jews
Johnson, Robert 65f.
Jones, David 60
Jones, Mary 80f.
Jones, Thomas (of Creaton)
    83
Jones, Thomas (of Denbigh)
    110
Jowett, J. (of Sleaford) 145f.
Judaism, British 174-191
    Great London Synagogue 188
Justification 15

Kent, Duke of 179
King, John 139
Kingswood School 207
Knight, James 56, 216
Knight, Joel Abraham 56
Knight, Titus 56
Knill, Richard 65
Knox, Alexander 93

Lady Huntingdon's Connexion
    10f., 13, 40, 42, 51,
    72, 212
Lambert, George 63, 169
Langley, John 116
Laqueur, Thomas 34f.
Latimer, Hugh 154
Law, George Henry 105
Leeds 67f.
Leifchild, John 94

Lively, R. L. 144
Llanfihangel y Pennant (Wales)
    80
Lloyds of London 88
Lock Hospital 52, 125, 162,
    209, 214
London Asylum for the Deaf
    and Dumb 217
London Board of Congregational
    Ministers 74, 165ff.
London Missionary Society 10,
    23, 25, 28, 40-78, 81,
    84f., 93, 149f., 151f.,
    156, 163, 175-178, 181,
    185f., 194f., 198f., 201f.,
    203, 205ff.
    Activities (domestic and in-
        terdenominational) 53ff.
    Committee for Jewish Af-
        fairs 176ff.
    Denominational Patronage 44ff.
    Evolution into a Congrega-
        tional Mission 71f.
    External relations with other
        missionary societies: Bap-
        tist Missionary Society
        61-64; Church Missionary
        Society 68-71; Wesleyan
        Methodist Missionary So-
        ciety 64-68
    Founding 40ff.
    Fundamental Principle 45f.,
        55, 74, 77f., 84
    Jews Chapel 181f., 186f.
    London Society for Promoting
        Christianity Amongst the
        Jews, Founding of 175ff.
    Mission ship "Duff" 58, 63,
        69
    Religious Tract Society,
        Founding of 150
    Sheffield Auxiliary 74
London Secretaries Association
    64, 68f., 75
London Society for Promoting
    Christianity Amongst the
    Jews 29, 54, 168, 174-
    191, 194f., 201, 203,
    205ff.
    Activities (domestic and in-
        terdenominational) 182f.
    Denominational Patronage 178f.
    Evolution into an Anglican

Mission 185ff.
Founding 174ff.
French Church (Spitalfields)
181
Fundamental Principle 179ff.
Olney Auxiliary 180
Palestine Place (London)
183, 187
London Society for Visiting the
Sick and Distressed 117
London Tavern 88, 160
Love, John 42, 47, 213
Luddite Riots 110
Luther, Martin 154
Lutherans 4, 69, 94, 186,
215
Savoy Lutheran Chapel (Lon-
don) 69, 85
Lutterworth Press 168

Macaulay, Zachary 89, 152,
170
Macbride, J. D. 134f.
McGavin, William 155f.
Madan, Martin 212
Maltby, Edward 104f.
Mann, Isaac 74
Marsden, Samuel 69
Marsh, Herbert 104f., 109,
120
Marsh, William 179
Marshman, J. C. 75
Mary, Queen 167
Mason, H. C. 217
Mason, John M. 31
Maxwell, Lady 213
Medley, Samuel 13
Melanchthon, Philipp 154
Methodist Missionary Society
see Wesleyan Methodist
Missionary Society
Methodists, English Calvinistic
5f., 11, 18, 72, 201
Methodists, Welsh Calvinistic
11, 82
Methodists, Wesleyan 5f.,
10, 18, 24, 32, 40, 45,
47f., 49ff., 57, 59f.,
64-68, 74, 82, 89, 135,
151f., 164, 166, 178,
181, 197, 201, 216
Chapels:

City Road 50
Foundery 5
Queen Street 68
Metrical Psalms see Bibles
Middleton, Charles 179, 213
Middleton, Erasmus 214
Millennialism 4, 28-30, 40
and the Jews 29, 36, 174f.,
185
Mills, Samuel 152, 213, 216
Milne, William 113
Milner, George 141
Milner, John 215
Milner, Joseph 4f., 14f.,
104, 165, 200
Milnerian Controversy see
Religious Tract Society
Missionary Magazine 208
Missionary Society see Lon-
don Missionary Society
Mitchell, G. B. 180
Moderate Calvinism see Cal-
vinism
Molther, P. H. 5
Moravians 4f., 40, 175
More, Hannah 148, 150, 158
Cheap Repository Tracts
148
Morgan, Edward 83
Mules, Charles 109f.

Napoleon 28, 157
Naval and Military Bible So-
ciety 24, 82f., 138
Netherlands Missionary Society
53
New South Wales 69
New York Missionary Society
53
Newman, John 200
Newman, William 151, 213f.
Newport Pagnell Academy 13,
209
Newton, John 7, 13, 15, 24,
28, 170, 216
Noel, Baptist 91, 138f., 141,
167, 215
Norris, Henry Handley 105,
108, 132, 190

Open Communion see Com-

munion
Otaheite 69
Otter, William 90, 104
Overton, J. H. 200
Owen, John (of Paglesham)
      85f., 88, 95, 101, 108,
      110, 117f., 127, 206,
      214
Owen, John (the Puritan) 157
Oxford Movement 93, 200,
      205
Oxford University see Uni-
      versity of Oxford

Paine, Tom 107
Palestine Place see London
      Society for Promoting
      Christianity Amongst the
      Jews
Palmer, C. N. 173
Palmer, Edward 163
Pan-Evangelicalism, Theories
      of 30-33
Paul 30
Pawson, John 50, 76
Pearce, Samuel 49, 58f.
Peel, Robert 90
Pentycross, Thomas 60
Perceval, Spencer 90, 139
Percy, W. (of Bromwich)
      217
Perfection, Doctrine of 5
Peto, Henry 163
Philips, George Washington
      135f., 138f., 146
Philo-Judean Society 190
Platt, T. Pell 138, 141, 146
Platt, W. F. 56
Porteus, Beilby 89, 100ff.,
      119, 214
Pratt, Josiah 71, 86f., 95,
      198
Prayer Book and Homily So-
      ciety 109
Prayer Call Movement 23f.
Predestination 16f.
Predestined Reprobation 162
Pre-Millennialism 30
Presbyterians 11, 72, 129,
      201
   Chapels:
   Artillery Street (London)

42, 47, 213
Clyde Street (Anderston)
      213
Crown Court (London) 28
Miles Lane (London Bridge)
      178
Pretyman-Tomline, George
      105
Priestley, Joseph 26f.
Pringle, Alexander 139
Protestant Dissenters Magazine
      44
Protestant Society 118, 132
Pusey, Edward 200

Quakers see Society of
      Friends
Quinland, Maurice 156

Raffles, Thomas 13, 178
Raikes, Robert 26
Randolph, John 103, 110, 119,
      182f., 187, 214
Rankin, Thomas 76
Rauceby Society 8, 52
Record Newspaper 133
Redemption 17
Reed, Andrew 201
Reform Bill 137, 197
Religious Tract Society 24,
      28, 54, 81ff., 148-173,
      174, 178f., 194f., 197,
      199f., 202f., 205ff.
   Activities (domestic and in-
      terdenominational) 156ff.
   Anti-Catholic Broadsheets
      Controversy 166ff.
   Bible Society, Founding of
      83ff.
   Demoninational Patronage
      150ff.
   Founding 148ff.
   Fundamental Principle 153f.
   Hawker Controversy 161f.
   Milnerian Controversy 165ff.
      202
   Tract selection 154f.
Reprobation, Predestined 17
Reyner, Joseph 58
Richardson, Thomas 91
Richmond, Legh 141, 152ff.,

156, 158f., 167, 170, 179, 209, 214f.
Dairyman's Daughter 152f., 158f., 214
Rippon, John 74
Roberts, John 100
Robinson, Robert 18, 211
Robinson, Thomas 27
Roby, William 57
Rogers, Hugh 132
Romaine, William 206, 209
Roman Catholic Emancipation 123, 137, 154, 161, 166ff., 172, 196
Roman Catholics 90, 97, 107, 123, 126, 129, 134f., 137, 139, 157, 161, 165, 166ff., 184, 196, 200f., 202, 215
Rouse, Ruth 13
Rowlands, Daniel 11
Royal Academy (London) 206
Royal Military Academy 114
Ryland, John Collett 13, 24, 211, 213
Ryland, John, Jr. 18, 56, 74, 151, 178

Saddington, Thomas 170
St. James Episcopal Chapel (Edinburgh) 126
St. Paul's Coffee House 150
St. Saviours Grammar School 152
Salisbury 160
Salter's Hall (London) 27, 208
Sarum 108
Scotland 111f., 123ff., 155f.
Scott, John 215
Scott, Thomas 52, 82, 89, 179, 209, 216
Scott, Walter 207
Seceders see United Secession Church
Serampore (India) 42, 48f., 63, 140
Seward, William 3
Sharp, Granville 85, 89, 112, 210
Shaw, Robert 90
Shore, John 87f., 89, 100,

103f., 106ff., 117, 125ff., 140, 214
Shrubsole, William 214f.
Sibthorpe, Humphrey 215
Sibthorpe, Richard Waldo 167, 173, 215
Sidmouth's Bill 103, 137
Sierra Leone Colony 34, 41, 205, 211
Sikes, Thomas 101, 103ff., 108
Simeon, Charles 7, 17, 69, 85, 89, 95, 104, 141, 162, 170, 179
Simpson, David 12, 30
Sinclair, George 139
Slatterie, Joseph 13, 169
Sloper, Robert 169
Smith, John Pye 178
Smith, Robert 66
Smithfield Martyrs 167
Smyth, Charles 7
Society Established in London for the Support and Encouragement of Sunday Schools 25f.
Society for Distributing Evangelical Tracts Gratis 170, 217
Society for Promoting Christian Knowledge 82f., 99ff., 105f., 109f.
Society for Promoting Religious Knowledge 24, 148
Society for the Abolition of the Slave Trade 25, 34
Society for the Propagation of the Gospel 60
Society for the Reformation of Manners 24
Society for the Relief of Poor Pious Clergymen 209
Society of Friends 85, 90, 94, 97, 107, 116, 118, 134f., 136, 180f., 197, 200f., 202, 209f.
Socinian Controversy see British and Foreign Bible Society, Test Controversy
Socinianism 107f., 115, 131ff., 157, 202, 210
Southsea Islands 188
Spa Field's Chapel (London)

43, 56, 83, 216
Spear, Robert 159
Spener, Jacob 4
Spitalfield Benevolent Society
205
Stapleford 110
Steinkopf, C. F. 69, 85, 87,
90, 124, 128, 152, 215f.
Stephen, James 194
Stepney College 214
Steven, James 42
Steven, Robert 71, 97, 213,
216
Stewart, James Haldane 135,
144, 167
Stokes, George 165
Sunday School Movement
25ff., 35, 149, 159,
195, 206f., 212
Sunday School Society see
Society Established in
London for the Support
and Encouragement of
Sunday Schools
Sundius, Christopher 47, 65,
169, 216
Surrey Chapel 12f., 51, 150,
212f.
Sutcliffe, John 49, 58
Swedenborg, Emanuel 117
Swedish Missionary Society
53

Tarn, Joseph 88, 91, 95,
170, 216f.
Tavistock 92
Taylor, Isaac 206
Taylor, Thomas 59
Teignmouth, Lord see John
Shore
Terpstra, Chester 56
Test Act, Repeal of 8, 28,
118, 123, 131f., 137,
196
Test Controversy see British
and Foreign Bible Society
Thompson, Andrew 129
Thornton, Henry 89
Thornton, John 82
Thorpe, William 125f., 130
Thurlow, Thomas 208
Tindal, Matthew 154

Toleration Act 10
Toplady, August 6, 16
Total Depravity, Doctrine of
6
Towers, John 56, 217
Towne, Thomas 169
Townsend, George 57
Townsend, John 47, 217
Tract Society see Religious
Tract Society
Tractarianism see Oxford
Movement
Travancore (India) 53
Trevecca College 6, 208,
217
Trinitarian Bible Society 139f.,
167, 205
Truro Grammar School 205,
212
Turner, Daniel 18
Twining, Thomas 87
Tyndale, Thomas 118

Unitarians 11, 28, 90, 108,
118, 123, 131ff., 161,
200f., 202
United Secession Church 11,
54, 130
Universalism, Hypothetical
17
University of Aberdeen 86,
211, 212, 217
University of Cambridge 90,
104f.
Colleges:
Corpus Christi 214
Emmanuel 42, 208
Queens 104, 152
St. Johns 51
Trinity 208, 217
University of Edinburgh 42,
206, 208, 210f., 217
University of Glasgow 213,
216
University of Michigan 186
University of Oxford 90, 104f.
Colleges:
Christ Church 212
Jesus 90
Lincoln 179, 209
Magdalen 215
Magdalen Hall 134, 162,

209, 212
Oriel 206, 209
Queens 205
St. Johns 212
Trinity 208, 214
Urwick, William 198
Utilitarianism 197

Van Buren, President 210
Van Ess, Leander 126f.
Van Mildert, William 101,
    107f.
Vansittart, Nicholas 104
Vason, George 48, 58
Vaughan, James 70, 77
Vazeille, Jane 216
Venn, Henry, Sr. 7, 12f., 24
Venn, Henry II 141
Venn, John 208
Ventnor (Isle of Wight) 110
Victoria, Queen 179
Village Itinerancy Society
    208, 211
Von Schirnding, Baron 175

Walker, John 51, 60
Walkerites 60
Wallbridge, Elizabeth 153,
    158f.
Wallis, Beiby 210
Walsh, J. D. 7, 22, 173,
    204
Ward, William (of Myland)
    103f.
Ward, William (of Serampore)
    63
Wardlaw, Ralph 142
Warwickshire Association of
    Ministers for the Spread
    of the Gospel 41, 206
Watson, Richard 76
Watts, Isaac 157
Waugh, Alexander 42, 217
Wawm, John Dale 118
Way, Lewis 179, 188
Webster, Thomas 152
Welsh Calvinistic Methodists
    see Methodists
Wesley, Charles 5
Wesley, John 3ff., 9f., 15,
    21, 24f., 47, 50, 67, 216

Wesleyan Methodist Missionary
    Society 49, 67f., 207
Wesleyan Methodist Tract So-
    ciety 169
Wesleyan Methodists see Meth-
    odists
West, George 51
Westminster Confession 129
White, George 117
Whitefield, George 3f., 9ff.,
    15, 17, 21, 30, 149,
    206, 210, 215
Whitefieldites 10f., 24
Whitefield's Tabernacle 42,
    215, 217
Widow's Friend Society 205
Wilberforce, William 27f.,
    59, 83, 85, 89, 97f.,
    109, 152, 157, 162, 179,
    196f., 210, 214
    Practical View 152, 157,
    214
Wilcox, John 152
Wilkinson, Rebecca 94, 148
Wilks, Matthew 13, 42, 57,
    169f., 215, 217
Williams, Edward 13, 17, 57
Williams, Thomas 56
Williams, William 133f.
Wills, Thomas 60
Wilson, Daniel 32f.
Wilson, Roger Carus 110
Wilson, Walter 19
Wilson, William Carus 117
Winkworth, William 51
Winter, Cornelius 212
Women, Evangelical 114f.
Woodd, Basil 71, 89, 217
Wordsworth, Christopher 103f.

Young Men's Christian Associa-
    tion 195

Zinzendorf, Nicholas 4f., 31,
    203
Zion's Trumpet, 206

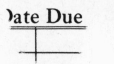

Date Due